Hazard Prevention through Effective Safety and Health Training

Joel M. Haight, Editor

American Society of Safety Engineers
Des Plaines, Illinois, USA

Library of Congress Cataloging-in-Publication Data (applied for)

Managing Editor: Michael F. Burditt, ASSE
Editor: Jeri Ann Stucka, ASSE
Text design and composition: Cathy Lombardi
Cover design: Image Graphics

Printed in the United States of America

18 17 16 15 14 13   6 5 4 3 2 1

HAZARD PREVENTION THROUGH EFFECTIVE SAFETY AND HEALTH TRAINING

Contents

FOREWORD

EFFECTIVE SAFETY TRAINING IS critical to accident prevention. Current estimates identify 80–90 percent of all accidents are caused by unsafe acts. OSHA believes training is essential to protecting workers from injuries and illnesses, and more than 100 OSHA standards contain training requirements. OSHA recommends employers use a risk-based approach to prioritizing training. OSHA's Voluntary Protection Program (VPP) guidelines specify training as necessary to reinforce and complement management's commitment to prevent exposure to hazards. As Dr. Ferguson points out:

> A fundamental premise of the safety and health training included as part of the VPP Safety and Health Management System is that all employees must understand their safety and health responsibilities, the hazards to which they may be exposed, and how to prevent harm to themselves and others from such exposures. Without such an understanding, employees will not be able to perform their responsibilities for safety and health effectively.

A listing of all the mandatory and implicit training required by OSHA is available in OSHA 2254, *Training Requirements in OSHA Standards and Training Guidelines.*

As Charles Stanfill points out in the chapter, "EPA Safety and Health Training Requirements," it is sometimes difficult in regard to environmental regulations, "...to ascertain the distinction between employee safety and the public's safety." This results from the fact that environmental law applies to anyone coming in contact with certain products and hazardous substances. He further points out the important fact that, based on a memorandum of understanding between the two agencies, the EPA and OSHA, there are "several training requirements addressed in various OSHA standards. Those that involved hazardous waste, hazardous substances, and waste products tend to be the most prominent." Dr. Stanfill discusses EPA/OSHA training requirements for asbestos, hazardous waste operations and emergency response standards, hospital/medical/infectious waste incineration, oil spills, pesticide safety, and radiation training, as well as others. He also reviews *recommended* training for mold assessment and remediation, the National Pollutant Discharge Elimination System (NPDES), as well as Clandestine Laboratory Site Safety Officers training offered by the DEA. Major resources for environmental educational training are also discussed.

NIOSH and ANSI Z490 training requirements are discussed in Chapter 3. NIOSH offers a continuing education program for hazardous substance in cooperation with the National Institute of Environmental Health Sciences (NIEHS). Currently there are two types of hazardous substance training programs: a continuing education training program, and an academic training program for safety and health professionals responsible for responding to hazardous substance spills and releases, as well as managing, controlling, cleaning up and remediating areas affected by incidents involving hazardous substances. Both programs are offered through the 12 NIOSH Education and Research Centers.

The final NIOSH training program discussed is emergency responder training. Begun in 2012, the program is offered through a cooperative agreement with the International Association of Fire Fighters (IAFF). A primary emphasis of the program is the health and safety of first responders, given their exposure to hazardous toxic materials.

The second half of Chapter 3 is devoted to discussing the ANSI/ASSE Z490.1-2009, "Criteria for Accepted Practices in Safety, Health, and Environmental Training." The Z490 Standard lists the criteria necessary for effective management of SH&E training, recognizing that training is part of the SH&E management system. For training to be effective, results should be demonstrable and measurable. In developing training, the knowledge, skills, and abilities of employees should be enhanced so that workers will be able to identify and understand the hazards of their jobs while using proper control measures. The systematic process for training development recommended in Z490-2009 includes: a needs assessment; written learning objectives and their prerequisites; training course design; a strategy for evaluation; completion criteria, which specifies a minimum level of accomplishment; and a process for continuous improvement of training.

The important provisions of the Z490 Standard that are so important to developing effective training which are discussed by Dr. Stanfill are: training delivery, training evaluation, documentation and record keeping, and confidentiality and availability of training records.

The author of Chapter 4, "Safety and Health Training Theories and Applications," posed this question, "If you were hiring a safety instructor, what knowledge and skills would you look for? An excellent communicator ... someone who can design web-based instruction ... has a degree in adult education...or someone who is bi-lingual?" The need for skilled trainers is greater than ever, because of the impact injuries can have on quality of life, healthcare and workers' compensation insurance costs. Companies today want trainers to have a variety of technical skills that will engage and motivate workers to want to learn about safety. To further reiterate the need for good training skills, some performance-based OSHA standards require subject-matter competencies in order to teach them. Even OSHA's voluntary training model encourages the use of adult learning principles, such as needs assessments and developing training objectives. These critical topics, along with the following, are covered in this chapter:

- Adult learning theories – how people learn;
- How to increase learner motivation;
- Ways to determine if training is the solution to performance problem or injury; and
- Using learning styles to make training sessions more interactive.

Ms. Simmons commented, "As a practicing safety trainer for the past 25 years, I have used the information and tools in this chapter to:

1. "Promote safe work practices and behaviors that have made a positive impact on injury rates; and
2. "Help companies comply with OSHA's training regulations to prevent citations.

"Having this background has given me the ability to teach workers from diverse educational backgrounds and work in variety of environments ranging from administrative to manufacturing settings. Even though the technology used to train employees has evolved over the past 10 years, adult learning principles have remained consistent. This chapter is designed to enhance the knowledge and skills of anyone providing safety instruction in the workplace."

Use of Terminology Notice. This chapter includes examples that refer to the term Material Safety Data Sheet (MSDS), which in use was prior to the final adoption of OSHA's Globally Harmonize System term

SDS (Safety Data Sheet). For the purposes of this chapter, either term can be used in the scenarios presented.

The next chapter, "Presentation and Documentation of Safety and Health Training," provides often-overlooked information that is critical for continuity of training and for improving training delivery. This is particularly true in the case of well-written lesson plans. Following a valuable discussion of lesson plans, the author, Fred Fanning, discusses collaborative and active learning. In collaborative learning, instructors become coaches and facilitators. This requires some adjustments for instructors. Fanning writes:

> To do this effectively, instructors must be able to consider that adult students know a great deal about the world, and perhaps even the subject being taught. With a little help, the students might be able to figure the material out on their own with more retention and better understanding than an instructor could ever provide.

In collaborative/active learning, students take responsibility for their learning. Students can also serve as facilitators in developing ideas for presenting training. Different aspects of collaborative training are discussed, including changing roles from participant to observer.

Trainers should consider the benefits of active learning, because many studies have shown that traditional passive (lecture) learning results in only about 20-percent retention. The author shares some interesting and informative tips on how to structure active learning sessions.

Some training documentation requirements are too often overlooked, such as what should be included in the training documentation method used, and the method of evaluation. Readers are reminded that OSHA requires that training records for the Hazard Communication Standard (HCS) be kept for the length of employment, plus 30 years.

The last three chapters cover important training management practices and principles: cost analysis and budgeting, benchmarking, and best practices. Effective safety and health training requires resources for development and delivery. Cost analysis and budgeting is critical to leveraging training dollars to provide the most comprehensive training possible. As Brent Altemose, the author of the chapter on budgeting and cost analysis, notes, "The advent of computer-based training and other technology training techniques has made cost analysis more critical, because the cost of such programs varies widely." Methods for collecting data on training costs are discussed in detail, with the cost to develop the program being significant. The author provides a useful worksheet on development, implementation, and other life cycle costs (which are discussed).

The benefits portion of cost/benefit analysis provides a revealing list of both tangible and intangible benefits, including increased productivity or improved organizational reputation. A useful example of net present worth cost analysis is HazCom training. Some of the choices that may need to be made in managing a safety and health budget are also explored. The author concludes his discussion with a thoughtful analysis on continuous improvement of training programs.

In the next chapter, "Safety and Health Training Benchmarking and Performance Criteria," Richard Stempniak and Linda Tapp begin by metrics for measuring training effectiveness. They then provide answers to the question, "Why Assess?", followed by a discussion of the different types of assessment. Benchmarking, which as the authors point out, is a type of assessment is discussed, as are the types of benchmarking. The chapter ends with an interesting discussion of acceptable training evaluation approaches as proscribed by ANSI Z490.1-2009. In the final chapter, "Best Practices in Safety and Health Training," the authors discuss important considerations that need to understood for effectively training training adults and the distinction between training and educating. They then discuss how to integrate training into a company's strategic plan. Key training highlights of two important standards, ANSI Z10-2005, and OHSAS 18001—2007 are discussed. The authors conclude with an insightful discussion of considerations for selecting training staff.

ABOUT THE EDITOR

In 2009, Joel M. Haight, Ph.D., P.E., was named Branch Chief of the Human Factors Branch at the Centers for Disease Control and Prevention (CDC)—National Institute of Occupational Safety and Health (NIOSH) at their Pittsburgh Office of Mine Safety and Health Research. He continues in this role. In 2000, Dr. Haight received a faculty appointment and served as Associate Professor of Energy and Mineral Engineering at the Pennsylvania State University. He also worked as a manager and engineer for the Chevron Corporation domestically and internationally for eighteen years prior to joining the faculty at Penn State. He has a Ph.D. (1999) and Master's degree (1994) in Industrial and System Engineering, both from Auburn University. Dr. Haight does human error, process optimization, and intervention effectiveness research. He is a professional member of the American Society of Safety Engineers (where he serves as Federal Liaison to the Board of Trustees and the ASSE Foundation Research Committee Chair), the American Industrial Hygiene Association (AIHA), and the Human Factors and Ergonomics Society (HFES). He has published more than 30 peer-reviewed scientific journal articles and book chapters and is a co-author and the editor-in-chief of ASSE's *The Safety Professionals Handbook* and the John Wiley and Sons, *Handbook of Loss Prevention Engineering*.

ABOUT THE AUTHORS

Brent A. Altemose, M.S., CIH, CSP, is President and Principal Consultant, SABRE Health & Safety LLC, Easton, PA.

David F. Coble, M.S., CSP, is President of Coble, Taylor & Jones Safety Associates in Cary, NC.

Fred E. Fanning, M.Ed., M.A., is the Director, Program Integration and Logistics Operations for the U.S. Department of Energy in Washington, D.C.

Lon Ferguson is a Professor in the Safety Sciences Department at Indiana University of Pennsylvania (IUP). Dr. Ferguson has both his B.S. and M.S. in Safety Sciences from IUP, and his doctorate is from the University of Pittsburgh.

Phyllis A. Simmons, M.A., CSP, is a safety consultant and President of Creative Safety Designs in San Leandro, CA.

C. Keith Stalnaker, Ph.D., is Professor in the Department of Occupational Safety and Health at Columbia Southern University in Orange Beach, AL.

Charles V. Stanfill, Jr., is Safety Director at the North Carolina Department of Environment and Natural Resources.

Richard A. Stempniak, CMfgE, is an Associate Professor of Technology (Industrial) at the State University of New York College at Buffalo.

Linda M. Tapp, M.S., ALCM, CSP, is President of Crown Safety LLC.

OSHA Safety and Health Training Requirements

1

Lon Ferguson

LEARNING OBJECTIVES

▌ Be able to utilize three methods recommended by OSHA for prioritizing training needs.

▌ Be able to identify examples of both mandated and implied training requirements in OSHA standards.

▌ Learn how to use the OSHA Voluntary Training Guidelines to determine if training is needed.

▌ Be able to identify training needs and content, training goals and objectives, and develop learning activities. Conduct the training, evaluate its effectiveness, and develop recommendations to improve the training program.

▌ Learn to use a variety of OSHA resources available to develop and implement safety and health training, such as the OSHA Training Institute, the Resource Center Loan Program, Susan Harwood Grants Program, OSHA Web site and e-Tools, and the OSHA Outreach Training Program.

THE OCCUPATIONAL SAFETY AND HEALTH ACT of 1970 (OSH Act) does not directly address the responsibility of employers to provide health and safety information and instruction to employees. However, Section 2 of the OSH Act does encourage employers and employees to reduce workplace safety and health hazards through the institution of new and existing programs, and by specifically providing for training programs to increase the number and competence of personnel engaged in the field of occupational safety and health (OSHA 1970).

In terms of employer training responsibilities and duties, Section 5(a)(2) of the OSH Act requires each employer to "comply with occupational safety and health standards promulgated under this Act," and currently more than 100 of these standards contain training requirements (OSHA 1970). These training requirements reflect the Occupational Safety and Health Administration's (OSHA) belief that training is an essential part of every employer's safety and health program for protecting workers from injuries and illnesses (NIOSH 2004).

This is also reflected in OSHA enforcement activities in the construction industry: in 2008, two of the top ten most frequently cited violations [29 CFR Sections 1926.503, and 1926.454] were directly related to training (OSHA 1995 and 1996a).

In Title 29 of the *Code of Federal Regulations*, Section 1908.2, Consultation Agreements–Definitions, OSHA defines training as the planned and organized activity of a consultant to impart skills, techniques, and methodologies to employers and their employees to assist them in establishing and maintaining employment and a place of employment that is safe and healthful (OSHA 2000). While businesses sometimes object to the specific wording of an OSHA standard, there is little written in occupational safety and health

1

literature stating that the OSHA-mandated training requirements are unnecessary or generally unreasonable (Saccaro 1994, 50–51).

From a legal perspective, the adequacy of employee training has become an issue in contested cases where the affirmative defense of unpreventable employee misconduct is pursued. Under case law well-established in the Occupational Safety and Health Review Commission, an employer may successfully defend itself against an otherwise valid citation by demonstrating that all feasible steps were taken to avoid the occurrence of the hazard, and that actions of the employee involved in the violation were a departure from a uniformly and effectively enforced work rule of which the employee had either actual or constructive knowledge. The adequacy of the training and education given to employees in connection with a specific hazard is a factual matter that can be decided only by considering all the facts and circumstances surrounding the alleged violation (OSHA 1998, 2).

Legally mandated training is an important component in a company's safety training program, but it should not be the foundation of the program. This legally mandated training should be viewed as minimal standards; training to merely avoid citations will not decrease the rate and severity of injuries, nor does it satisfy the spirit of the OSH Act (OSHA 1970). Companies can buy training programs that cover many of the OSHA training requirements. These programs are designed to meet the minimum training requirements established by OSHA. However, the programs do not address the specific company procedures, manufacturing processes, or hazards that are necessary for successful training. There are sure to be major gaps in a safety training program if the goal is merely compliance with government safety regulations, while company-specific safety hazards are left unaddressed (Saccaro 1994, 50–51).

THE ROLE OF TRAINING IN ACCIDENT PREVENTION

Current estimates identify that 80–90 percent of all accidents are caused in part by unsafe acts (Lawton and Parker 1998). Training, or the lack of training, may play a role in the occurrence of unsafe acts, and therefore play a role in accident prevention. There is very little disagreement in the role that training plays in reducing unsafe acts, but the more pressing problem for many employers is deciding which employees have the greatest need for training.

In OSHA's publication, *Training Requirements in OSHA Standards and Training Guidelines*, two methods for prioritizing training needs are discussed (OSHA 1998). The first method is to identify employee populations that are at higher levels of risk The nature of the work will provide an indication that such groups should receive priority for training on occupational safety and health risks. This risk can be influenced by conditions under which the work is performed, such as noise, heat or cold, or safety or health hazards in the surrounding area.

The second method of identifying employee populations at high levels of risk is to examine the incidence of accidents and injuries. Within the company, workers' compensation data and/or OSHA record-keeping logs (OSHA Form 300, Log of Work-Related Injuries and Illnesses) and reports (OSHA Form 301, Injury and Illness Incident Report) can be used to justify and define the role of training for targeting preventive follow-up action (OSHA 2004b). A thorough accident investigation can identify not only specific employees who could benefit from training, but also identify companywide training needs.

On a national level, federal as well as professional safety societies can be used to provide injury and illness data. Research from these data sources has identified several variables as being related to a disproportionate share of injuries and illnesses at the work site. These variables should be considered when identifying those with the greatest need for training (OSHA 1998, 7):

- the age of the employee—younger employees have higher incidence rates
- the length of time on the job—new employees have higher incidence rates
- the size of the firm—in general terms, medium-size firms have higher incidence rates than smaller or larger firms

- the type of work performed—incidence and severity rates vary significantly by the Standard Industrial Classification (SIC) Code
- the use of hazardous substances by SIC Code (OSHA 2010f)

Determining the content of training for employees at higher levels of risk is similar to determining what any employee needs to know. A job hazard analysis is a useful tool for determining training content from job requirements. This procedure examines each step of a job, identifies existing or potential hazards, and determines the best way to perform the job in order to reduce or eliminate the hazards (OSHA 1998, 7).

FUTURE OUTLOOK

In 1999, the National Institute for Occupational Safety and Health (NIOSH), the National Institute of Environmental Health Sciences (NIEHS), and OSHA sponsored a national conference to discuss emerging issues in the occupational safety and health field with a focus on training effectiveness. Specifically, this conference focused on the following (NIOSH 2004, 1):

- issues concerning the changing workplace and workforce
- methodologies for training
- evaluation of training
- systems of safety, including training
- policies and resources to meet projected training needs

What follows are some of the major findings from this conference related to training needs and challenges, and training policy and regulations.

Needs and Challenges

Although the reported number of workplace fatalities in the United States has decreased over the past decade, according to the Bureau of Labor Statistics (BLS), the number of reported fatalities is still substantial— 4547 fatalities in the United States in 2010 (BLS 2011). Therefore, improving training program quality and the effectiveness of training efforts, together with comply-

ing with the relevant OSHA training regulations, are important interventions aimed at workplace hazard prevention and control.

The acknowledged need for training is also being influenced by performance-based training, which is not mandated by law but is based on the need to improve job performance. In addition, workplace and workforce changes that are responding to advances in technology, demographic shifts, and global economic factors all act to complicate the task of training (NIOSH 2004, 2–4).

Examples of workplace changes in the United States include the shift from a manufacturing economy to one that is dominated by services and a reduced management-to-worker ratio. Since occupational hazards in the service sector tend to be more variable, training may have to change to incorporate alternative approaches to ensure learning of safe work practices. As an organization becomes flatter, the workers can be expected to play a greater role in OSH efforts. This implies that these same workers must receive appropriate training and information about hazards, control measures, and preventive actions commensurate with their safety and health program responsibilities (NIOSH 2004, 5–6).

Policy and Regulations

OSHA recognizes training as a critical action to take in further reducing workplace injuries and illnesses in the United States. This is especially true when training is combined with other workplace interventions, such as safety programs and procedures. However, OSHA also has found the effectiveness of OSH training as a sole intervention is less certain and more limited (NIOSH 2004, 11–13).

As a result of the 1999 NIOSH, NIEHS, and OSHA Training Conference, there were three major findings related to policy, regulation, and standards. The first was the need to prioritize training with a focus on directing OSH training at those conditions that represent the highest risk of work-related injury and illness. Three methods for prioritizing training were discussed earlier in this chapter. OSHA has also been gathering empirical evidence on the benefits of training (lives saved, injuries avoided, and reduced costs to business) through OSHA Consultation Safety and Health Program Evaluations completed at sites requesting consultation services. Data from these program evaluations support the premise that companies demonstrating a strong emphasis on worker training had the most effective occupational safety and health programs (NIOSH 2004, 11–13).

The second major finding was the need to set at least voluntary standards for acceptable OSH training program practices. This also included establishing competencies of those delivering OSH training. It was believed that these standards would help provide a certain level of quality control (NIOSH 2004, 12). OSHA has, in fact, developed Voluntary Training Guidelines, which are discussed later in this chapter.

The third major finding was the need to provide OSH training to all levels of the workforce to promote total staff knowledge of the training goals and to reinforce its objectives. As mentioned earlier, this is also important as organizations become flatter and additional safety and health responsibilities are placed on workers at all levels. To address this issue, OSHA is providing support for direct training and education of workers through grants to various nonprofit organizations, offering course s at OSHA Training Institute Educations Centers, and disseminating training products through distance learning technology, CD-ROMs, and the Internet (NIOSH 2004, 12).

OSHA Training Requirements
OSHA Revisions to the Voluntary Protection Programs to Provide Safe and Healthful Working Conditions

Section IV of the Revisions to the Voluntary Protection Programs to Provide Safe and Healthful Working Conditions outlines the requirements of a safety and health management system for all VPP participants. The four basic requirements are in line with the Voluntary Safety and Health Program Management Guidelines originally developed in 1989 (OSHA 1989). A summary of the four elements in the VPP Safety and Health Management System include (OSHA, 2009b):

- management leadership and employee involvement—integrating the OSH program

with the overall management system, clearly establishing policies with goals and objectives, responsibility/authority, and accountability for OSH activities, and involving workers in hazard recognition and control activities
- work-site analysis—analyzing the workplace conditions and work practices to identify hazards, policies, and procedures for the purpose of anticipating harmful occurrences (i.e., inspections and job hazard analysis)
- hazard prevention and control—eliminating or controlling hazards via engineering, administrative, work practices, or PPE
- safety and health training—addressing the responsibilities of all personnel at all levels of the organization

According to these guidelines, training is necessary to reinforce and complement management's commitment to prevent exposure to hazards. The guidelines do not suggest that elaborate or formal training programs solely related to safety and health are always needed. In fact, integrating safety and health protection into all organizational activities is the key to its effectiveness. Safety and health information and instruction is often most effective when incorporated into other training about performance requirements and job practices, such as management training on performance evaluation, problem solving, and employee training on the operation of a particular machine or the conduct of a specific task (OSHA 2009b).

A fundamental premise of the safety and health training included as part of the VPP Safety and Health Management System is that all employees must understand their safety and health responsibilities, the hazards to which they may be exposed, and how to prevent harm to themselves and others from such exposures. Without such an understanding, employees will not be able to perform their responsibilities for safety and health effectively. For this to happen, the training must ensure the following (OSHA 2009b):

- Managers and supervisors understand their safety and health responsibilities and are able to carry them out effectively. These responsibilities may include identifying unrecognized potential hazards, maintaining physical safeguards in their work areas, and reinforcing employee training on the nature of potential hazards and on needed protective measures, such as work practices and personal protective equipment.

- All employees are made aware of hazards and are taught how to recognize hazardous conditions and the signs and symptoms of work-related illnesses. All employees are also provided with information and training in the safety and health program and the provision of applicable standards.
- All employees learn the safe work procedures to follow in order to protect themselves from hazards. This includes what is being done to control these hazards and the protective measures the employee must follow to eliminate or reduce exposure to these hazards.
- All employees and visitors on site understand what to do in emergency situations.
- All employees required to wear personal protective equipment must understand why it is required, its limitations, how to use it properly, and how to maintain it.

An important part of training is the need to evaluate employee understanding of the safety and health information covered. It is a major mistake to assume that the mere act of training ensures practical comprehension; there must be some means of verifying comprehension. As part of the Construction Safety and Health Outreach Program, the OSHA Office of Training and Education publishes *Tools for a Safety and Health Program Assessment*. This publication identifies three key components for assessing safety and health training (OSHA 1996b, 10–11):

1. Ensuring that all employees understand hazards

   Documentation:

   - Does the written training program include training for all employees in emergency procedures and in all potential hazards to which the employees may be exposed?

   - Do training records show that all employees received the planned training?
   - Do the written evaluations, test results, and other forms of training indicate the training was successful in meeting training objectives?

   Interviews:

   - Can employees identify the hazards they are exposed to, why those hazards are a threat, and how they can help protect themselves and others?
   - If PPE is used, can employees explain why they use it and how to use and maintain it properly?
   - Do employees feel that health and safety training is adequate?

   Site conditions and root causes of hazards:

   - Have employees been injured or made ill by hazards of which they were unaware, or whose dangers they did not understand, or from which they did not know how to protect themselves?
   - Have employees or rescue workers ever been endangered by employees not knowing what to do in a given emergency situation?
   - Are there hazards in the workplace that exist, at least in part, because one or more employees have not received adequate hazard control training?
   - Are there any instances of employees not wearing the required PPE properly because they have not received appropriate training?

2. Ensuring that supervisors understand their responsibilities

   Documentation:

   - Do training records indicate that all supervisors have been trained in their responsibilities to analyze work to identify hazards, to maintain physical protections, and to reinforce employee training and work practices through performance feedback and, where necessary, enforcement of safe work procedures and safety and health rules?

Interviews:

- Do supervisors know their safety and health responsibilities?
- Do employees confirm that supervisors are carrying out their safety and health responsibilities?

Site conditions and root causes of hazards:

- Has a supervisor's lack of understanding of safety and health responsibilities played a part in creating hazardous activities or conditions?

3. Ensuring that managers understand their safety and health responsibilities

Documentation:

- Do training plans for managers include training in safety and health responsibilities?
- Do records indicate that all line managers have received this training?

Interviews:

- Do employees confirm that managers know and carry out their safety and health responsibilities?

Site conditions and root causes of hazards:

- Has a manager's lack of understanding of safety and health responsibilities played a part in creating hazardous activities or conditions?

The documentation of safety and health training discussed above is a critical consideration in all safety and health training. At a minimum, this documentation should include the name of the worker, job title, personal identifier such as clock number, date, list of topics covered, length of training, and the trainer's name and signature. The documentation records can provide evidence of the employer's good faith and compliance with OSHA standards and also answer one of the first questions an accident investigator may ask: "Was the injured employee trained to do the job?" (Reese 2003, 238–239).

OSHA Voluntary Training Guidelines

In an attempt to assist employers with their occupational safety and health training activities, OSHA has developed a set of training guidelines. OSHA does not intend to make these guidelines mandatory and they are available for review in OSHA Publication 2254, *Training Requirements in OSHA Standards and Training Guidelines*. OSHA encourages a personalized approach to the training programs at individual work sites. Therefore, the guidelines are general enough to be used in any area of occupational safety and health training, and allow employers flexibility to determine for themselves the content and format of training (OSHA 1998).

The OSHA training guidelines recommend the following seven steps when developing safety and health training:

1. Determining if training is needed

Training is not a panacea for all safety and health problems. In general, training is most effective when addressing problems related to a lack of knowledge, unfamiliarity with equipment or processes, or incorrect execution of a task. However, training is less effective for problems arising from an employee's lack of motivation or lack of attention to the job, and training should not be used as a substitute for engineering or other administrative controls (OSHA 1998). Methods for addressing the unmotivated employee were discussed in an earlier chapter.

2. Identifying training needs

The first step in identifying training needs is to identify what the employee is expected to accomplish. The second step is to identify in what ways, if any, the employee's performance is deficient. To avoid unnecessary training and meet the needs of the employees, training must focus on those areas where improved performance is needed. A valuable tool available to the safety professional to identify deficiencies in employee performance is a job hazard analysis. The information obtained from the job hazard analysis can then be used as the content for the training activity.

Other means suggested by the guidelines for developing training content include (OSHA 1998):

a. Using company accident and injury records to identify how accidents occur and what can be done to prevent them from recurring.

b. Requesting employees to provide written descriptions of their jobs. These should include the tasks performed and the tools, materials, and equipment used.

c. Observing employees at the work site as they perform job tasks. Safety and health hazards can be identified through the employees' responses to such questions as, have they had any near-miss incidents, do they feel they are taking risks, or do they believe that their jobs involve hazardous operations, substances, and so forth.

d. Examining similar training programs offered by other companies in the same industry, or obtaining suggestions from such organizations as the National Safety Council, the American Society of Safety Engineers, or federal safety and health agencies such as OSHA and NIOSH.

e. Reviewing the specific federal or state safety, health, and environmental standards applicable to a business can also provide direction in developing training content.

3. Identifying training goals and objectives

Well-written instructional objectives will identify as precisely as possible what individuals will do to demonstrate that the objective has been reached. These objectives will be clear, measurable, and describe the important conditions under which the individual will demonstrate competence. The objectives will also define what constitutes acceptable performance (OSHA 1998).

4. Developing learning activities

Learning activities enable those being trained to demonstrate that they have acquired the desired skills and knowledge. To be effective, these activities should simulate the actual job as closely as possible. This is especially true if a specific process is to be learned, in which case the activities should be arranged in the same sequence in which the tasks are performed on the job. These training activities can include such things as lectures, role playing, self-paced instruction, and demonstrations. There are a few factors that will influence the type of learning activity selected. One of these factors is the training resources available to the employer. Another factor is the kind of skills or knowledge to be learned (OSHA 1998).

5. Conducting the training

A critical part of conducting the training is knowing your audience. This will be accomplished if the prior steps are done properly. The trainer must also get the audience to buy into the training. Specifically, the trainees must be convinced of the importance and relevance of the training material. When this is achieved, the audience is much more likely to pay attention and learn the material. When conducting the training, it should be presented so that its organization and meaning are clear to the employees. The OSHA training guidelines suggest one way to accomplish this is to do the following:

a. provide overviews of the material to be learned

b. relate the new information or skills to the employee's goals, interests, or experience

c. reinforce what the employees learned by summarizing the program's objectives and key points.

The training content, the nature of the workplace, federal and state regulations, and the resources available for training will help employers determine the frequency of training activities, the length of the sessions, the instructional techniques, and the individuals best qualified to complete the training (OSHA 1998).

6. Evaluating training program effectiveness

A critical component to a training program is the development of a method to measure the effectiveness of the training. The development of such a method should be considered at the same time the course content and objectives are being developed. As mentioned earlier, all good objectives are measurable, and the evaluation of the training will help determine how effective the trainer was in meeting the training objectives.

If done properly, this evaluation will also provide an indication on the trainees' improved performance on the job. The OSHA training guidelines provide the following examples of methods for evaluating training programs (OSHA 1998):

   a. student surveys (opinions/perceptions)

   b. supervisors' observations

   c. workplace improvements—the ultimate success of a training program may be changes throughout the workplace that result in reduced injury or accident rates.

A more specific discussion on evaluation of training as well as examples of the above evaluation tools will be included in the chapter titled, "Benchmarks and Performance Appraisal Criteria" in this section.

   7. Improving the training program

If the evaluation shows that the training did not meet its objectives, it may be necessary to revise the training program. One way to accomplish this is to repeat the steps in the training process by starting with the first step of determining if training is needed. The OSHA training guidelines suggest asking the following questions as part of improving the training program (OSHA 1998):

- If a job hazard analysis was conducted, was it accurate?
- Was any critical feature of the job overlooked?
- Were the important gaps in knowledge and skills included?
- Was material already known by the employees intentionally omitted?
- Were the instructional objectives presented clearly and concretely?
- Did the objectives state the level of acceptable performance that was expected of employees?
- Did the learning activity simulate the actual job?
- Was the learning activity appropriate for the kinds of knowledge and skills required on the job?
- When the training was presented, was the organization of the material and its meaning made clear?

- Were the employees motivated to learn?
- Were the employees allowed to participate actively in the training process?
- Was the employer's evaluation of the program thorough?

OSHA MANDATED AND IMPLICIT TRAINING REQUIREMENTS

Many of the standards promulgated by OSHA explicitly require the employer to train employees in the safety and health aspects of their jobs. An example of a standard that mandates training is 29 CFR 1910.178 (l)(1)(i), which states the following: "Prior to permitting an employee to operate a powered industrial truck (except for training purposes), the employer shall ensure that each operator has successfully completed the training required by this paragraph (l), except as permitted by paragraph (l)(5)" (OSHA 2006).

Other OSHA standards imply training by making it the employer's responsibility to limit certain job assignments to employees who are certified, competent, or qualified—meaning that they have had special previous training. An example of a standard that implies training is 29CFR 1926.1053(b)(15), which states that ladders shall be inspected by a competent person for visible defects on a periodic basis and after any occurrence that could affect their safe use (OSHA 1991).

A listing of all the mandatory and implicit training required by OSHA is available in OSHA 2254, *Training Requirements in OSHA Standards and Training Guidelines* (OSHA 1998). This is the most recent OSHA publication on training requirements in OSHA standards; some changes have been made in the regulations since 1998.

OSHA TRAINING RESOURCES
OSHA Directorate of Training and Education

The OSHA Directorate of Training and Education (DTE) is responsible for managing OSHA's national training and education policies and procedures. OSHA's DTE offers a variety of resources to help companies satisfy safety training requirements. The training guidelines developed by the DTE were discussed earlier

(OSHA 2009c). Other training resources provided by the DTE include the Resource Center Loan Program (OSHA 2008a), the Susan Harwood Grants Program (2009a), OSHA Training Institute, OSHA Training Institute Education Centers (OSHA 2009d), and the OSHA Outreach Training Program (OSHA 2010a). What follows is a brief discussion of these training resources and what they offer a safety and health professional.

Resource Center Loan Program

The Resource Center Loan Program was developed by the OSHA Directorate of Training and Education to respond to the many requests for safety and health training materials. The resource center has a collection of books and over 600 videos covering 100 occupational safety and health topics. Currently, these training materials are made available to the following: OSHA national, regional, and area office employees, employees of state plan states, Consultation Program employees, Voluntary Protection Program site employees, OSHA federal agency trainers, OSHA grantees, and OSHA outreach trainers within the United States. For those who are eligible to use these training materials, there are no direct fees charged by the center with the exception of paying the cost of return shipping. Those interested in using training material should make their requests at least fifteen days prior to the start of the training. The typical loan period used by the center is fourteen days, which includes days for shipping. *The Resource Center Loan Program Catalog*, which explains in detail the policies for borrowing training materials as well as a complete listing of subject titles, is available from the OSHA Web site (OSHA 2008a).

Susan Harwood Grants Program

OSHA offers grants to nonprofit organizations to train workers in the recognition, avoidance, and prevention of safety and health hazards in their workplaces through the Susan Harwood Grants Program. Each nonprofit organization awarded a grant is responsible for the following: developing a training program that addresses one of the safety and health topics identified by OSHA, recruiting individuals for the training, conducting the training, and following up

with trainees to find out what changes were made to reduce hazards in their workplaces as a result of the training. Additional information on the Susan Harwood Grants Program is available at OSHA's Web site.

In general, the grant program focuses on four areas:

1. Educating workers and employers in small businesses (250 or fewer employees).
2. Training workers about new OSHA standards.
3. Training at-risk workers and employer populations.
4. Training workers about high-risk activities or hazards identified by OSHA through the Department of Labor's Strategic Plan.

Examples of safety and health topics that have been funded through the grant program in recent years include crane safety, combustible dust, emergency preparedness and response, and the OSHA record-keeping process (OSHA 2009a).

OSHA Education Centers and Outreach Training Programs

Prior to 1992, the OSHA Training Institute (OTI) served as OSHA's primary training provider for federal and state compliance officers and state Consultation Program staff. The institute also offered training to private-sector employees on a space-available basis. However, during the 1980s, demand for training from private-sector employees increased substantially and the OTI did not have the capacity to handle this demand. As a result, in October of 1992, the OTI Education Center Program was established to meet the expanding need for OSHA training to private-sector employees. These Education Centers support OSHA's training and education mission by providing the following (Barnes 2003, 36–37):

- basic courses that teach students to recognize, avoid, and prevent unsafe and unhealthful working conditions
- enhance the agency's community outreach efforts, including Spanish-language courses and youth initiatives
- specialized local instruction tailored to specific regional industry needs

Initially, the OTI Education Center Program started with 4 education centers, but has now expanded to 27 centers, comprised of 45 member organizations, with at least one in each of OSHA's regions. This expansion allowed OSHA to nearly double its training capability to meet the increasing demand for OSHA training. In fact, in 2007 alone, more than 27,346 students were trained at education centers (OSHA, 2009c). The education centers offer numerous short courses, online training, on-site training for organizations, and training in Spanish, with a complete listing available from the OSHA Web site within the Office of Training and Education section (OSHA, 2009b). The courses available from the OTI range from 5 to 70 contact hours, while the Education Center courses typically range from 6 to 30 contact hours, with continuing education units (CEUs) available for all courses. Courses are both lecture-based and web-based, with a blended course being a combination of both.

Based on course enrollments, two of the most popular courses taught by the Education Centers are #500, "Trainer Course in Occupational Safety and Health Standards for the Construction Industry" and #501, "Trainer Course in Occupational Safety and Health Standards for General Industry." Students completing these courses and passing a test become authorized by OSHA to participate in the Outreach Training Program. The general industry outreach trainers are authorized to conduct 10- and 30-hour general industry outreach courses and receive OSHA course completion cards to issue to the participants.

To stay current on OSHA, general industry outreach trainers must attend #503, "Update for General Industry Outreach Trainers" every four years to maintain their status as authorized general industry outreach program trainers, or they may retake #501 to maintain their trainer status. Construction industry outreach trainers are authorized to conduct 10- and 30-hour construction industry outreach courses and receive OSHA course completion cards to issue to attendees. To stay current on OSHA, construction outreach trainers must attend #502, "Update for Construction Industry Outreach Trainers" every four years to maintain their status as authorized construction outreach program trainers, or they may retake #500

to maintain their trainer status (OSHA 2010a). More information on these outreach trainer courses is available on the OSHA Training Institute Education Centers Web site (OSHA, 2009d).

OSHA Outreach Training Program

Through OSHA's Outreach Training Program, individuals are permitted to obtain course completion cards verifying their participation in 10- and 30-hour general industry and construction courses. This outreach program has grown rapidly in recent years, with over 680,000 students trained and 43,000 classes offered in 2008. Over the past three years, 1.6 million students were trained with 80 percent working in the construction industry (OSHA 2011a). What follows is a brief overview of the 10- and 30-hour courses:

10-HOUR GENERAL INDUSTRY COURSE

The 10-hour general industry course is intended to provide a variety of training on safety and health to entry-level workers in general industry. This course emphasizes hazard identification, avoidance, control, and prevention. The program guidelines for the 10-hour course require a minimum of one hour in each of the following topics, except for the Introduction to OSHA, which must be two hours (OSHA 2011b):

- an introduction to OSHA (OSH Act; General Duty Clause, employer rights and responsibilities, whistleblower rights, record-keeping basics, inspections, citations, value of safety, OSHA Web site and 800 number)
- walking and working surfaces, including fall protection
- fire and emergency preparedness (exit routes, emergency action plans, fire prevention plans, and fire protection)
- electrical
- personal protective equipment
- hazard communication

In addition, the guidelines require two hours from at least two of the elective topic areas and two hours from any other general industry hazards or policies or from the elective list below, with a minimum of 30 minutes spent on topics covered:

- hazardous materials
- materials handling
- machine guarding
- ergonomics
- introduction to industrial hygiene
- bloodborne pathogens
- fall protection
- safety and health programs

30-HOUR GENERAL INDUSTRY COURSE

The 30-hour general industry course is intended to provide a variety of training on safety and health to those workers with at least some safety and health responsibilities within general industry. The course emphasizes hazard identification, avoidance, control, and prevention, as well as specific OSHA standards. The program guidelines for the 30-hour course require coverage of each of the following topics (OSHA 2011b):

- An introduction to OSHA (OSH Act; General Duty Clause, inspections, general safety and health provisions, citations and penalties, record keeping, value of safety, and OSHA Web site) – 2 hours
- Managing safety and health – 2 hours
- Walking and working surfaces, including fall protection – 1 hour
- Fire and emergency preparedness (exit routes, emergency action plans, fire prevention plans, and fire protection) – 2 hours
- Electrical – 2 hours
- Personal protective equipment – 1 hour
- Materials handling – 2 hours
- Hazard communication – 1 hour

The remaining time is spent on the coverage of a minimum of five elective topics (which must add up to at least ten hours, with a minimum of 30 minutes for any topic) from the list below, along with seven optional hours related to any general industry hazards or policies and/or expanding on the mandatory or elective topics:

- hazardous materials
- permit required confined space

- powered industrial vehicles
- lockout/tagout
- fall protection
- machine guarding
- welding, cutting, and brazing
- introduction to industrial hygiene
- bloodborne pathogens
- ergonomics
- safety and health programs

10-HOUR CONSTRUCTION INDUSTRY COURSE

The 10-hour construction industry course is intended to provide a variety of training on safety and health to entry-level workers in the construction industry. This course emphasizes hazard identification, avoidance, control, and prevention. The program guidelines for the 10-hour course require a minimum of the following (OSHA 2011a):

- An introduction to OSHA – 2 hours (OSH Act; General Duty Clause, record keeping, general safety and health provisions, citations, competent person, value of safety, and OSHA Web site)
- Four hours total in each of the OSHA Focus Four Hazards—falls (minimum of 1 hour and 15 minutes), electrocution (minimum of 30 minutes), struck-by (minimum of 30 minutes), and caught in/between (minimum of 30 minutes)
- Personal protective equipment – 30 minutes
- Health hazards in construction – 30 minutes

In addition, the guidelines require two hours of electives in at least two of the topics below with at least 30 minutes per topic, the remaining four optional hours can be spent on any other construction industry hazards or policies, or on the following electives:

- hand and power tools
- materials handling
- excavations
- cranes, derricks, hoists, elevators, and conveyors
- stairways and ladders
- scaffolds

30-HOUR CONSTRUCTION INDUSTRY COURSE

The 30-hour construction industry course is intended to provide a variety of training on safety and health to those workers with at least some safety and health responsibilities within the construction industry. The course emphasizes hazard identification, avoidance, control, and prevention, as well as specific OSHA standards. The program guidelines for the 30-hour course require coverage in the following topics (OSHA 2011a):

- An introduction to OSHA – 2 hours (OSH Act; General Duty Clause, record keeping, general safety and health provisions, citations, safety programs, value of safety, and OSHA Web site)
- Managing safety and health – 2 hours
- OSHA Focus Four Hazards – 6 hours—falls (minimum of 1 hour and 15 minutes), electrocution (minimum of 30 minutes), struck-by (minimum of 30 minutes), and caught in/between (minimum of 30 minutes)
- Personal protective equipment – 2 hours
- Health hazards in construction – 2 hours
- Stairways and ladders – 1 hour

The remaining time is spent on the coverage of a minimum of six elective topics (which must add up to at least twelve hours) from the list below, along with three hours of optional topics from any of the required areas or other construction industry standards or practices, with a minimum of 30 minutes per topic:

- ergonomics
- powered industrial vehicles
- excavations
- fire protection and prevention
- materials handling, storage, and disposal
- hand and power tools
- welding and cutting
- scaffolds
- cranes, derricks, hoists, elevators, and conveyors
- concrete and masonry
- steel erection
- safety and health programs
- confined space entry
- motor vehicles (roll-over protection, overhead protection, and signs, signals, and barricades)

OSHA Web Site and Web-Based Training (eTools)

OSHA recognizes the usefulness of distributing information through the Internet for accessing standards, directives, and other official documents with links to other agencies and private sources categorized by topic. Currently, the following electronic products are available from OSHA (OSHA 2010b):

- safety and health topics
- eTools
- PowerPoint presentations

A discussion follows of the web-based tools that are especially applicable to safety and health training.

Safety and Health Topics

The primary purpose of safety and health topics is to provide easy access to current technical information that will assist employees and safety and health professionals in reducing occupational injuries and illnesses. To maintain the quality of information on these topics, the references are selected by editors who are safety and health professionals. These editors are also assisted by editorial boards to keep the topic pages current (OSHA 2010c).

OSHA currently has more than 160 topics. Examples of topics include: accident investigation, alcohol, bioterrorism, combustible dust, dry cleaning, electricity, solvents, and teen workers. A complete listing of all topics is available at the OSHA Safety and Health Topics web page (www.osha.gov/SLTC/index.html). From a safety and health training aspect, the safety and health professional can use these topics to:

- review occupational safety and health information that is categorized on over 60 technical subjects
- identify ways to recognize, evaluate, and control general workplace hazards as well as hazards specific to an industry
- access a variety of reference materials such as OSHA and non-OSHA documents, standards, compliance guidance, training slides, course handouts, video clips, and links to other Internet sites.

eTools

Electronic Tools (eTools) are interactive web-based training tools on a variety of occupational safety and health topics. Highly illustrated and interactive, they allow users to answer questions and get reliable advice on how OSHA regulations apply to their work site. Many of the eTools can be downloaded using a supplied Microsoft Windows installer program for online use; some are also available in Spanish. Examples of eTool topics are anthrax, evacuation plans, lockout/tagout, machine guarding, nursing homes, and silica. A complete listing of available eTools is available on the OSHA eTools and Electronic Products for Compliance Assistance Web site (OSHA 2010d).

PowerPoint Presentations

OSHA has developed Microsoft PowerPoint presentations on a variety of occupational safety and health topics that are particularly useful for training courses. These PowerPoint presentations can be downloaded and used for safety and health training. Examples of topics where PowerPoint presentations are available include asbestos, crane, derrick, and hoist safety, ergonomics, eye and face protection, fall protection, powered industrial trucks, and radiation. A complete listing of available PowerPoint presentations is available at the OSHA Multimedia Web site and on the OSHA Training and Reference Library Web site (OSHA 2009c).

OSHA Publications

OSHA has numerous publications related to safety and health training that can be downloaded in either HTML or PDF formats from the OSHA Publications Web site (OSHA n.d.). These publications include booklets, fact sheets, guidance documents, pocket guides, posters, QuickCards, and QuickTakes. Two very useful training publications are OSHA 2019, *OSHA Publications and Audiovisual Programs* (OSHA 1998a) and OSHA 2254, *Training Requirements in OSHA Standards and Training Guidelines* (OSHA 1998b), which was discussed earlier in this chapter. A complete listing of available training aids and materials from OSHA is available from the OSHA Outreach Training Program Web site (OSHA 2010a).

CONCLUSION

Since the passage of the OSH Act in 1970, safety and health training has played a major role in both OSHA regulatory and enforcement activities. Currently there are more than 100 OSHA standards that contain training requirements and, in 2008, two of the top ten most frequently cited serious violations in the construction industry were directly related to training in fall hazards and scaffolding (OSHA 2010c). OSHA has also expanded the number of OTI Education Center Programs from four to twenty-seven centers over the past twenty years. This has resulted in a tremendous increase in the number of individuals being trained as part of the OSHA Outreach Training Program, from 305,000 cards being issued in 2003 to 680,000 cards issued in 2008 (OSHA 2009c).

Based on the above, it is the author's belief that the role of safety and health training within OSHA will continue to expand in the twenty-first century. Safety and health professionals must continue to stay abreast of these regulatory influences on safety and health program activities as well as on the profession as a whole.

REFERENCES

Barnes, Jim. 2003. "Focus on Education Centers." *Job Safety & Health Quarterly* (Summer/Fall) 14(4):36–37.

Bureau of Labor Statistics (BLS). 2011. *Census of Fatal Occupational Injuries Charts, 1992-2010 (Preliminary Data)* (accessed October 6, 2011). www.bls.gov/iif/oshwc/cfoi/cfch0009.pdf

Lawton, Rebecca, and Dianne Parker. 1998. "Individual Difference in Accident Liability: A Review and Integrative Approach." *Human Factors* 40(4):655–682.

National Institute for Occupational Safety and Health (NIOSH). 2004. Publication No. 2004-132, *Report from the 1999 Workplace Safety & Health Training: Putting the Pieces Together and Planning for the Challenges Ahead*. Cincinnati, OH: NIOSH.

National Safety Council (NSC). 2007. *OSHA's "Top 10" for 2007* (retrieved December 2007). www.nsc.org/plus

Occupational Safety and Health Administration (OSHA). 1970. *Occupational Safety and Health Act*. www.osha.gov/pls/oshaweb/owadisp.show_document?p_table+OSHACT&p_id=2743

———. 1989. *Safety and Health Program Management Guidelines; Issuance of Voluntary Guidelines*. www.osha.gov/pls/oshaweb/owadisp.show_document?p_id=12909&p_table=FEDERAL_REGISTER

_____. 1991. 29 CFR 1926.1053(b)(15), *Safety and Health Regulations for Construction; Stairways and Ladders; Ladders* (accessed June 16, 2011). gpoaccess.goc/cgi/text/text_rdx?c=ecfr&sid=70ba0712041e435f395b18f409e17308&rgn=div8&view=text&node=29:8.1.1.1.1.24.19.4&idno=29

_____. 1995. 29 CFR 1926.504, *Fall Protection; Training Requirements.*

_____. 1996a. 29 CFR 1926.454, *Scaffolds; Training Requirements.*

_____. 1996b. *Tools for a Safety and Health Program Assessment.* www.osha.gov/doc/outreachtraining/htmlfiles/evaltool.html

_____. 1998a. OSHA 2019. *OSHA Publications and Audiovisual Programs* (accessed June 16, 2011). www.osha.gov/Publications/osha2019.pdf

_____. 1998b. *OSHA 2254: Training Requirements in OSHA Standards and Training Guidelines.* www.osha.gov/Publications/osha2254.pdf

_____. 2000. 29 CFR 1908.2, *Consultation Agreements; Definitions.* www.osha.gov/pls/oshaweb/owadisp.show/document?p_table=STANDARDS&p_id=9686

_____. 2004a. *OSHA Forms for Recording Work-Related Injuries and Illnesses.* www.osha.gov/recordkeeping/new-osha300form1-1-04.pdf

_____. 2004b. 29 CFR 19001.1, *Draft Proposed Safety and Health Program Rule*, Docket No. S&H-0027. www.osha.gov/dsg/topics/safetyhealth/nshp.html

_____. 2006. 29 CFR 1910.178(l)(1)(ii), *Occupational Health and Safety Standards; Powered Industrial Trucks* (accessed June 16, 2011). www. gpoaccess.gov/cgi/text/text-idxc=ecfr&sid=64a653e603c51230209639b4c9629cb&rgn=div8&view=text&node=29:5.1.1.1.8.4.37&idno=29

_____. 2008a. *Resource Center Loan Program.* www.osha.gov/dcsp/ote/resource-center/loan.html

_____. 2008b. *29 CFR 1910, Occupational Safety and Health Standards.* www.osha.gov/pls/oshaweb/owadisp.show_document?p_table=STANDARDS&p_id=9686

_____. 2009a. *OSHA Susan Harwood Training Grant Program.* www.osha.gov/dte/sharwood/index.html.

_____. 2009b. *Revisions to the Voluntary Protection Programs to Provide Safe and Healthful Working Conditions.* www.osha.gov/pls/oshaweb/owadisp.show_document?p_id=18042&p_table=FEDERAL_REGISTER&p_id=21385

_____. 2009c. *OSHA Directorate of Training and Education.* www.osha.gov/dcsp/ote/index.html

_____. 2009d. *OSHA Training Institute Education Centers.* www.osha.gov/fso/ote/training/edcenters/background.html

_____. 2010a. *OSHA Outreach Training Program - How to Become an Authorized Trainer.* www.osha.gov/dte/outreach/construction_ generalindustry/authorized.html

_____. 2010b. *OSHA eTools and Electronic Products for Compliance Assistance.* www.osha.gov/dts/osta/oshasoft/

_____. 2010c. *Safety and Health Topics.* www.osha.gov/SLTC/index.html

_____. 2011a. *OSHA Outreach Training Program.* www.osha.gov/dte/outreach/construction_general industry/index.html

_____. 2011b. *OSHA Outreach Training Program-Program Guidelines.* www.osha.gov/dte/outreach/construction_generalindustry/guidelines.html

Reese, Charles D. 2003. *Occupational Health and Safety Management: A Practical Approach.* Boca Raton, FL: Lewis Publishers.

Saccaro, Joseph A. 1994. *Developing Safety Training Programs: Preventing Accidents and Improving Worker Performance Through Quality Training.* New York: Van Nostrand Reinhold.

EPA SAFETY AND HEALTH TRAINING REQUIREMENTS

2

Charles Stanfill, Jr.

LEARNING OBJECTIVES

▐ Become familiar with regulatory and nonregulatory environmental safety training issues.

▐ Learn about regulatory and non-regulatory training requirements and resources available to the safety professional.

▐ Gain an understanding of the interaction among OSHA, EPA, and other training requirements for environmental safety issues.

WHAT'S IN A NAME? Safety Department. Safety Compliance. Risk Management. Safety and Loss Control. Environmental, Health, and Safety. Regardless of the departmental name used within a company or public agency, or the title used by any manager, today's safety professional has increased responsibility for environmental issues. As far back as 1996, the *Accident Prevention Manual for Business and Industry, Administration and Programs* noted that, "managers responsible for occupational safety and health are increasingly affected by developments in environmental law" (Krieger and Montgomery 1996). As green building practices, and the green industry in general, gain acceptance in today's business world, and as companies raise their social consciousness, safety and health professionals "are often assigned environmental responsibilities as well as safety responsibilities" (Ayers 2010). For additional information on this issue, refer to the "Sustainability for the Safety, Health, and Environmental Professional" chapter in this Handbook.

When dealing with environmental regulations, it is sometimes difficult to ascertain the distinction between employee safety and the public's safety. Because environmental law calls for the protection of anyone coming in contact with certain products and hazardous substances, safety professionals benefit from having a basic understanding of environmental regulations that impact their business, products, and services.

Due to a memorandum of understanding (MOU) between the Occupational Safety and Health Administration (OSHA) and the U.S. Environmental Protection Agency (EPA) to coordinate environmental enforcement activities, several environmental activities have training requirements addressed in various OSHA standards. Those that involve hazardous waste, hazardous substances, and waste products tend to be the most prominent. This means that occupational safety, health, and environmental compliance issues are becoming even more intertwined. With Homeland Security issues such as chemical, biological, and biochemical threats getting increased attention from both the public and private sector, safety professionals are or will be tasked for greater involvement.

This chapter introduces the reader to a variety of environmental training issues and provides information regarding required and recommended training. Where available, references and resources for environmental training are provided.

To make this chapter as effective and user-friendly as possible, regulatory citations for promulgated EPA and OSHA standards will be provided so that readers can selectively choose to review those that apply to their workplace situation.

THE ENVIRONMENTAL PROTECTION AGENCY

The EPA was established in December 1970 in response to the growing public demand for cleaner water, air, and land. As new threats became known (hazardous and toxic spills, sewage, and wastewater spills), additional responsibilities were placed with the EPA to assist in those areas.

Following the terrorist attacks of September 11, 2001, the EPA was designated by a Presidential Decision Directive as the lead federal agency for reducing the vulnerability of the chemical industry and hazardous materials sector of our nation's infrastructure. The U.S. EPA maintains ten regional offices, each of which is responsible for several states and territories. Most states also have a regulatory agency that is responsible for environmental enforcement. (See Appendix A at the end of the chapter for a listing of the EPA regional offices.)

According to its history statement, "The U.S. Environmental Protection Agency was established in 1970 to consolidate in one agency a variety of federal research, monitoring, standard-setting and enforcement activities to ensure environmental protection. EPA's mission is to protect human health and to safeguard the natural environment—air, water, and land—upon which life depends" (www.epa.gov/history/timeline/index.htm). Since the EPA's inception, environmental programs have expanded to include programs for:

- air quality
- effluents
- pesticides
- water
- noise abatement
- solid waste
- radiation
- toxic substances

By memorandums of agreement, regulations, and other avenues, several environmentally related training issues are found in the U.S. Energy Department, the Federal Emergency Management Agency (FEMA), the U.S. Nuclear Regulatory Commission (NRC), OSHA, and other agencies. The states also have state-managed environmental programs with varying degrees of training requirements, recommendations, and resources. State OSHA and environmental programs may also have unique training requirements. Check the state where the operations are conducted to become aware of all environmental training requirements that may impact that facility and operations. A listing of state agencies responsible for environmental enforcement is available at the EPA Web site.

If an employer has overseas operations, then familiarity with the environmental, safety, and health regulations of any country where the operation is domiciled is important.

EPA/OSHA REQUIRED TRAINING
Asbestos

During the late 1960s, asbestos became a safety and health issue in the United States as evidence emerged indicating that asbestos fibers were a dangerous health risk. In the 1970s, the U.S. government initiated action to address the risks associated with asbestos; in the 1980s, health concerns led to the new industry of asbestos abatement.

Training issues surrounding asbestos are dictated by the job functions performed while working with or around asbestos-containing material (ACM). The job functions are designated as Class I, II, III, or IV work, and they are further defined in 29 CFR 1926.1101. Accordingly, training issues became paramount for those employees who worked with or around ACM. The main areas and training needs for those working with ACM can be found at the citations listed below:

Asbestos Abatement

- Training for asbestos operations, including repair, removal, enclosing, or encapsulating ACM, is covered in 40 CFR Part 763, Subpart E, and 29 CFR Part 1926.1101.
- Appendix B of the *Inspection Procedures for Occupational Exposure to Asbestos*, OSHA Directive CPL 2-2.63 (REVISED) (1995), includes a summary and comparison of OSHA and EPA training requirements.

Asbestos Awareness

- Employee information and training is covered in 40 CFR 763.92(a)(1) and OSHA 29 CFR 1910.1001(j)(7)(i). This training must be provided according to OSHA standards, but only to "employees who are exposed to airborne concentrations of asbestos at or above the PEL and/or excursion limit." The employer must ensure employee participation in the program. An annual retraining requirement is included in the standard for those with exposure.
- OSHA 29 CFR 1910.1001(j)(7)(iv) requires that awareness training must be provided to housekeeping staff working near asbestos-containing material or presumed asbestos-containing material (PACM).

Asbestos-Competent Person

The training varies according to the type of asbestos work being performed (as defined in 29 CFR Part 1926.1101). For Class I and II work, personnel must have training in a special course that meets the criteria of EPA's Model Accreditation Plan (40 CFR 763) for supervisor, or its equivalent. For Class III and IV work, the training must be provided in a manner consistent with EPA requirements for training of local education-agency maintenance and custodial staff as set forth in 40 CFR 763.92 (a)(2).

Asbestos Operations and Maintenance

Standards 40 CFR 763.92(a)(1), 40 CFR 763.92(a)(2), 29 CFR 1910.1101, and 29 CFR 1926.1101(k)(9) require asbestos training for the various types of asbestos operations and maintenance activities.

In addition, the employer shall maintain all employee training records for one year beyond the last date of employment of that employee.

Hazardous Waste Operations (HAZWOPER) and Emergency Response Standards

Found at 29 CFR 1910.120(a)(1)(i-v) and 29 CFR 1926.65 (a)(1)(i-v), HAZWOPER began as the Comprehensive Environmental Response, Compensation and Liability Act (CERCLA). This act was amended by the Superfund Amendments and Reauthorization Act (SARA) on October 17, 1986. SARA eventually became known as the HAZWOPER rule.

HAZWOPER training is required to ensure that employees are trained to perform the emergency response and clean-up activities associated with the release of hazardous materials expected of them in a safe manner. Employers must train their employees in accordance with paragraph 29 CFR 1910.120(e) and 1926.65. The training must occur during times that the employee is paid for work.

Training requirements are determined by the type of response activity an employee will be involved with during a spill. The various types of response categories covered in the OSHA requirements are listed below:

HAZWOPER Categories

- General Site Workers (40 hours of training). These are usually equipment operators, general laborers, and supervisory personnel who are engaged in hazardous substance removal or other activities that expose or potentially expose them to hazardous substances and health hazards.

- Occasional Site Workers (24 hours of training). These are workers who are occasionally on site for a specific, limited task such as, but not limited to, groundwater monitoring, land surveying, or geophysical surveying, and who are unlikely to be exposed over the permissible exposure limits and the minimum of one day actual field experience under the direct supervision of a trained, experienced supervisor.
- Supervisors (40 hours of training). On-site management and supervisors directly responsible for, or who supervise, employees engaged in hazardous waste operations. These individuals are also to receive 40 hours initial training and three days of supervised field experience. This particular training may be reduced to 24 hours and one day under certain circumstances. See 29 CFR 1910.120(e)(4).
- OSHA 29 CFR 1910.120(e)(8) states that employees specified in paragraph (e)(1) of this section, and managers and supervisors specified in paragraph (e)(4), shall receive 8 hours of refresher training annually.
- Treatment, storage, and disposal operations (24 hours of training). 29 CFR 1910.120(p)(7)(i) notes that "The employer shall develop and implement a training program which is part of the employer's safety and health program, for employees exposed to health hazards or hazardous substances at Treatment, Storage and Disposal (TSD) Facilities operations. . ." In addition to the initial training, for facility employees regulated under the Resource Conservation and Recovery Act (RCRA), refresher training shall be for 8 hours annually. A written certificate attesting that the employees have successfully completed the necessary training must be provided. It is the responsibility of the employer to develop this training, whether internally or through a third party.
- Hazmat Technicians (24 hours of training). These are individuals who respond to releases

or potential releases for the purpose of stopping the release. Employees with less aggressive responsibilities, such as performing defensive actions (First Responder Operations Level) or being able to recognize a spill and initiate the facility's Emergency Response Plan (First Responder Awareness Level), are required to receive 8 hours and "as necessary" initial training, respectively.

- Incident Command System (ICS) (16 hours of training). Due to the nature of spill response, where typically multiple agencies respond, such responding employees must have an understanding of the ICS. Additionally, it is possible for a first responder at the awareness level to be called upon to assume the duties of incident commander (IC) until a more senior and appropriately trained individual arrives at the response site. In that case, the IC shall have received at least 24 hours of training equal to the first responder operations level and additional competencies as listed in 29 CFR 1910.120(q)(6)(v)(A)-(F). FEMA has an online training course that is a good beginning to understanding the ICS (www.fema.gov/IS100b/index.htm).
- Hazardous Waste Refresher Training. Employees who have taken the 24- or 40-hour OSHA HAZWOPER course are required to maintain their certification by taking an 8-hour annual refresher course. Annual refresher courses are also required for First Responder Operations Level (4 hours) and Awareness Level (as needed) responders.
- The U.S. Department of Transportation in 49 CFR Part 172, Subpart H, requires employees who work with or transport hazardous materials be provided various types of training noted in 49 CFR Part 172.704. Training requirements include general awareness/familiarization training, function-specific training, safety training, security awareness training, and in-depth security training. Some of the training can be satisfied through proper documentation

of related OSHA- or EPA-required training (29 CFR 1910.120).

Some useful resources for HAZWOPER, Haz Mat, and RCRA operations are also found in OSHA Directive CPL-02-02-071 (OSHA 2003). Additional guidance for HAZWOPER training is located in the following resources:

- Nonmandatory Appendix E for 1910.120 and 1926.65 (Training Curriculum Guidelines).
- Chapter 4, "Training," of the four-agency document, *Occupational Safety and Health Guidance Manual for Hazardous Waste Site Activities* (NIOSH 1985). It provides a chart listing the required training by job category.
- Chapter 4, "Training," in EPA publication 9285.1-03, *Standard Operating Safety Guides*, which provides a more detailed explanation of the various levels of training for workers at EPA-regulated sites (EPA 1992).

Hospital/Medical/Infectious Waste Incinerators

EPA 40 CFR 60.53(c) deals with operator training and qualification requirements for these incinerators.

In 1998, a MOU between EPA and the American Hospital Association (AHA) was signed to reduce the amount of pollution generated by the healthcare provider industry. The hospital safety practitioner should be aware of EPA 40 CFR 60 Subpart E—*Standards of Performance for Hospital/Medical/Infectious Waste Incinerators for Which Construction is Commenced After June 20, 1996.* The Texas Commission on Environmental Quality (TCEQ) has developed a useful flowchart in PDF format to assist in understanding the requirements (www.tceq.state.tx.us.assets.public/permitting/air/Rules/Federal/60/ec/f60ec.pdf).

Lastly, the Joint Commission on Accreditation of Healthcare Organizations is a resource the healthcare safety professional should use for areas of recommended training.

Lead

Employees who may be exposed to lead in the workplace, whether in general industry or construction, are required to maintain training depending upon tasks and exposure levels. These include:

- Awareness: OSHA 1910.1025(l) and 1926.62(l). Each employer who has a workplace in which there is a potential exposure to airborne lead at any level shall inform employees of the content of Appendices A and B of this regulation.
- Abatement: OSHA 1926.62(l) describes the training of employees who have a daily exposure to lead at or above the action level. EPA 40 CFR 745.225-226 describes the accreditation of training programs for lead-based paint in target housing and child-occupied facilities. Currently, contractors performing this type of work in child-occupied facilities and in pre-1978 housing must be certified as a lead-safe certified contractor and use lead-safe work practices. The certification includes an 8-hour training course from an accredited trainer. (A 4-hour refresher course may be substituted if an eligible renovation course has previously been completed.) The location of accredited trainers is available from the EPA Web site.

Oil Spills

EPA 40CFR 109.5(d)(1) specifies that an oil-discharge response operating team must consist of trained personnel. The response team can be from the public or private sector.

Training elements for oil storage facilities that must comply with the Spill Prevention, Control and Countermeasures regulation of the Clean Water Act are found at 40 CFR Subchapter D, Part 112.

Following the April 20, 2010, Gulf of Mexico oil spill and subsequent clean-up operations, training requirements were added for the different classes of responders, including volunteers. If a company allows employees to volunteer for such community service projects, the company's professional safety staff must

If you are:	You must receive:
Doing work that does NOT involve materials contaminated by the spill	45 minutes of site training [Module 2 or equivalent Site Health Safety and Environment (HSE) Orientation or equivalent]
Doing work picking up tar balls and other oil-contaminated debris on beaches and along the shoreline	4 hours of site training [Module 3 – Shoreline Spilled Oil Response] NOTE: These workers will be supervised by someone with 40 hours of hazardous waste operations training.
Doing work at decontamination areas, handling or cleaning oily boom and equipment, or using vacuum trucks and portable skimmers to clean up weathered oil along the shoreline	45 minutes of site training [Module 2 or equivalent Site Health Safety and Environment (HSE) Orientation] and 40 hours of hazardous waste operations training. NOTE: These workers will be supervised by someone with 40 hours of hazardous waste operations training. BP is not providing the 40-hour hazardous waste operations training.

FIGURE 1. Oil-spill training requirements (*Source:* www.osha.gov/oilspills/ training.html)

ensure that volunteers are aware of the necessary training requirements. The relevant training categories and desired training requirements are shown in Figure 1.

Job-specific training requirements related to the various on-shore and off-shore job tasks for an oil-spill response can be found on the EPA Web site.

Pesticide Safety Training for Workers

All of the training issues surrounding the various types of duties and timelines for training an employee who applies or handles a pesticide regulated by the Federal Insecticide, Fungicide, and Rodenticide Act (FIFRA) are listed in 40 CFR 170.130, as well as the required content of the training program. The regulation addresses the requirements of the trainer and the content to be provided to workers who use and apply pesticides, as well as workers who are exposed to pesticides. Training requirements (initial and continuing education) are also imposed by different agencies within the various states. The National Pesticide Information Center (NPIC) is a respectable online resource one can use to identify training requirements for states and territories of the United States. The NPIC site provides links for

each state's agency that regulates pesticide use and application for both individuals and corporations (npic.orst.edu/state_agencies.html#).

Risk Management Plan–40 CFR Part 68

With passage of the Clean Air Act Amendments of 1990, (Section 112r), the EPA was required to publish regulations and guidance for the prevention of accidental chemical releases at facilities using substances that pose a significant risk if released. The regulations are available at www.epa.gov/emergencies/lawsregs. htm#fraccident.

The regulations require companies, regardless of size, that use certain listed, regulated flammable and toxic substances to have a risk management program (RMP) in place. The RMP process is similar in scope to the OSHA process safety management process. Training requirements for the RMP are based on defined criteria and apply to companies meeting the Program Level 2 and Level 3 classifications. The various program levels and a decision tree can be found at www.epa.gov/emergencies/docs/chem/Chap-02-final.pdf.

Training requirements for the RMP Program 2 level are found in 40 CFR 68.54 (a)-(d) and 40 CFR 68.71 for the Program 3 level. Both program levels have requirements for refresher training at least every three years.

Radiation Protection

The U.S. Department of Energy governs the majority of training requirements associated with ionizing radiation.

The general training requirements for radiation workers are covered in 10 CFR 19. It requires that all individuals who, in the course of employment, are likely to receive an annual dose of radiation in excess of 100 millirems must receive adequate training to protect themselves.

Title 10 of the Code of Federal Regulations covers training requirements for various occupational areas using or involved with ionizing radiation. Some of the more common ones include:

- 10 CFR 34: Licenses for industrial radiography and radiation safety
- 10 CFR 35.900: Medical use of by-product material, including training requirements for:
  - the radiation safety officer
  - employees performing various laboratory processes and diagnostics using radioactive materials
  - employees using various diagnostic equipment, imaging and localization studies and procedures using radioactive devices
- 10 CFR 50.120: Training and qualification of nuclear power plant personnel
- 10 CFR 76.95: Training for employees who operate, maintain, or modify gas diffusion plants
- 10 CFR 835.901: Radiation safety training for Department of Energy employees
- 10 CFR 1046.12-DOE: Protective force personnel physical fitness training

OSHA 29 CFR 1926.53(b) indicates that individuals performing, "any activity that involves the use of radioactive materials or X-rays, whether or not under license from the Nuclear Regulatory Commission, shall be performed by competent persons specially trained in the proper and safe operation of such equipment."

Additional information regarding training for exposure to radioactive materials is found in the OSHA HAZWOPER standard.

Consideration should be given to the following training for employees working around or near ionizing or nonionizing radiation:

- training in principles of radiation protection
- training in shielding design
- training in shielding evaluation
- the specific type of machine application
- training in basic radiological health
- radiation instrument calibration

Resource Conservation and Recovery Act (RCRA)

RCRA has training requirements that cover both large- and small-quantity generators of waste, as regulated by the EPA in 40 CFR Part 265. Safety practitioners need to know if their company generates waste, and if so, in what quantities. Additional awareness of storage times and disposal locations may also be a factor in determining training requirements. This knowledge helps to establish the type of RCRA training needed. Topic areas to consider include:

- Large Quantity Generator (LQG): EPA 40CFR 262.34(a)(4)
- Small Quantity Generator (SQG): EPA 40CFR 262.34(d)(5)(iii)
- RCRA requirements for treatment, storage, and disposal facilities (TSDF): EPA 40CFR 264.16 and 265.16

Hazardous Waste Treatment, Storage, and Disposal Facilities–Solid Waste

Personnel training is covered by 40 CFR 264.16(a)(1). Facility personnel must successfully complete a program of classroom instruction or on-the-job training that teaches them to perform their duties in a way that ensures the facility's compliance with the requirements of this part. The owner or operator must ensure that this program includes all the elements described in the document required under paragraph (d)(3) of this section. *Note:* Part 270 of this chapter requires that owners and operators submit, with Part B of the RCRA permit application, an outline of the training program used (or to be used) at the facility and a brief description of how the training program is designed to meet actual job tasks.

Spill Management Facility Response Planning

EPA 40 CFR 112.21 describes the requirements for facility response training, along with and drills/exercises for facilities required to comply with the Spill Prevention, Control, and Countermeasures requirements in this section.

Universal Waste Handlers

EPA 40 CFR 273.16 states that the employer must inform all employees who handle or have responsibility for managing universal waste about the proper handling and emergency procedures appropriate to the type(s) of universal waste located at the facility.

Underground Storage Tank Training

EPA 40 CFR 280 TNRCC describes the requirements for contractors and supervisors who install and/or repair underground storage tanks.

RECOMMENDED TRAINING
Bioterrorism (Including Biological and Chemical Response) Training

The U.S. Department of Homeland Security Web site provides information on the following training:

- training resources, grants, and requirements (www.dhs.gov/files/training/prepresrecovery. htm)
- response and recovery (www.dhs.gov/ xfrstresp/training)

- first responder training resources (www.dhs. gov/dhspublic/display?theme=63&content= 3547)

Clandestine Methamphetamine Laboratories

This is a unique and growing area that has safety implications for all (i.e., law enforcement, emergency medical and fire department personnel, as well as those conducting regulatory environmental activities) who respond to the site of a clandestine methamphetamine ("meth") laboratory. Although this activity is not specifically referred to by name in the OSHA standard, the safety training information in the hazardous waste clean-up operations standard (OSHA 1010.120) is required to be followed for meth-lab responses and remediation. Training in the ICS is also recommended, as several agencies are involved in responding to meth labs. The U.S. Drug Enforcement Agency (DEA) offers a 40-hour training class to law-enforcement officers that is designed to certify attendees as Clandestine Laboratory Site Safety Officers. The DEA training meets the 40-hour OSHA HAZWOPER training requirement. Training in hazard assessment, PPE assessment and use, budgeting, clean up, and site security issues are good starting points.

Mold Assessment and Remediation

At the time of this writing, there are no specific OSHA or EPA training requirements for mold remediation. However, there are recommendations for PPE when working around known or suspected mold growth, and OSHA has indoor air-quality standards as well. Both OSHA and the EPA have resources available to assist in identifying training for mold-related issues.

The reader should refer to OSHA Safety and Health Information Bulletins on mold and EPA Office of Radiation and Indoor Air publications 402-F-93-005 and 402-K-01-001).

National Pollutant Discharge Elimination System (NPDES)

The NPDES program covers animal-feeding operations, combined sewer overflows, pretreatment, sanitary sewer overflows, and stormwater issues. Safety training for these areas is not located in a single resource, requiring the safety practitioner to be aware of the types of operations being conducted by the employer and to use OSHA training to ensure safe operations at NPDES sites. EPA provides NPDES training courses and workshops, but primarily for any administrative procedures surrounding the permitting process. Additionally, some states accept various OSHA-required training as fulfillment of the water/wastewater operator license/certification training requirements.

Regulatory Inspections and Assessments

State and private employers that conduct regulatory inspections need to ensure that hazard assessments are conducted and appropriate training is provided.

Green Building/Green Industry/ Environmental Sustainability

The need for safety training in the green industry is becoming increasingly apparent. In a January 2010 online science blog, NIOSH noted that: "Safety and health should be considered an essential component for all green job training, in addition to training on the skills workers need to complete job tasks" (NIOSH 2010b). NIOSH has also addressed this issue in an online publication, *Prevention through Design: Green, Safe and Healthy Jobs* (NIOSH 2010a).

As environmental sustainability issues move into the business world and stakeholders express a desire for corporate social responsibility, safety and health (S&H) professionals may find themselves with increased environmental responsibilities and will need to identify areas of training that address sustainability issues and environmental management systems (EMS). S&H professionals who have environmental management responsibilities will want to become familiar with the latest environmental management standard, ISO 14001. Employees of an ISO 14001-certified company that performs operations having the potential to create a negative environmental impact must be trained according to section 4.4.2 of the ISO 14001 standard.

ENVIRONMENTAL EDUCATIONAL TRAINING RESOURCES

While there are many companies and consultants that offer training and education on environmental issues, several links on the EPA Web site can assist in locating both private and government-supported environmental training topics. The EPA Web site also offers educational and informational resources and databases for environmental topics.

Examples of the training resources accessed from the EPA Web site include the following:

- CERCLA Education Center (Superfund Training). The CERCLA Education Center (CEC) is a unique training forum implemented by the EPA's Office of Solid Waste and Emergency Response (OSWER) Technology Innovation Office (TIO). It offers EPA on-scene coordinators (OSC), remedial project managers (RPM), site-assessment managers (SAM), and other environmental professionals' training courses on the many aspects of Superfund and the latest environmental technologies. The courses provide basic definitions and procedures, and detailed presentations on EPA's role with other federal agencies as well. CEC courses have been developed cooperatively by TIO, the Office of Emergency and Remedial Response, the Office of Acquisition Management, the Office of Enforcement and Compliance Assurance, and the Office of Research and Development. Site managers from many EPA regions also provided technical advice, comment, and support.

Environmental Response Training Program (ERTP) Courses

The Environmental Response Training Program is directed by the EPA's Environmental Response Team Center and derives its authority to develop and present various technical, health, and safety courses from CERCLA. The program is designed to train personnel from federal, tribal, state, and local government agencies in hazardous waste site investigation and remediation practices and procedures, as well as emergency response to hazardous chemical releases. Registration, required for taking the courses, can be accomplished on the Web site (www.ertpvu.org).

ADDITIONAL RESOURCES FOR EPA TRAINING

National Institute for Occupational Safety and Health (NIOSH)

Through university-based Education and Research Centers (ERCs), NIOSH supports academic degree programs and research-training opportunities in the core areas of industrial hygiene, occupational health nursing, occupational medicine, and occupational safety, plus specialized areas relevant to the occupational safety and health field. There are seventeen regional ERCs throughout the country. (NIOSH resources are more fully discussed in the next chapter.)

The Occupational Safety and Health Education and Research Centers were established by NIOSH to ensure an ample supply of well-trained professionals in the area of occupational safety and health.

In addition to the academic training programs, NIOSH supports ERC short-term continuing education (CE) programs for occupational safety and health professionals, and others with worker safety and health responsibilities. A current CE course schedule for all NIOSH Education and Research Centers can be found on the NIOSH ERC Web site (www.niosh-erc.org), or use the toll free number, 1-800-35-NIOSH (1-800-356-4674), or contact the NIOSH Publications Office. The reader should refer to the next chapter in this section for additional details and resources associated with NIOSH.

Trainex

Note: This information is for the convenience of the reader. Neither the author, the EPA, nor ASSE endorse any private-sector Web site, product, or service.

Trainex (www.trainex.org), in partnership with the Interstate Technology Regulatory Council and the EPA, is a provider that offers a range of training courses and information to the EPA, other federal agencies, and state, tribal, and local staff involved in hazardous waste management and remediation. Both classroom and Internet-based courses are available.

Many EPA and other federal offices provide training relevant to hazardous waste remediation, site characterization, risk assessment, emergency response, site/incident management, counterterrorism, and the community's role in site management and clean up. Some of the courses that have been provided by Trainex are listed in Appendix B at the end of the chapter. It provides insight to the reader into the varied array of environmental topics that are available beyond the basic Superfund courses.

Additional environmental training resources include:

- *Nonprofit course providers.* These include University of California, Berkeley; Georgia Tech; the University of Kansas; and the University of Utah.
- *Publications.* Various publications related to training requirements and resources for hazard communication, hazardous waste operations, RCRA, respiratory protection, and other topics are available from the OSHA Web site (www.osha.gov/pls/publications/pubindex.list).
- *EPA Education Center.* The EPA Education Center (www.epa.gov/teachers) is designed for teachers and educators. It has several useful resources that can be utilized by the environmental trainer. The resources are valuable training aids when the trainer needs to provide an overview of environmental issues to employees, management, and clients.
- *Miscellaneous Resources.* Appendix C at the end of this chapter lists EPA-hosted or EPA-sponsored Web sites that contain information related to a variety of environmental safety training. Some are at no cost for those who meet the criteria.

PROFESSIONAL ORGANIZATIONS FOR THE ENVIRONMENTAL SAFETY TRAINER

ASSE and ANSI collaborated on the consensus standard, ANSI/ASSE Z490.1-2001, *Criteria for Accepted Practices in Safety, Health, and Environmental Training* (ASSE 2001) to provide safety professionals with training methodologies they can use with assurance.

There are several accreditation and certification programs for trainers (Nilson 2001). There are also several corporate agencies that provide a safety training designation upon completion of their paid course.

Three environmental training certification programs related to occupational safety are listed here. Included for the reader's use is some brief information about the programs. Again, neither the author, the EPA, nor ASSE endorses any Web site, product, or service.

The National Environmental, Safety and Health Training Association

Founded in 1977 with support and assistance from the EPA, the National Environmental, Safety and Health Training Association is an international, nonprofit educational and professional society dedicated to promoting competency and excellence in education and training, with an emphasis on environmental, safety, and health training. The Certified Environmental Safety & Health Trainer designation (CET) is a voluntary credentialing system based on the certification guidelines published by the Council of Engineering and Scientific Specialty Board (CESB). Certification requires measuring instructional knowledge (as one competency indicator) and confirming technical knowledge in the following areas:

- emergency response
- management and transportation of hazardous materials and waste
- occupational safety and health
- radiation protection
- wastewater treatment
- water treatment

National Association of Safety Professionals

The National Association of Safety Professionals (www.naspweb.com) Board of Certification provides third-party validation of your specific safety training, planning, or inspection/auditing knowledge, based upon the qualifications recommended by ANSI, OSHA, and the Courts. It offers the Certified HAZWOPER Training Specialist (HTS) certification for environmental safety training.

Institute of Hazardous Materials Management

The Institute of Hazardous Materials Management (IHMM) (www.ihmm.org) was founded as a non-profit organization in 1984, and launched the Certified Hazardous Materials Manager (CHMM) Program in June of that year. The Certified Hazardous Materials Manager Program is accredited by The Council of Engineering and Scientific Specialty Boards.

CONCLUSION

The key points in this chapter include the need for students and safety professionals to understand the interrelationship between OSHA training requirements and EPA training requirements. Several EPA training requirements are covered in the OSHA standard. The safety practitioner needs to be aware of the interconnectivity between the two agencies with regard to safety training issues.

REFERENCES

American Society of Safety Engineers (ASSE). 2001. *ANSI/ASSE Z490.1-2001. Criteria for Accepted Practices in Safety. Health, and Environmental Training*. Des Plaines, IL: ASSE.

Ayers, David, M.S., CSP, CHHM. "Environmental Aspects & Impacts." *Professional Safety Magazine*. February, 2010.

Environmental Protection Agency (EPA). 2006. *CFR Title 40: Protection of Environment* (retrieved August 2006). www.epa.gov/epahome/cfr40.htm

National Institute of Occupational Safety and Health (NIOSH). 1985 (October). *Occupational Safety and Health Guidance Manual for Hazardous Waste Site Activities* (Publication No. 85-115). Cincinnati, OH: NIOSH.

_____. 2010a. *Going Green: Safe and Healthy Jobs* (accessed October 20, 2011). www.cdc.gov/niosh/blog/nsb 010410_green.html

_____. 2010b. *Prevention through Design: Green, Safe and Healthy Jobs* (accessed February 19, 2010). www.cdc.gov/niosh/topics/PtD/greenjobs.html

National Safety Council (NSC). 1996. *Accident Prevention Manual for Business & Industry: Administration & Programs*. 10th ed. Gary R. Krieger and John F. Montgomery, eds. Itasca, IL: NSC.

Nilson, Carolyn, ed. 2001. *Training and Development Yearbook*. Paramus, NJ: Prentice Hall.

Occupational Safety and Health Administration (OSHA). 1995. *Guidance Manual for Hazardous Waste Site Activities* (accessed June 20, 2010). www.osha.gov/Publications/ complinks/OSHG-HazWaste/4agency.html
_____. 2003. *OSHA Directive Number CPL 02-02-071. Technical Enforcement and Assistance Guidelines for*

Hazardous Waste Site and RCRA Corrective Action Clean-up Operations. Washington, D.C.: Department of Labor.
Schroll, R. Craig. "Emergency Response Training—How to Plan, Conduct & Evaluate for Success." *Professional Safety Magazine*. December 2002.

APPENDIX A: EPA REGIONAL OFFICES

Region 1 (CT, MA, ME, NH, RI, VT)
Environmental Protection Agency
1 Congress St. Suite 1100
Boston, MA 02114-2023
www.epa.gov/region01/
Phone: (617) 918-1111
Fax: (617) 565-3660
Toll free within Region 1: (888) 372-7341

Region 2 (NJ, NY, PR, VI)
Environmental Protection Agency
290 Broadway
New York, NY 10007-1866
www.epa.gov/region02/
Phone: (212) 637-3000
Fax: (212) 637-3526

Region 3 (DC, DE, MD, PA, VA, WV)
Environmental Protection Agency
1650 Arch Street
Philadelphia, PA 19103-2029
www.epa.gov/region03/
Phone: (215) 814-5000
Fax: (215) 814-5103
Toll free: (800) 438-2474
Email: r3public@epa.gov

Region 4 (AL, FL, GA, KY, MS, NC, SC, TN)
Environmental Protection Agency
Atlanta Federal Center
61 Forsyth Street, SW
Atlanta, GA 30303-3104
www.epa.gov/region04/
Phone: (404) 562-9900
Fax: (404) 562-8174
Toll free: (800) 241-1754

Region 5 (IL, IN, MI, MN, OH, WI)
Environmental Protection Agency
77 West Jackson Boulevard
Chicago, IL 60604-3507
www.epa.gov/region5/
Phone: (312) 353-2000
Fax: (312) 353-4135
Toll free within Region 5: (800) 621-8431

Region 6 (AR, LA, NM, OK, TX)
Environmental Protection Agency
Fountain Place 12th Floor, Suite 1200
1445 Ross Avenue
Dallas, TX 75202-2733
www.epa.gov/region06/
Phone: (214) 665-2200
Fax: (214) 665-7113
Toll free within Region 6: (800) 887-6063

Region 7 (IA, KS, MO, NE)
Environmental Protection Agency
901 North 5th Street
Kansas City, KS 66101
www.epa.gov/region07/
Phone: (913) 551-7003
Toll free: (800) 223-0425

Region 8 (CO, MT, ND, SD, UT, WY)
Environmental Protection Agency
999 18th Street Suite 500
Denver, CO 80202-2466
www.epa.gov/region08/
Phone: (303) 312-6312
Fax: (303) 312-6339
Toll free: (800) 227-8917
Email: r8eisc@epa.gov

Region 9 (AZ, CA, HI, NV)
Environmental Protection Agency
75 Hawthorne Street
San Francisco, CA 94105
www.epa.gov/region09/
Phone: (415) 947-8000
(866) EPA-WEST (toll free in Region 9)
Fax: (415) 947-3553
Email: r9.info@epa.gov

Region 10 (AK, ID, OR, WA)
Environmental Protection Agency
1200 Sixth Avenue
Seattle, WA 98101
www.epa.gov/region10/
Phone: (206) 553-1200
Fax: (206) 553-0149
Toll free: (800) 424-4372

APPENDIX B: SAMPLING OF TRAINING COURSES OFFERED BY TRAINEX

2nd Civilian-Military Anthrax Response Technical Workshop

Application of Transport Optimization Codes to Groundwater Pump-and-Treat Systems

ASTM Phase I/Phase II Training

Bevill Amendment and Phase IV LDR Rule Workshop (U.S. EPA - Region 4)

Continuing Challenge Hazmat Workshop

Data Quality Objective Process Workshop

Data Validation Course

DOT Training for Offerers of Bulk and Non-bulk Hazmat Packages

Environmental Stability of Chemicals in Sediments

ESAT Project Officer Training

Hazard Ranking System

Identification of Regulated Hazardous Waste Course (U.S. EPA - Region 4)

Introduction to Environmental Management Systems

Management of Ordnance and Explosives at Closed, Transferred and Transferring Ranges (CTT) and Other Sites

Microbiology Workshop

Oilfield Production Facility Training

OSC Readiness Training

Permeable Reactive Barriers (In Situ): Application and Deployment

Pollution Prevention (P2) Training (U.S. EPA - Region 4)

Quality Assurance Project Plans (QAPPs) Workshop (U.S. EPA - Region 4)

Quickscore/Superscreen Training Course

RCRA Brownfields Prevention Initiative (U.S. EPA - Region 4)

RCRA Hotline Modules

RCRA Organic Air Standards Permitting and Compliance Training (U.S. EPA - Region 4)

RCRA Miscellaneous Units Permit And Compliance Training Course (U.S. EPA - Region 4)

RCRA Reforms Corrective Action Conference (U.S. EPA - Region 4)

RCRA Seminar (U.S. EPA - Region 4)

Risk Communication and Decision Making (U.S. EPA - Region 4)

Spill Prevention Control and Countermeasure

Temporary Relocation

Urban Rivers Forum Meeting

Achieving Data Quality - Developing & Review of Quality Assurance Project Plans (QAPPs)

Asthma Summit

Basic Inspector Training (BIT) (U.S. EPA - Region 10)

Community Involvement Outreach and Training Week (U.S. EPA - Region 4)

Customer Service/Communication Skills (U.S. EPA - Region 4)

Data Quality Objectives (DQO) Managing Uncertainty and Systematic Planning for Environmental Decision Making

Designing Your EMS: A Federal Facilities Workshop

Drum Job 101

EPA Region 10 Sponsored McCoy RCRA Seminar

EPA Region III Emergency Preparedness and Prevention Conference

Five Year Review Training (U.S. EPA - Region 4)

Hazardous Waste Operations and Emergency Response 8-Hour Refresher

In-situ Contaminated Sediment Capping Workshop

Leadership 2000 (U.S. EPA - Region 4)

Managing Conflict (U.S. EPA - Region 4)

Mobile 6 Modeling Course - Various Locations

National Superfund Radiation Meeting

On-Site Insight Training

Planning and Using Data for Site Assessment

PREscore Training Course

Quality Management Plan Workshop

Radiochemistry Workshop

RCRA Corrective Action Streamlined Orders (Internet-based seminar)

RCRA Corrective Action Workshop

RCRA Orientation/Permit Writers (U.S. EPA - Region 4)

Region 4 Brownfields Workshop

RevTech Conference - Cleaning Up Contaminated Properties for Reuse and Revitalization: Effection Technical Approaches and Tools

SPCC Inspector Training Short (8-Hour) Course

Superfund Hotline Training Modules

Triad Experts Training

Vapor Intrusion into Indoor Air: Introduction to OSWER Guidance (Internet-based seminar)

APPENDIX C: RESOURCES FOR ENVIRONMENTAL SAFETY TRAINING

Air Pollution Training Institute (APTI)	www.epa.gov/air/oaqps/eog
Alternative Dispute Resolution Training	www.epa.gov/adr/cprc_training.html
American Indian Environmental Office (AIEO)	www.epa.gov/aboutwpa/oia.html#aieo
Asbestos - National Directory of AHERA Accredited Courses (NDAAC)	www.epa.gov/asbestos/pubs/ncaac.html
CAMEO Training (Computer Aided Management of Environmental Operations)	www.epa.gov/emergencies/content/cameo/index.html
CERCLA Training Modules	www.epa.gov/wastes/inforesources/pubs/training/olaw.pfd
Chemical Information Exchange Newtork (CIEN) Project	jpl.estis.net/commuities/cien
CLU-IN Courses and Conferences	www.clu-in.org/courses
Drinking Water Academy	www.epa.gov/learn/training/dwatraining/
Evaluation Training	www.epa.gov/evaluate/training.htm
FIELDS Training–Region 5	www.epa.gov/region5fieldshtm/training.htm
Multi-Agency Radiation Surveys and Site Investigation Manual (MARSSIM) Training	www.epa.gov/radiation/marssim/training.html
National Association for Remedial Project Managers (NARPM) Training Program	www.epa.gov/oamsrpod.hcsc/NARPM
National Center for Environmental Assessment	cfpub2.epa.gov/ncea/basicinfo.htm
National Center for Environmental Economics (NCEE)	yosemite.epa.gov/ee/epa/eed.nsf/Webpages/homepage
National Enforcement Training Institute (NETI)	www.epa.gov/compliance/training/neti/index.html
Office of International Affairs	epa.gov/aboutepa/oia.html
Oil Spill Training	www.epa.gov/oem/content/learning/respmgmt.htm
On-Scene Coordinators	www.epa.gov/osweroe1/content/nrs/nrsosc.html
Pesticides: Safety Training	www.epa.gov/pesticides/health/worker.htm
Quality Assurance Training (Region 1)	www.epa.gov/region1/lab/qa/training.html
Quality System Training Program	www.epa.gov/quality/train.html
RCRA Compliance Assistance Training	www.epa.gov/compliance/assistance/bystature/rcra
RCRA Corrective Action Training Curriculum	www.epa.gov/epawaste/hazard/correctiveaction/curriculum/index.htm
RCRA Training Module–Solid Waste and Emergency Response	www.epa.gov/wastes/inforesources/pubs/training/hwid05.pdf
RCRA State Authorization Training Manuals	www.epa.gov/wastes/laws-regs/state/revision/training.htm
RCRA Training Modules	www.epa.gov/epawaste/inforesources/pubs/rmods.htm
Regional Environmental Justice (EJ) Training Contacts	www.epa.gov/compliance/neti/training/index.html
Regional Information Sensitivity (RIS) Training (Procedures for CBI) Region 4	www.epa.gov/region4/ris_training
Risk Assessment Training (NCEA)	cfpub.epa.gov/ncea/pdfs/ncea_brochure.pdf
Risk Management Workshops (ORD)	www.epa.gov/ttbnrmrl/index.htm
Science Advisory Board Ethics Training	www.epa.gov/sabproduct/nsf/Web/ethics?OpenDocument
Site Assessment: OnSite Tutorials	www.epa.gov/athens/learn2model/part-two/onsite/i_onsite.htm
Superfund Analytical Services Sample Documentation Training (FORMS II Lite)	www.epa.gov/superfund/programs/clp/f2ltrain.htm
Superfund Job Training Initiative (SuperJTI)	www.epa.gov/superfund/community/sfjti/
Superfund Training and Learning Center	www.epa.gov/superfund/training/index.html
Superfund Training Opportunities	www.epa.gov/superfund/training/index.htm
Superfund: Hazard Ranking System (HRS) Courses	www.epa.gov/training/hrstrain/hrstrain.htm
Superfund: Natural Resources Damages	www.epa.gov/superfund/programs/nrd/train/index.htm
Superfund, TRI, EPCRA, RMP and Oil Information Center	www.epa.gov/superfund/contacts/infocenter
Technology Innovation Program	www.epa.gov/etop/cont_tip.html
Toxics Release Inventory (TRI)	www.epa.gov/tri/report/training/index.htm
Toxics Release Inventory Training Modules	www.epa.gov/tri/training.2011
Waste, Pesticides and Toxics Training (Region 5)	www.epa.gov/region5/waste/training/
Water Program - National Pollutant Discharge Elimination System (NPDES) Training	cfpub.epa.gov/npdes/outreach.cfm?program_id=0&otype=1
Water Program - Training Opportunities	www.water.epa.gov/learn/training/index.cfm
Water Quality Standards Academy (WQSA)	wwwn.epa.gov/learn/training/standardsacademy.didex.html
Watershed Academy	www.epa.gov/learn/training/standardsacademy.didex.html

NIOSH, ANSI-Z490 AND ADDITIONAL TRAINING REQUIREMENTS

3

David Coble

LEARNING OBJECTIVES

▌ Identify the occupational safety and health training available from NIOSH Education and Research Centers.

▌ Search the NIOSH Web site for further details on training available from the NIOSH Education and Research Centers.

▌ Be able to prepare state-of-the-art occupational safety and health training systems that will conform to the ANSI national consensus standard for accepted practices in safety, health, and environmental training.

ON DECEMBER 29, 1970, President Richard M. Nixon signed the Occupational Safety and Health (OSH) Act, passed by the 91st Congress. (The Occupational Safety and Health Act of 1970, along with the amendments made to it in 1998, can be accessed on the OSHA Web site (www.osha.gov) by clicking on the A-Z index link, then clicking on the letter "O" at the top of the page and scrolling down to OSH Act of 1970.) The law went into effect four months later, on April 28, 1971. The Occupational Safety and Health Act created five new federal government agencies:

1. The Occupational Safety and Health Administration (OSHA)
2. The Occupational Safety and Health Review Commission (OSHRC)
3. The National Advisory Committee for Occupational Safety and Health (NACOSH)
4. The Workers' Compensation Commission (WCC)
5. The National Institute for Occupational Safety and Health (NIOSH)

The purpose of the Occupational Safety and Health Act, as stated in Section 2(b) was "to assure so far as possible every working man and woman in the nation safe and healthful working conditions, and to preserve our human resources." One action intended by the writers of the OSH Act to continually assure safe and healthful workplaces was the creation of the National Institute for Occupational Safety and Health (NIOSH). NIOSH was established in Section 22 of the OSH Act and assigned its main goal, the prevention of injury and illness, in a three-pronged approach:

• identifying occupational hazards by conducting research and field studies of hazards

- conveying the results of that research and the field studies to OSHA and the Mine Safety and Health Administration (MSHA), as well as other federal agencies and safety and health professionals working in the field
- providing training programs based on the results of NIOSH's research and study

This last objective, which can be found at Section 21 of the Occupational Safety and Health Act, states that

(a) The Secretary of Health and Human Services, after consultation with the Secretary [here meaning the Secretary of Labor] and with other appropriate Federal departments and agencies, shall conduct, directly or by grants or contracts (1) education programs to provide an adequate supply of qualified personnel to carry out the purposes of this Act, and (2) informational programs on the importance of and proper use of adequate safety and health equipment.

(b) The Secretary [of Labor] is also authorized to conduct, directly or by grants or contracts, short-term training of personnel engaged in work related to his responsibilities under this Act.

(c) The Secretary [of Labor], in consultation with the Secretary of Health and Human Services, shall (1) provide for the establishment and supervision of programs for the education and training of employers and employees in the recognition, avoidance, and prevention of unsafe or unhealthful working conditions in employments covered by this Act, and (2) consult with and advise employers and employees, and organizations representing employers and employees as to effective means of preventing occupational injuries and illnesses.

Primarily as a result of the OSH Act (but also in response to the high cost of injuries and illnesses), awareness of occupational hazards and interest in worker protection increased in both the public and private sectors. Because of studies conducted by NIOSH, it became apparent by the mid-1970s that there was a shortage of qualified specialists in industrial hygiene and safety qualified to achieve the goals of the OSH Act, which included:

- ensuring that employers were meeting OSHA's standards
- improving worker health and safety

TRAINING AND EDUCATION PROVIDED BY THE NATIONAL INSTITUTE FOR OCCUPATIONAL SAFETY AND HEALTH

In an effort to meet these challenges and to alleviate the manpower shortages in the safety, occupational health, and industrial hygiene fields, initially NIOSH established twelve Educational Resource Centers, now called Education and Research Centers, at selected universities across the country during the mid-1970s. [Information regarding NIOSH training and education can be found at the Centers for Disease Control (CDC) Web site at www.cdc.gov/niosh/training.] NIOSH gradually implemented and sponsored five broad areas of education and training:

- continuing education short courses
- training project grants
- academic degree programs in safety, industrial hygiene, occupational nursing, and medicine
- hazardous substance training programs
- emergency responder training programs

NIOSH also began sponsoring other, even more specific, training and education, including spirometry training programs and programs addressing safety and health in mining.

Education and Research Centers

At the outset, these twelve Education and Research Centers (ERCs), received five years of funding. NIOSH intended to provide seed money for academic institutions to develop or expand existing occupational health and safety degreed curricula and programs, as well as to provide continuing education courses for safety professionals, industrial hygiene professionals, nurses, physicians, and other specialists currently practicing in the occupational safety and health field. The ERCs are currently funded through monetary grants from NIOSH and by those who pay for the ERC's services (Buckheit 2010). Further information on the seventeen ERCs presently in operation, and their contact information as of May 19, 2010, can be found in the appendix to this chapter and at www.cdc.gov/niosh/oep/centers.html and niosh-erc.org.

ERCs are valuable resources to NIOSH in three of its five broad areas of training and educational activities.

Achieving Academic Degrees in Safety and Health

The first type of NIOSH training assists students in their pursuit of academic degrees in occupational safety and health. ERCs fund and otherwise support programs for students attempting to earn academic degrees in four core areas: industrial hygiene, occupational health nursing, occupational medicine, and occupational safety. ERCs also similarly assist students involved in specialized fields (called *component areas*) that are relevant to occupational safety and health, such as ergonomics, epidemiology, and toxicology. Each ERC is required to support two degree programs from the four core areas. Stipends and traineeships are made available to qualified applicants for advanced degrees in one of these academic areas. In addition to two degree programs, each ERC must sponsor an approved component area of education—epidemiology, toxicology, ergonomics, or some other related field of study.

DEGREE ACADEMIC PROGRAMS

The academic degree programs supported by each ERC sometimes change. The most current listing of ERC academic assistance is available at www.cdc.gov/niosh/oep/centers.html.

According to Kathleen Buckheit (2010b), Continuing Education Director of the ERC at the University of North Carolina, Chapel Hill, the most commonly offered degree program among ERCs are:

Industrial Hygiene: This degree teaches students to anticipate, recognize, evaluate, and control hazards related to employee health that arise in the workplace. It can also prepare experienced industrial hygienists

for research and teaching careers in occupational health and industrial hygiene. The typical curriculum includes sample collection, analysis, statistical modeling, and interpretation of exposure data for the purpose of identifying the relationship between exposure and disease.

Occupational Health Nursing: This degree encourages practice and research in nursing that relates to worker safety and health.

Occupational Epidemiology: This degree trains those who will develop and apply the theory, methods, and intent of epidemiology to promote and protect worker safety and health.

Occupational Safety: This degree educates those who will study, research, and apply the techniques for recognizing, evaluating, and controlling workplace hazards.

Ergonomics: This degree educates those who will study, research, and apply biomechanics, engineering, and the relationship workers have with their environments.

Occupational Medicine: This degree trains medical doctors who will specialize in the recognition, evaluation, and treatment of occupation-related injuries and illnesses.

The ERCs also offer other academic degrees, including industrial hygiene research, occupational epidemiology, toxicology, occupational injury prevention, agriculture health and safety, hazardous waste, and occupational health psychology. These degrees are offered through traineeships funded by NIOSH. Further information about the degrees promoted by ERCs can be obtained from the individual ERC (Buckheit interview 2010a).

Continuing Education (CE)

The second broad area of NIOSH training and education is continuing education. The NIOSH definition for continuing education is "[a] specific plan for preparing, distributing and conducting courses, seminars, and workshops to provide short-term continuing education courses for physicians, other industrial safety and health professionals, paraprofessionals and technicians, including personnel of labor-management health and safety committees." NIOSH supports ERC short-term continuing education courses for occupational safety and health professionals and others with worker safety and health responsibilities. A wide variety of personnel attend ERC continuing educational courses, including safety personnel, industrial hygienists, nurses, doctors, engineers, employees, union officials, union members, human resource specialists, production supervisors, managers, executives, quality-control specialists, environmental specialists and professionals, ergonomists, and others. A current continuing education course schedule for all NIOSH Education and Research Centers can be accessed at the NIOSH ERC Web site (www.niosh-erc.org/), by contacting NIOSH toll free at 1-800-35-NIOSH (1-800-356-4674), or by contacting the NIOSH Publications Office. Many of the seventeen ERCs sponsor a variety of safety and health courses customized for particular companies, employers, or industries. ERCs also hold courses that are open to the public. Not all ERCs offer all topics, but new topics continue to be added throughout the year. Among the many subjects included in continuing education are:

- OSHA's 10-hour and 30-hour courses for General Industry and Construction
- Fundamentals of Safety
- Fundamentals of Industrial Hygiene
- Industrial Hygiene Sampling Techniques
- Occupational Health Nursing
- Occupational Medicine
- Asbestos
- Lead Abatement
- Contractor Safety Management
- Safety and Health Auditing
- OSHA Injury and Illness Recordkeeping
- Toxicology
- Electrical Safety
- Machine Guarding and Lockout/Tagout
- Safety and Health Management Systems

Another important aspect of continuing education is interdisciplinary education, a hallmark of each ERC and required of them all. Because of the expanding roles of occupational safety and health practitioners, many safety and health professionals are receiving training in other disciplines so that they can function adequately while meeting new job responsibilities. The crossover has become extensive—occupational physicians and nurses take safety-related courses, safety professionals study ergonomics, and industrial hygienists learn about safety and health management. The ERCs' continuing education programs have been charged with providing the continuing education needed for professionals to upgrade their skills and knowledge in other program areas and disciplines (Buckheit interview 2010a).

Hazardous Substance Training Programs

The third area of NIOSH training and education deals with hazardous substances. Although NIOSH ERCs are not required to offer this program, it is available. In 1988, NIOSH entered into an Interagency Agreement with the National Institute of Environmental Health Sciences (NIEHS). The purpose of the agreement was to develop and conduct a continuing education program for hazardous substances. The authority for this agreement and the resulting training was established in Section 311 (a)(1)(B) of the Comprehensive Environmental Response, Compensation and Liability Act (CERCLA) of 1980, as amended by Section 209 of the Superfund Amendments and Reauthorization Act (SARA) of 1986. Furthermore, in 1993, in response to urging by professional personnel, the hazardous substance training program was expanded to include graduate-level academic training. The NIEHS Superfund Basic Research Program (www.niehs.nih. gov/research/supported/srp) provides financial support for this training through additional grants to the NIOSH Education and Research Centers.

According to the Superfund Amendments and Reauthorization Act, enacted on August 17, 1986, as well as the NIOSH Web site at www.cdc.gov/niosh/ oep/training.html#erc (scroll down to ERC Hazardous Substance Training Programs Target Audience), this training targets primarily:

- health and environmental agency personnel at the state and local levels

- any other professional personnel involved in the management and control of hazardous substances

According to the same Web page, this training is intended to assist employees of state and local agencies, and other professionals in this field, in meeting certain requirements of laws and codes such as OSHA 29 CFR 1910.120 (*Hazardous Waste Operations and Emergency Response*), CERCLA, SARA, and National Fire Protection Codes concerned with a response to emergencies involving hazardous substances. These professionals respond to incidents involving hazardous substances, including releases of hazardous substances, and they travel to hazardous waste sites around the country that must be monitored, controlled, and, sometimes, cleaned up and remediated. These personnel are in continual need of training through both brief courses and degree programs.

There are two types of hazardous substance training programs.

HAZARDOUS SUBSTANCE CONTINUING EDUCATION PROGRAM

The hazardous substance training (HST) program includes the following elements:

- training activities coordinated with the agencies responsible for training of personnel, for enforcement, and for clean up, as dictated by CERCLA and SARA requirements, as well as with other related groups
- specific plans of instruction developed and implemented to assist in adequately training personnel throughout the duration of approved clean-up or remediation projects
- a project director who is expected to demonstrate leadership and competence in conducting training concerning the handling, managing, and evaluation of hazardous substances. This person should have a level of education and experience in the hazardous substance field adequate for the project.
- a project staff able to demonstrate proper experience and technical expertise in the area

of hazardous substances, as well as to develop the necessary curricula while providing quality training
- short courses and continuing education courses developed for state and local health and environmental professionals, among others, who are involved in evaluating, managing, controlling, and handling hazardous substances
- a thorough evaluation of the hazardous substances training program, including a determination of whether the needs of these professionals are being met

HAZARDOUS SUBSTANCE ACADEMIC TRAINING PROGRAM (HSAT)

The purpose of the hazardous substance academic program is to prepare occupational safety and health professionals who specialize in hazardous substances for the responsibilities they accept in responding to hazardous substance spills and releases, as well as in managing, controlling, cleaning up and remediating areas affected by incidents involving hazardous substances. This program is intended to be a specialty area within the existing ERC industrial hygiene core programs.

The key program elements of the HSAT include:

- an assessment of the needs of government and private professionals who practice in the area of hazardous substances
- a training plan developed to satisfy the needs of these individuals
- a formal curriculum that includes a minimum level of coursework that must be met before receiving a degree
- a program director and staff whose experience makes them competent to manage the program
- a formal plan for evaluating the overall effectiveness of the training

A listing of hazardous substance training program directors can be found at www.cdc.gov/niosh/oep/hstcontacts.html.

Two Other Broad Areas of NIOSH-Sponsored Training

Two other broad areas of NIOSH-sponsored training are not administered by the Education and Research Centers, but rather by other universities or associations: training project grants (TPGs) and emergency responder training programs.

Training-Project Grants

Training-project grants are awarded by NIOSH at academic institutions primarily providing single-discipline graduate training in the industrial hygiene, marine safety, occupational health psychology, occupational health nursing, occupational medicine, and occupational safety fields, as well as in closely related occupational safety and health fields. Typically these grants are awarded to colleges and universities wishing to provide a single degree in a safety- and health-related field. They are usually awarded for three to five years and are renewable. A current list of training-project grants is available at www.cdc.gov/niosh.oep/trngrnt.html.

Any public or private institution of higher learning located in a state, in the District of Columbia, or in a U.S. territory that is able to demonstrate its competency in the field of occupational safety and health education is eligible to apply for a training-project grant.

Each April an announcement of available training funds is published in the *Federal Register*. More information on the training grants can be obtained from:

Grants Management Officer,
Procurement and Grants Office
Centers for Disease Control and Prevention
Acquisitions and Assistance Field Branch
626 Cochrans Mill Road
PO Box 1870
Pittsburgh, PA 15236
412-386-6428

Emergency Responder Training Program

The last broad area of NIOSH-sponsored training involves emergency responders. Primarily in response to the terrorist attacks of September 11, 2001, NIOSH began, in the 2002 fiscal year, to support training for emergency responders through a cooperative agreement with the International Association of Fire Fighters (IAFF). The IAFF has implemented a comprehensive nationwide Emergency Responder Training Program for firefighters, paramedics, and other first responders employed in over 30,100 fire departments throughout the United States. National Fire Protection Association data for the year 2008 indicated that 77,900 firefighters were injured while on duty. In 2009, the NFPA reported that 82 firefighters died while on duty (NFPA 2010). Thousands of other first responders are exposed to hazardous toxic materials that increase their long-term risk of cancer, respiratory ailments, leukemia, and other diseases.

A primary emphasis of the Emergency Responder Training Program is the health and safety of first responders. Chief among the training efforts is the recruit training initiative (RTI), an initiative intended to provide training to new first-responder recruits nationwide, as well as in the New York City and Washington metro regions in response to the terrorist attacks. Each year, in approximately 165 courses, the IAFF trains over 5000 first-responder firefighters.

The objectives of this training program include:

- conducting hazardous materials training at the first-responder level to ensure that first responders have the knowledge, skills, equipment, and materials to adequately and safely respond to emergency situations
- providing workshops to help current emergency responder instructors maintain their skills, and to train new instructors, ensuring an adequate supply of instructors for the future
- conducting analysis intended to identify the risks of hazardous materials at the local level, with the goal of assessing the level of training needed
- continually updating the first-responder training program to meet local needs
- initiating marketing and outreach efforts that use a variety of media to ensure that training reaches its intended audience
- implementing a thorough quality-assurance effort in order to maintain the program at a high level of quality

Contact Information:

> International Association of Fire Fighters
> 1750 New York Avenue, NW
> Washington, DC 20006
> IAFF Web site: www.iaff.org
> IAFF HazMat Training Department
> 1750 New York Avenue, NW
> Washington, DC 20006

CONCLUSION

NIOSH offers a wide variety of training and education, including continuing education courses, academic degree programs at selected universities, training project grants, and specific programs, including training about hazardous materials and emergency response. This section summarizes these offerings. To inquire about current training and education available, visit the NIOSH Office of Extramural Programs Web site at www.cdc.gov/niosh/oep/training.html#erc.

A SUMMARY OF AMERICAN NATIONAL STANDARD ANSI/ASSE Z490.1-2009–CRITERIA FOR ACCEPTED PRACTICES IN SAFETY, HEALTH, AND ENVIRONMENTAL TRAINING

Safety and health professionals generally agree upon a few basic elements that must be incorporated into any effective safety and health management system. Those basic elements include:

- management support, commitment, leadership, and action
- employee involvement and acceptance
- hazard recognition, evaluation, and control
- training and education

On September 19, 1997, the charter was accredited by ANSI for the preparation of the American National Standard ANSI/ASSE Z490.1, *Criteria for Accepted Practices in Safety, Health, and Environmental Training*. A need was recognized by the safety, health, and environmental (SH&E) profession to improve training regarding safety, health, and environmental management. To be effective, such training must provide man-

agement, workers, and SH&E professionals with the knowledge, skills, perspective, and abilities to recognize, evaluate, and control hazards in order to protect themselves and others while in the workplace.

Development of the standard began in April 1996, when the ASSE conducted focus-group meetings in Houston, Chicago, and Gaithersburg, Maryland. More than 100 training experts, representing businesses, industry associations, professional societies, providers of training, and organizations both large and small, participated. ASSE needed to know whether there was a need for a national training standard. ANSI/ASSE Z390.1-1995, *Accepted Practices for H2S Training*, was approved just before these focus groups began meeting, demonstrating the industry's support for the development of training standards.

After three years of development, approximately 48 organizations and a number of individuals developed ANSI/ASSE Z490.1-2001. During the standard's process of enactment, each ASSE chapter president and governmental affairs chairperson was asked to review the drafts and comment upon them. ASSE's practice specialty administrators also reviewed the drafts and added their comments. Finally, nearly 1500 copies of the draft standard were made available for public review, resulting in a dramatic response and a much higher quality standard.

The ANSI/ASSE Z490.1-2001 standard was developed in order to improve the consistency and quality of training development, delivery, evaluation, and management. Members of the ANSI/ASSE Z490.1-2001 committee had as their goal the combination of accepted practices from the training and education industry with accepted practices of professionals involved in safety, health, and environmental management.

In May 2009, an updated ANSI/ASSE Z490.1 standard was issued. Numerous changes that were primarily intended to improve readability and understanding were made in the explanatory section of the standard. A comparison of the changes from 2001 to 2009 is available from the American Society of Safety Engineers in the *Comparison Document of Z490.1 American National Standard Criteria for Accepted Practices in Safety, Health and Environmental Training* published in November 2009 (ANSI/ASSE 2009).

The purpose and scope of Z490.1-2009 is established in Paragraph 1 of the standard: "the establishment of criteria for effective development, delivery, evaluation, and management of training in safety, health, and environmental management, and the description of accepted practices in such training."

Please note that there are other chapters in this book that address the "how-tos" of training, including training course design, delivery of training, evaluation of training, and numerous others. Please refer to those chapters for more specific information.

Management and Administration of SH&E Training

Section 3 of Z490.1-2009 lists the criteria necessary for effective management of SH&E training, recognizing that training and education are a part of the SH&E management system and must be integrated into it. Effective management of SH&E training and education includes:

- responsibility for the training program
- accountability for proper administration of the program
- resources adequate for trainers and trainees to complete training and education
- personnel qualified to design, develop, and deliver training and education by use of appropriate techniques
- strategies for meeting learning goals
- evaluation sufficient to assure the effectiveness of training and education
- oversight of the training process sufficient to assure its consistency, quality, and constant improvement

SH&E training historically has been most effective when integrated into organizational goals and objectives rather than as a stand-alone training event. Any organization can enroll its employees in the course "Control of Hazard Energy during Servicing and Maintenance of Equipment, Processes and Machinery" (popularly known as "Lock, Tag and Try"), but this training is most effective when integrated into overall goals and policies for machine guarding, electrical safety, production strategies, quality systems, and cost control.

In paragraph 3.2, the Z490.1-2009 standard describes proper management of a SH&E training system as beginning with a needs assessment, the establishment of learning objectives, and a written plan that documents methods of training and education.

Other key criteria that must be managed properly are:

- training development
- course content and format
- resource materials
- indicators of satisfactory completion of training and education
- evaluation of training and education effectiveness
- submission of documentation of training and education

Management at any organization providing SH&E training must report adequate numbers and expertise of personnel who administer and support training and education, as well as adequate budgets for training and education, supporting technologies (including presentation equipment and practice equipment), adequate time investment, and suitable facilities and materials, including classrooms, handouts, and lesson plans.

Training Development

Training must be developed to meet and improve the organization's safety, health, and environmental goals. The knowledge, skills, and abilities of employees should be enhanced so that workers will be able to identify and understand the hazards of their jobs while using proper control measures. In order to accomplish this, Z490.1-2009 recommends a systematic process of training development that includes:

1. *An Assessment of the Need for Training.*
   Training may not be the correct response to an organization's needs. In some cases, improved equipment design, new tools, personal protective equipment, or other physical change (or merely greater accountability) may be a more appropriate response.

The training needs assessment should inquire into:

- the nature of the audience to be trained

- the things trainees are expected to know and do as a result of their training
- job procedures and job hazard analyses
- the communication abilities of trainees, including their native language and their ability to see or hear
- the nature of any prior training given to the trainees
- regulations, laws, and standards concerned with the training

2. *Learning Objectives and Their Prerequisites.* Goals and objectives should be in written form and should describe:

- the target audience
- the knowledge, abilities, and skills that employees must learn
- the knowledge, abilities, and skills that training will impart
- how to ascertain whether training has had its desired effect

The results of the training should be demonstrable and measurable. If an employer wishes to train a small group of maintenance employees how to use ladders safely, the goals of the training should specify whether it will include both portable and fixed ladders, as well as special ladders such as those used in the maritime industry or rolling ladder stands. The goals should specify whether training will deal simply with the proper use of ladders or whether it will also include proper inspection of ladders. They should specify whether the effectiveness of the training will be measured by a written test, an oral test, or by direct observation of the newly trained employees' use of ladders—or by a combination of the three.

Prerequisites should include prior formal training, certifications or licenses, level and length of experience, knowledge of equipment, tools and processes, and so on.

3. *Design of Training Course.* When designing the course, consider delivery methods, course content, instructional materials, trainer materials, the physical environment of the training, the time needed, the qualifications necessary

for the trainers, and methods by which to evaluate the effectiveness of the training.

Delivery methods might include classroom time, on-the-job training, formal lecturing, computer-based simulation, peer discussion, multimedia demonstrations, hands-on practice, distance learning, and much more. Usually, a variety of methods work best to keep trainees' attention; and some delivery methods work better than others during instruction about certain types of material. All methods must include plans for collecting adequate, timely feedback; for answering questions and concerns; and for assessing the receptivity of trainees to the training. Various methods could include techniques that develop attendees' interest, such as trivia questions, history lessons, competitive knowledge-based games, and use of the facilities for real observations related to the subject at hand. If an instructor is presenting a course on electrical safety, attendees could be asked to identify electrical hazards in the classroom and to explain how any potential electrical hazards are being controlled.

Course content should consist of the information needed by the trainees and should be based on such elements as:

- organizational policies
- procedures and practices
- current and state-of-the-art peer-reviewed literature
- recognized scientific and professional principles
- knowledge and judgment of experts in the subject
- site-specific issues and concerns
- regulatory requirements

Instructional materials should be pertinent to the targeted audience, to the method of delivery, and to the learning objectives. These materials might include a trainer's guide; attendee handouts; multimedia aids such as video, PowerPoint, flip charts, or whiteboards; "show and tell" devices; tools and equipment able to give trainees hands-on practice and experience; copies of regulatory standards; and the organization's written policies and procedures.

A trainer's lesson plan, guidebook, or outline should be developed and should include:

- an agenda
- training goals
- prerequisites
- a schedule for presentation, breaks, meals, and so on
- a list of training aids
- copies of handouts
- requirements for the physical environment, such as classroom size, style of seats, lighting level (including individual lamps for students if required), computer access, available equipment, and any other physical necessities
- methods for evaluating the effectiveness of training, such as critique sheets, tests, or demonstration requirements
- a list of accessible reference documents

Be sure to include the date the trainer's guide was prepared or revised, and by whom.

The physical environment must take into account the number of trainees per class; whether interactive discussion will be encouraged (which affects classroom seating arrangements); any necessity for watching or using machines, equipment, tools, or similar items; and any multimedia needs.

The design of the course is also based on the time allocated for delivering the information. In some cases, government regulations or certifying organizations specify a minimum time. Training classes may be spread over days and weeks or can be delivered in one time block. Human resource requirements for staffing and running the organization must be taken into account. In addition, some topics will generate more questions and the need for individual tutoring than will others. Decide whether time for questions and tutoring should be reserved beforehand or taken as necessary after the training. Methods and times of testing must also be considered.

With more qualified trainers comes better training. Indicate any necessary requirements of trainers, such as certifications, licenses, degrees, experience, background, expected delivery techniques, and anything else required to abide by regulations.

4. *A Strategy for Evaluation.* Determining how well course attendees understood, accepted, and are prepared to apply their training is difficult at best. Adult trainees do not comprehend oral presentations as well as they do hands-on practice. Methods of evaluation might include written tests, oral tests, demonstrations by course attendees, observations by supervisors while in the field, written reports in which attendees describe what they learned, or other such methods. Multiple evaluation techniques may be needed.

5. *Completion Criteria.* The development of the training must include a minimum level of accomplishment below which training is not considered complete, and the training plan must specify procedures to follow when an attendee does not successfully complete the course. Satisfactory completion of a training curriculum should include, as applicable

- minimum attendance requirements, such as attendance during a certain number of hours or a percentage of the entire course
- minimum passing test scores
- certain mandatory times of attendance
- any requirements for demonstration of proper tool or equipment usage
- any required exercises, drills, or role-playing

6. *Continuous Improvement.* The final parameter for development discussed in Z490.1-2009 is continuous improvement. All training must be revised and upgraded periodically. The best way to learn what needs upgrading is to scrutinize the contents of attendee course evaluations. Develop an evaluation form and allow attendees adequate time to fill it out—preferably as the course progresses, but certainly by the end of the course—and review the evaluations. Qualified personnel should review all training courses annually or even more frequently.

Training Delivery

This section of Z490.1-2009 describes requirements for acceptable trainers and delivery of training content. The minimum qualifications of the trainers must be specified during the training development plan and should include:

Trainers' Expertise in the Subject Matter. At a minimum, establish any certifications, licenses, degrees, continuing education, length of experience, skills, abilities, and technical knowledge needed by trainers.

Trainers' Delivery Skills and Abilities. Trainers should have a thorough knowledge of adult learning methods as well as of delivery techniques. This is usually best evaluated by references who are able to give feedback about previously conducted training.

Trainers' Current Status of Required Skills and Knowledge. All those involved in training must stay current in their profession and its subject matter. This can be evaluated by discovering how often trainers deliver courses on the subject matter, to whom training has been delivered, and how competency is maintained (whether by attending continuing education seminars, by publishing articles and books, by speaking at conferences and meetings, by teaching higher education courses, or by consulting with organizations), as well as by reviewing references from those who have attended previous training courses.

Documentation of Trainers' Abilities. Z490.1-2009 specifies that documentation of trainers' abilities is necessary, but it does not specify any particular method of documentation. Documentation may include curriculum vitae; biographical experience sheets; résumés; continuing education transcripts; a written biography; or copies of certifications, registrations, or licenses.

Delivery of the training itself must be carefully planned and managed. Trainers must be evaluated to assure that they understand course learning objectives, are famiiar with specific course materials, display necessary expertise, use appropriate delivery techniques (those suitable for the audience—neither offensive nor distasteful), and are familiar with the principles of adult learning. Ensure that the trainer has customized the training to the audience receiving it.

To facilitate acceptable delivery of training, the training environment and location should be free of obvious hazardous conditions and should have access to potable water and restrooms while maintaining a suitable climate (including temperature and air quality) with sufficient lighting, seating, and work space, as well as planned emergency evacuation routes and procedures. Also consider the necessity for snacks and meals and whether all phones and pagers should be turned off or placed on silent mode, as well as the timing and length of any breaks. Ensure an adequate supply of training materials; handouts; back-up multimedia equipment, such as spare projector bulbs and extension cords; adequate electrical power; furniture, such as tables and chairs; and computers, along with telephone lines or Internet connections, if needed.

The room or training area must be arranged so that all attendees can see and hear the instructor. Trainees with special needs must be considered.

Most adult attendees will want to learn and have a successful training experience. In return, the trainer must treat trainees with respect and fairness; recognize and respond appropriately to each individual's learning styles and abilities; and exercise good professional judgment when responding to difficult, unexpected situations or individuals. The pace of the training should match the audience's ability to internalize the training. In most cases, attendee participation should be encouraged and welcomed. Trainers should answer *all* questions and answer them respectfully, even when it means searching out answers later and conveying them to questioners by other means.

Training Evaluation

The tools and techniques for training evaluation should apply equally to trainers, trainees, training, and the training management system. Trainers' abilities to effectively impart and transfer knowledge, skills, and abilities to trainees must be evaluated. Trainees' understanding and use of the training content must be evaluated—perhaps by having attendees perform tasks correctly. The training and its environment must be evaluated. The system that manages the needs assessment, planning, delivery, and evaluation must also be evaluated periodically. The key question to be answered is: Are the organization's goals being met?

Each training event should include evaluation tools, which must be prepared during the training development. Tools should be reliable and act as valid measures, and they must be based on accepted practices. Reliable, valid measures are those that give consistent feedback over time, reflecting the knowledge, skills, and abilities that are the goals of the training.

The selection of the evaluation approach is based on the training audience, the expected outcomes of the training, and the established learning objectives. Evaluation approaches might include:

Reaction Surveys. Sometimes called critique sheets or course evaluations, these are questionnaires that attendees can fill out to subjectively evaluate the trainer's abilities, the training location, the trainer's delivery technique, the training environment, the pace of the training, the course's content, and all other aspects of the training.

Evaluation of Knowledge, Skills, and Abilities. This might include a written test, an oral test, the completion of an assigned project (such as a written paper), the design of a tool or device, demonstration of a new skill in the real or simulated work setting, observation over time by a supervisor or auditor, a decrease in the number of unwanted events, or an increase in the number and quality of proactive metrics for safety, health, and environmental management activities.

Quantitative Measurements. These can include a pre-test and a post-test to measure improvement, linking performance to training. In many cases, this helps identify gaps that impede the value and application of training, such as the availability of appropriate equipment, conflicting direction from a supervisor, or the lack of management support, leadership, and accountability.

Organizational Results. Another evaluative technique compares the results of those trained with those who have not yet been trained. To accomplish this, a control group of workers who have not yet been trained is compared with the trained group. Measurements to compare the trained group with the control group can include:

- increasingly safe behaviors (also called actions) or decreases in unsafe behaviors
- increasing use of preventative measures, controls, and devices

- fewer near hits, injuries, illnesses, and other unwanted events
- diminishing costs and workers' compensation claims
- higher returns on investment
- fewer observable regulatory noncompliance findings

Overall, the evaluation must be used to continuously improve the content of the training course and its delivery methods, materials, and environment.

Documentation and Record Keeping

A favorite expression of many SH&E professionals is, "What has not been documented has not been done." The final paragraph of Z490.1-2009 provides guidance for documenting training. Some regulatory standards, such as OSHA's standard for personal protective equipment [29 CFR 1910.132(f)(4)], require that training be documented. Best practice is for all training to be documented. The most effective method of managing evidence of completed training is documenting the who, when, what, and so on, of all training.

The record-keeping management system for documentation of training should, according to Z490.1-2009, ensure that records are:

- readily retrievable, identifiable, and orderly
- current, accurate, legible, and dated
- retained for a reasonable time specified by a "record retention policy" developed with the assistance of legal counsel, ensuring that records are properly controlled
- in compliance with all regulatory and legislative requirements

The most important uses of the training records include:

- allowing management to assess the extent of the training system requirements and allowing auditors to discover who is being trained, whether the training is timely, whether training make-up sessions will adequately allow everyone opportunity to attend training, and whether regulatory requirements are being met

- safeguarding against governmental regulatory actions or other liability claims

Development Records

Records documenting training development should identify the targeted audience, the learning goals and objectives, the personnel and organization used to develop the training curriculum and materials, and the qualifications of those who designed and developed the training curriculum and materials, as well as including copies of the actual materials used and plans for evaluating the effectiveness of the training course.

Delivery Records

When training courses are being delivered, several pieces of information should be documented, including the date, location, and duration of the training, the name and description of the course, the names and qualifications of those delivering the course, copies of the materials used and of handouts provided to attendees, the names (preferably the signatures) of the attendees, and some indication of which attendees successfully completed the training. Z490.1-2009 also recommends a unique identifying number for each attendee.

Evaluation Records

The forms used by attendees to evaluate the training should be retained for use in evaluating the training management system as well as for regular evaluation of continuing improvement of a particular course.

Records Confidentiality and Availability

Regulations that require records to be kept should be met. Regulatory requirements might stipulate that the records be readily available for a government inspector while remaining confidential and protecting trade secrets. Some sort of statement should be made in the written management training system document about to whom the records may be disclosed.

Certificates

Certificates for training completion, while not always required, should be provided to attendees as documentation. However, should they be issued, best practice is for certificates to include trainees' names; the course name; the date; the total number of hours of instruction; a statement that attendees successfully completed the course; the names and addresses of those who provided training; some indication of whether a refresher course is required or suggested, and at what time interval; the training's expiration date, if applicable; trainees' individual identification numbers; the level of training attended or the type of certification achieved, if applicable; any other information required by government regulations; and the number of continuing education credits or units (often called CEUs) earned. CEUs are required by many professions to indicate that professionals who hold certifications, licenses, and other designations are maintaining their professional knowledge and skills at an acceptable level. Some certifying or licensing bodies require that a minimum number of CEUs be acquired during a set period.

If continuing education credits or units are earned, credits must be in accordance with the certifying body's requirements and should be filed with the certifying body.

Annexes

There are three annexes (or appendices) to the Z490.1-2009 standard, as well as a checklist designed to assist on the day of training.

Annex A provides fourteen references for further information. These include ISO standards, such as 9001 and 14001; other ANSI standards, such as Z1.11; two NIOSH documents; one OSHA document (OSHA Publication 2254); one ASTD (American Society for Training and Development) document; and two books.

Annex B provides guidance for training course development, reiterating the Z490.1-2009 standard in a more step-by-step, "how-to" approach.

Annex C provides training delivery guidelines to assist trainers in delivering effective training. It also provides advice and guidance for traditional learning techniques, advanced technology training, and on-the-job training.

Day of Training Checklist

The last page of Z490.1-2009 is a two-page checklist of issues to manage on the day of training, including the training location's seating, lighting, temperature, and level of comfort; audiovisual equipment; training devices, materials, and supplies; what to do before attendees arrive; trainers' opening remarks; how to encourage participation; how to effectively present training material; proper documentation; and thanking the participants in such a way as to give a lasting impression.

CONCLUSION

ANSI Z490.1-2009, *Criteria for Accepted Practices in Safety, Health, and Environmental Training*, was prepared by a group of safety, health, and environmental management professionals whose intent was to cover all aspects of training, including development, delivery, evaluation, and management. To ensure quality training, review other chapters in this handbook that address training and education.

References

American National Standard Institute (ANSI). 2009. *ANSI Z490.1-2009 Criteria for Accepted Practices in Safety, Health and Environmental Training*. Des Plaines, IL: American Society of Safety Engineers.

American Society of Safety Engineers (ASSE). 2001. "ANSI Z490.1—2001 Approved." *The Advisor* (Fall) 1(1).

_____. November 2009. *Comparison Document of Z490.1 American National Standard Criteria for Accepted Practices in Safety, Health and Environmental Training*.

Buckheit, Kathleen. 2007. Personal Interview with Kathleen Buckheit, MPH, COHN-S/CM, FAAOHN, Director, Continuing Education, North Carolina Occupational Safety and Health Education and Research Center (January 30, 2007).

_____. 2010a. Email Correspondence with Kathleen Buckheit, MPH, COHN-S/CM, FAAOHN, Director, Continuing Education, North Carolina Occupational Safety and Health Education and Research Center (May 17, 2010).

_____. 2010b. Email correspondence with Kathleen Buckheit, November 29, 2010.

Centers for Disease Control & Prevention (CDC), National Institute for Occupational Safety & Health (NIOSH), *Education and Research Centers for Occupational Safety and Health*. www.niosh-erc.org

_____. NIOSH Office of Extramural Programs. *Training Programs*. www.cdc.gov/niosh/oep/training.html#erc

_____. NIOSH Office of Extramural Programs. *Hazardous Substance Training (HST) Program and Hazardous Substance Academic Training (HSAT) Program Grantees*. www.cdc.gov/niosh/oep/hstcontacts.html

_____. *Training*. www.cdc.gov/niosh/training

Kane, Steven F. *Use of the Z490 Voluntary National Consensus Standard to Improve Safety, Health, and Environmental (SH&E) Training*. Presentation by Steven F. Kane, CSP, PE, Chair, Z490 Committee at the ASSE Professional Development Conference. June 12, 2002. Nashville, TN.

National Fire Protection Association (NFPA). "Fire Service Statistics." www.nfpa.org/itemDetail.asp?categoryID=417&itemID=18246&URL=Research%20&%20Reports/Fire%20reports/Fire%20service%20statistics

National Institute for Occupational Safety and Health. 2010. *Education and Research Centers for Occupational Safety and Health 2010* (retrieved October 4, 2011). www.niosh-erc.org.

National Institutes of Health (NIH), National Institute of Environmental Health Sciences, Superfund Research Program. www-apps.niehs.nih.gov/sbrp

Occupational Safety and Health Administration (OSHA). www.osha.gov

Occupational Safety and Health Act of 1970, Public Law 91-596, 91st Congress, S.2193, December 29, 1970. www.osha.gov

Rogers, Bonnie. Telephone Interview with Bonnie Rogers, DrPH, COHN-S, LNCC, FAAN, Director of the University of North Carolina Occupational Safety and Health Education and Research Center. January 4, 2005.

APPENDIX

The following list of sixteen NIOSH Education and Research Centers is current as of May 19, 2010. For the most current information, go to www.cdc.gov/niosh/oep/centers.html.

Alabama Education and Research Center

University of Alabama at Birmingham
School of Public Health
1665 University Blvd.
Birmingham, AL 35294-0022
(205) 934-6208
Fax: (205) 975-6341
R. Kent Oestenstad, PhD, Director
Email: oestk@uab.edu

California Education and Research Center–Northern

University of California, Berkeley
School of Public Health
140 Warren
Berkeley, CA 94720-7360
(510) 643-4702
Fax: (510) 642-5815
John R. Balmes, MD, Director
Email: john.balmes@ucsf.edu

California Education and Research Center–Southern

University of California, Los Angeles
School of Public Health
650 Charles Young Drive South
Los Angeles, CA 90095-1772
(310) 206-6141
Fax: (310) 206-9903
John R. Froines PhD, Interim Director
Email: jfroines@ucla.edu

Cincinnati Education and Research Center

University of Cincinnati
Department of Environmental Health ML. Box 670056
3223 Eden Avenue
Cincinnati, Ohio 45267-0056
(513) 558-1751
Fax: (513) 558-2772
Carol Rice, Ph.D., CIH, Director
Email: alerdilr@ucmail.uc.edu

Colorado Education and Research Center

University of Colorado at Denver and Health Sciences Center
4200 E. Ninth Ave.
Denver, CO 80262
(303) 315-0880
Fax: (303) 315-7642
Lee S. Newman, MD, MA, FCCP, FACOEM, Director
Email: lee.newman@uchsc.edu

Harvard Education and Research Center

Harvard School of Public Health
Department of Environmental Health
665 Huntington Avenue
Bldg. 1, Rm. 1407
Boston, MA 02115
(617) 432-3323
Fax: (617) 432-3441
David C. Christiani, MD, Director
Email: dchris@hohp.harvard.edu

Illinois Education and Research Center

University of Illinois at Chicago
School of Public Health
2121 West Taylor St.
Chicago, IL 60612
(312) 996-7469
Fax: (312) 413-9898
Lorraine M. Conroy, ScD, CIH, Director
Email: lconroy@uic.edu

Iowa Education and Research Center

University of Iowa
College of Public Health
Department of Occupational and Environmental Health
100 Oakdale Campus - 126 IREH
Iowa City, IA 52242-5000
(319) 335-4428
Fax: (319) 335-4225
Craig Zwerling, MD, PhD, MPH, Director
Email: craig-zwerling@uiowa.edu

Johns Hopkins Education and Research Center

Johns Hopkins University
Bloomberg School of Public Health
615 North Wolfe Street Rm 7503
Baltimore, MD 21205
(410) 955-4037
Fax: (410) 614-4986
Jacqueline Agnew, PhD, Director
Email: jagnew@jhsph.edu

Michigan Education and Research Center

University of Michigan
School of Public Health
1420 Washington Heights
Ann Arbor, MI 48109-2029
(734) 936-0757
Fax: (734) 763-8095
Thomas G. Robins, MD, Director
Email: trobins@umich.edu

Minnesota Education and Research Center

University of Minnesota
School of Public Health
420 Delaware Street, S.E.
Minneapolis, MN 55455
(612) 625-5934
Fax: (612) 626-4837
Susan G. Gerberich, Ph.D., Director
Email: gerbe001@umn.edu

New York/New Jersey Education and Research Center

Mount Sinai School of Medicine
Department of Community and Preventive Medicine
P.O. Box 1057
One Gustave L. Levy Pl.
New York, NY 10029-6574
(212) 824-7018
Fax: (212) 996-0407
Philip J. Landrigan, MD, MSc, Interim Director
Email: phil.landrigan@mssm.edu

North Carolina Education and Research Center

University of North Carolina at Chapel Hill
School of Public Health
1700 Airport Rd., CB 7502
Chapel Hill, NC 27599-7502
(919) 966-1765

Fax: (919) 966-8999
Bonnie Rogers, DrPH, COHN-S, FAAN, LNCC,
    Director
Email: rogersb@email.unc.edu

South Florida Education and Research Center

University of South Florida
College of Public Health
13201 Bruce B. Downs Blvd., MDC Box 56
Tampa, FL 33612-3805
(813) 974-6629
Fax: (813) 974-4718
Thomas E. Bernard, Ph.D., Director
Email: tbernard@ health.usf.edu

Texas Education and Research Center

University of Texas Health Science Center at Houston
School of Public Health
P.O. Box 20186
Houston, TX 77225-0186
(713) 500-9464
Fax: (713) 500-9442
Sarah A. Felknor, PhD, Director
Email: sarah.a.felknor@uth.tmc.edu

Utah Education and Research Center

University of Utah
Rocky Mountain Center for Occupational and
    Environmental Health
391 Chipeta Way, Suite C
Salt Lake City, UT 84108
(801) 581-4800
Fax: (801) 581-7224
Kurt Hegmann, MD, MPH, Director
Email: kurt.hegmann@hsc.utah.edu

Washington Education and Research Center

University of Washington
Department of Environmental Health and
    Occupational Health Sciences
P. O. Box 354695
Seattle, WA 98105
(206) 685-7189
Fax: (206) 616-6240
Noah S. Seixas, PhD, Director
Email: nseixas@u.washington.edu

SAFETY AND HEALTH TRAINING THEORIES AND APPLICATIONS

4

LEARNING OBJECTIVES

▮ Be able to apply a knowledge of learning theories to select or develop appropriate training programs.

▮ Learn about factors that affect memory.

▮ Recognize the different categories of learning needed to teach problem-solving skills to beginning, intermediate, and advanced learners.

▮ Be able to identify motivational problems and implement strategies that will increase learners' interest in safety training.

▮ Learn how to conduct a performance and training needs assessment.

▮ Be able to analyze a target audience and develop training strategies based on audience characteristics.

▮ Master the terms goals and objectives, and be able to write course objectives.

Phyllis Simmons

MARIA IS A human resources manager for a law firm that employs 50 employees at one location. She is responsible for safety training in addition to her other responsibilities. Workers at her company are college-educated and computer-literate English speakers. Hazards at the firm consist of typical office hazards and those related to computer use. John, on the other hand, is a safety officer for a manufacturing company with 2000 employees who work at eight different geographic locations. Workers in his company speak four different languages, and their education levels range from seventh grade to college (the company also employs teenage workers during the summer). Hazards at the company include office hazards, chemical hazards, and hazards related to moving machinery. Each profile of the above-mentioned officials and their work environments reflects the diverse world in which today's trainers work. Even though Maria and John work in two different worlds, they have one thing in common—the need to understand how people learn best. Regardless of where trainers work, the fundamental philosophy stays the same: "If you know your audience, you will know what learners need and what motivates them."

IMPORTANCE OF LEARNING THEORIES AND TRAINING DEVELOPMENT

The first section describes learning theories, specifically cognitive, behavioral, and motivation theories that give trainers information about the learning process so they have a sound rationale for selecting training activities and materials. Many safety trainers purchase off-the-shelf training materials, and they may not be aware why certain learning activities have been selected by the

FIGURE 1. Chapter overview

designer. Theoretical principles are derived from the science behind how information is organized and presented. Once principles are learned, they can be applied to any type of work environment, especially those like Maria's and John's. Even though all workplaces are different, the principles about how people learn are the same.

In the second section, trainers will learn the mechanics of the training development process—performance assessment, training assessment, audience analysis, setting of goals and objectives—how to implement them. As Smith and Ragan (1999, 2) point out, "development is the systematic process of translating learning theories into plans for training materials, activities and evaluation." Although the two systems are different, they are dependent on each other. Theories are the foundation for training, and safety trainers are somewhat like architects in that, just as architects design houses based on sound engineering principles, trainers develop training based on established learning theories.

LEARNING THEORIES

This section will focus on three learning theories: *cognitive, behavioral,* and *motivational*. Each theory will help instructors create effective training programs regardless of whether they deliver training in the classroom or via technology. Learning theories are the foundation from which training is derived, and they have shaped learning as we know it today. Learning theories help trainers understand why certain

concepts are important and provide rationale as to why specific training activities are used.

Cognitive theories describe how people process and remember information. This area is where one can find answers to questions like How do people learn? and Why do workers sometimes forget information? Behavioral theory is especially important because it describes why it is important to reinforce principles after training. Behavior-based principles are used in companies to create a safety culture, and these principles have direct application to training. Equally important is motivation theory because it describes ways trainers can make safety training interesting and relevant to learners.

Cognitive Theory

In cognitive theory, the primary focus is on understanding the learner, specifically, (a) how people process information, (b) what affects memory, and (c) what type of strategies trainers should use to help employees learn safety information.

How the Brain Processes Information

Many theorists believe that memory has three components: sensory register, short-term memory, and long-term memory. Atkinson and Shiffrin (1968) designed an information-processing model describing how each system works and how those systems affect learning and the ability to recall information (see Figure 2).

A person's brain constantly receives information from the five senses and the environment, information that is transmitted to the first memory system called the *sensory register*. Information in this area is only held for a few seconds and is lost if the trainee does not actively pay attention to it. If the person pays attention to the information, then it is transmitted to the second part of the memory system called the *short-term memory*, or *working memory*.

Working memory holds information that is currently being used and is where most thinking and mental processing occurs (Woolfolk 1998). According to Bernstein et al. (2000), information is held in short-term memory—which has limited storage capacity—

for no more than 30 seconds. The best way to retain training information longer in short-term memory is through repetition (saying it over and over) or rehearsal (having the person mentally thinking about it). "Rehearsal is important because the longer an item remains in short-term memory, the greater the chance it will be transferred to long-term memory" (Slavin 2000, 178). Short-term memory is believed to have a limited storage capacity (5 to 9 bits of information), which is why people may feel overwhelmed or forget what was taught when they are given a large amount of information at one time, such as during new employee orientation. If large amounts of information must be presented all at once, it needs to be well organized and connected to information already in the trainee's long-term memory (Slavin 2000). Woolfolk (1998) recommends grouping individual ideas into meaningful categories (also called *chunking*) when people have to learn about several topics. When information is unorganized, the situation can cause confusion and frustration and negatively affect learner motivation. To better understand the power of chunking, read the following list of safety items new employees have to learn at John's manufacturing company—then, without looking, try to recall the safety items.

Safety orientation items (before chunking):

- gloves
- respirator
- keyboard tray
- fire extinguisher
- eyewash station
- glare screen
- safety glasses
- back belt
- wrist rest

Try the exercise again using the chunked list.

Safety items (after chunking):

Computer Safety Equipment

- glare screen
- keyboard tray
- wrist rest

Personal Protective Equipment

- back belt
- gloves
- respirator
- safety glasses

Safety Equipment

- eyewash station
- fire extinguisher

Notice how the information is now alphabetized and categorized by type of equipment, making it easier for people to process and remember. Chunking can also be done in visual form using symbols or pictures to convey messages, like the commonly used symbols

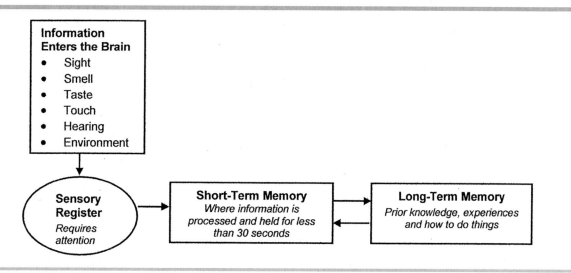

FIGURE 2. Information-processing model (Based on the Atkinson-Shiffrin model.)

in safety warning signs that are displayed in many companies. The brain processes mental images better than large amounts of text. The saying "A picture is worth a thousand words" holds true for learning and assimilating knowledge.

The third and most important memory system is called *long-term memory*. Theorists believe this memory system can hold an unlimited amount of information. It is the permanent storage system of the brain where prior knowledge is stored. In Figure 2 the arrows go in both directions between short-term and long-term memory, because to store new information in long-term memory, a person must draw on prior knowledge stored in this area (Ormrod 1998). Accessing prior knowledge is an important factor in learning and retention for both the trainer and trainee. Trainers, when they are aware of what learners already know, can use that information to help make the training more meaningful for the audience. Similarly, during the learning process, trainees will mentally search for prior knowledge to connect it to something familiar and meaningful to them. Long-term information is encoded in memory in three different ways, through *personal experiences*, *general knowledge*, and *procedural knowledge*, formally also known as episodic, semantic, and procedural memory systems, respectively. McCown, Driscoll, and Roop (1996) recommend training strategies for each area.

PERSONAL EXPERIENCES (EPISODIC MEMORY)

Personal experiences are usually stored in the form of mental images, including memorable events involving the five senses. For example, many people can recall the taste of their favorite childhood treat.

Training strategies: Because of the way personal experiences are stored in the brain, trainers should strive to make training sessions interesting and interactive. Instead of a lecture-only format, learners should be taught according to learning styles that involve the senses, such as discussions, hands-on activities, and visual-aids learning that facilitates long-term memory processing (James and Galbraith 1985). Slavin (2000) suggests using training activities that can create memorable events in the trainee's mind like visual aids, role playing, videos, and other forms of active learning.

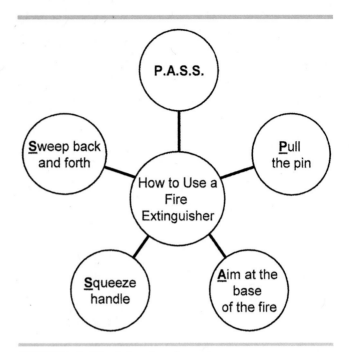

FIGURE 3. Mental network map

GENERAL KNOWLEDGE AND CONCEPTS (SEMANTIC MEMORY)

Many cognitive psychologists have hypothesized that general knowledge and concepts are organized in the brain like a network map (see Figure 3), and that people mentally connect similar concepts to each other. How people mentally organize information influences how they learn and retrieve information.

Training strategies: Find out what people already know and use that information to connect it to newer information. To access prior knowledge, trainers can use activities such as pre-tests, discussions, and asking questions during training.

PROCEDURAL KNOWLEDGE (PROCEDURAL MEMORY)

Procedural knowledge (how to do things) is acquired through practice, and if practiced enough, this knowledge can be retrieved automatically without conscious effort—like riding a bike, for instance. "When procedural knowledge becomes automatic it can also build problem solving skills because basic principles are embedded in long term memory" (McCown, Driscoll, and Roop 1996, 221).

Training strategies: Give participants time to practice procedural skills, especially when teaching important safety topics such as emergency response, first aid, and machine safety. Because of storage-space limitations in short-term memory, people can only learn so much at one time. Trainees need time to process the concepts that are being taught. Trainers can help by introducing redundancy into training sessions; they can, for example, present the ideas several times but in different ways. "Information encoded in different ways is more easily retrieved from long-term memory than just one way" (Ormrod 1998, 591). Another technique Ormrod recommends is pacing, in which the trainer pauses at 10-minute intervals to discuss the concepts that will activate mental processing.

Putting Theory into Practice: How to Help People Better Process and Retain Information

Based on the principles of information processing, here are more cognitive training strategies that can be used to help trainees better process and retain information.

Present information in an organized manner. According to cognitive principles, the brain seeks to arrange incoming information and put it in some type of order to help learners process materials more efficiently. Well-organized materials make it easier for a person to learn and recall information. Methods that trainers can use to organize instruction include the following (Ormrod 1998, Mayer 1989, Schunk 2004):

- Equipment and objects can be used as visual aids.
- Graphic organizers such as pictures, diagrams, and charts can also provide visual aids.
- Outlines or organization charts provide a framework for the training.
- Grouping concepts into modules (or sections) establishes links between concepts.
- Using paragraph headings with written material helps the learning process.
- Provide a chapter overview—Figure 1 was designed not only to help the reader understand the organization of this chapter, but also to provide him or her with a mental roadmap.

- Summarizing information at the end of instruction will help learners review and pull concepts together.
- Use acronyms—this is an abbreviation technique used to help learners remember names, concepts, and procedures. The acronym is the first letter of a word that, in aggregate, forms a familiar phrase; for example, the acronym PASS is used to help people remember how to use a fire extinguisher.
- Mayer (1989) found that supplementing verbal instruction with simple visual aids promotes greater long-term-memory storage and retrieval.

Integrate concepts into prior knowledge. One of the most important points stressed in cognitive theory is the use of prior knowledge. Information is better learned and retained if it can be integrated into existing knowledge and taught in a meaningful way. One way to do this is by using a technique called anchoring—linking new concepts to something familiar to the learner. For instance, when teaching employees how to read a material safety data sheet (MSDS), relate the process to something that is familiar, such as the labels on household cleaning products. MSDSs contain warnings and safety precautions similar to consumer labels, except they provide more extensive information. Connecting training content to learners' prior knowledge and familiar experiences is an effective way to help them learn and make the information more meaningful.

Another method a trainer can use to help workers access prior knowledge is through an *advanced organizer* (Ausubel 1977). The purposes of an organizer are (1) to connect new material to prior knowledge, (2) to remind learners of relevant information they already have, and (3) to direct the learners' attention to what is important in the upcoming material (Schunk 2004, Woolfolk 1990). Usually an advanced organizer is presented at the beginning of the instruction to provide the learner with a mental framework to facilitate encoding information into long-term memory. The following techniques are considered advanced organizers (Gredler 1997):

- Chapter overviews lay out a mental roadmap.
- Course outlines or knowledge maps (also called mind maps) graphically show concepts that will be discussed. (Figure 3 is an example of a knowledge map). To access prior knowledge, the trainer can leave the areas of the knowledge map blank and fill them in by asking participants what they already know about the subject. These maps can also be used to visually summarize information at the end of a training session.
- Analogies are images and concepts that compare new information to what trainees already know (Slavin 2000, 209). When using analogies, use examples that are familiar to the audience.
- Define concepts and terms early. For example, when training on ergonomics, trainers should define the term at the beginning of instruction and relate it to the daily, familiar activities of the workers.
- Pre-tests can be good learning motivators. Asking learners a few quiz questions at the beginning of the training will activate prior knowledge and catch their attention.

Make training interactive. Researchers have found that the more individuals pay attention to and interact with materials in a meaningful way, the more they remember and learn (Slavin 2000, Smith and Ragan 1999). Gaining the attention of learners is a necessary step in helping them enter information into their sensory registers. Active learning focuses on the learner and is more effective than passive teaching methods, such as lecture-only sessions. Active learning is a cognitive teaching method designed to help learners better process, store, and remember information. Learning activities that promote this process have one key ingredient—the learner is actively involved in the training. Activities such as discussions, problem solving, scenarios, quizzes, role playing, drills, hands-on training, case studies, and educational games promote learner participation. Workers generally find active learning more interesting and motivating as long as the activities have a point and are firmly connected to course objectives (Silberman 1995). Active learning makes training more meaningful, promotes deeper

cognitive thinking, and builds on prior knowledge. Silberman found active learning has at least seven characteristics.

1. Active learning concentrates on teaching learners critical items using real-world problems.
2. Active learning includes a balance of cognitive, behavioral, and motivational elements.
3. The active-learning principle influences the design of courses, including in them a variety of learning activities to peak interest and accommodate different learning styles.
4. Active learning provides opportunities for trainees to share their knowledge and experiences.
5. Active learning builds on prior knowledge by reintroducing concepts previously learned.
6. Active learning focuses on helping participants solve their problems.
7. Active learning in technology-based training contains interactive elements, such as quizzes, to promote cognitive processing. Live discussion on a subject, especially during a safety meeting, is a good way to make technology-based training more interactive.

Why Do People Forget Information?

As noted earlier in this section, memory is important for learning, and some information is naturally lost due to inattention. As a result, no one can remember everything. Researchers (Loftus and Loftus 1980, Schunk 2004) found several reasons why people forget:

- time (information decay)
- interference
- memory loss due to biological factors
- lack of motivation and the information not being meaningful to the learner
- the person has trouble accessing information from long-term memory
- the trainer presents too much information at one time—a situation known as information overload
- information is presented in an unorganized manner

Time is a critical factor when it comes to memory because some theorists believe that information can slowly dissipate and be forgotten if not used on a regular basis (Anderson 1990, Elliott et al. 2000). Decay can be lessened through effective presentation of the material and the amount of practice included during and after the training. Conducting interactive training, practice sessions, and refresher training is thus very important in fighting this decay of information.

Interference occurs when material that is being taught is very similar to another subject or gets mixed up with other information (Anderson 1995). New information cannot be stored because it conflicts with prior knowledge. For example, say a person receiving training on a new machine is familiar with the controls on an older machine. The person may experience interference in this situation (or move the controls incorrectly), because the controls, even though they may look familiar, could operate with different outcomes.

Putting Theory into Practice: How to Help People Remember Information

To help learners overcome these memory barriers, researchers (Slavin 2000, Driscoll 2000, Bernstein et al. 2000) suggest trainers use the following strategies:

- Try to connect the material to existing knowledge or something familiar to the learner.
- Integrate the practice of learned knowledge and skills into training sessions. People need to use the information or they may lose it.
- Make sure people understand the fundamentals before teaching them more complex subjects.
- Group similar ideas together or categorize the information. Build on themes and concepts. Chunking information (noted in the short-term memory section) into categories helps clarify thinking and aids memory. Use visual aids, pictures, and charts to organize information for learners.
- On critical safety topics, such as equipment lockout, spill response, and first aid/CPR (cardiopulmonary resuscitation), provide periodic reviews and drills so recall becomes automatic, especially during an emergency.

- When teaching concepts that interfere with each other, point out major differences and provide a checklist or job aid (such as a poster) if necessary.
- Make training interesting. Theorists suggest there is an area of the brain called the limbic system. It monitors incoming information, and when people experience pleasant emotions and feel relaxed during training, the brain is more receptive to retaining the material and transferring it to long-term memory (Lawlor and Handley 1996).

Teaching Higher-Level Problem Solving

So far this section has focused on basic cognitive principles and has provided training strategies for many safety topics. However, some safety topics require a higher level of cognitive thinking—topics such as ergonomic assessments, accident investigation, and emergency response. What is common to these types of classes is that learners need to activate a variety of information stored in their memory networks, to know how to apply it in different situations, and to be able to problem solve. Teaching these types of subjects can be challenging because there may be several possible solutions and ways to address a problem. When teaching more advanced and complex subjects, trainers can use the following strategies that are designed to promote higher-level thinking.

Putting Theory into Practice: Helping Learners Deal with Complex Problems

Knowing how to apply concepts from training to a variety of situations is called transfer learning. Some learners may have difficulty applying information if it is not taught in the context of their job. Transfer-of-learning problems can also be caused by motivational issues, language barriers, and target-audience appropriate training. To promote transfer of learning, researchers (Ormrod 1998, Smith and Ragan 1999, Bernstein et al. 2000) suggest that trainers practice the following:

- Create learning conditions that correspond to the workplace. Use real-life examples, equipment, and situations that trainees will likely encounter in the workplace.

- For learners who speak English as a second language, training may need to be provided in their native language to avoid misunderstandings and transfer-of-learning problems.
- Provide many opportunities for practice and problem solving. Encourage learners to bring up their own scenarios or case studies.
- Use a variety of examples, including challenging situations learners are likely to encounter and show them different ways to solve safety problems.

Teaching Beginner, Intermediate, and Advanced Courses

A worker's day is filled with many situations that call for complex decision making and problem solving. Many safety subjects involve the use of different cognitive skills, ranging from recalling basic facts (for example, what is an MSDS?) to making critical or emergency judgments (for example, rescuing a worker trapped in a confined space). Benjamin Bloom (1956) developed a six-level classification model that can be used to establish the course difficulty level as well as to teach problem-solving skills. His model is designed in hierarchal order, from skill building with knowledge, which is the first level, also called the beginner level, to the highest level, which is the evaluation level (advanced).

Each level of the hierarchy is defined in terms of learner comprehension (Gagne 1988, Cantonwine 1999):

> *Level 1: Basic knowledge.* Learners understand basic principles.
> *Level 2: Comprehension.* Learners understand information and can use it.
> *Level 3: Application.* Learners know how to use information in different situations.
> *Level 4: Analysis.* Learners can break a problem into smaller parts and use the principles to solve that problem.
> *Level 5: Synthesis.* Learners can put together different concepts to solve a problem.
> *Level 6: Evaluation.* Learners can use the principles to evaluate a situation and make the

appropriate decisions. At this level, learners are highly knowledgeable and can usually teach others.

This model has important training implications. Instructors can use the model to design different levels of training (basic to advanced). If training is to help prevent life-threatening injuries, it needs to be designed at a different level than training for basics. The class difficulty level can also affect learner motivation. For example, if most of the participants are highly knowledgeable in a subject area and the trainer makes the course too basic, then the participants will be bored and may not pay attention. Remember that attention is needed to activate short-term (working) memory. On the other hand, if many of the participants are novices and the course is taught at a high level, then the learners may become frustrated and be less motivated to learn. Figure 4 describes teaching strategies trainers can use to help learners actively process information in a way that involves a deeper level of problem-solving skills that can be used in a variety of situations.

Behavioral Theory

Whereas cognitive theory mainly focuses on the internal learning processes of a person, behaviorism studies how external factors influence human behavior and learning. The two behavioral theorists most relevant to safety training are B. F. Skinner and Albert Bandura. Skinner's work focused on understanding how learning and behavior can be influenced by external factors, such as positive reinforcement, and the how the environment can serve as a reinforcer. *Positive reinforcement* occurs when a reward follows a particular behavior, resulting in the increased likelihood of that behavior being repeated (Bernstein et al. 2000). Bandura's work (1986) focused on the influence of *modeling* (learning from observing others) and how it can shape and encourage similar behavior.

Putting Theory into Practice: Behaviorism and Safety Training

Skinner's principles of positive reinforcement (i.e., praise, rewards, and constructive feedback) are especially

LEVELS OF THINKING	COGNITIVE TEACHING STRATEGIES
Beginner Level	
1. Basic knowledge	**Teach fundamental principles.** Ask questions about the information presented.
2. Comprehension	**Test competency** and learners' understanding of the fundamentals before moving to higher levels. Ask them to explain the information in their own words: for example, Describe . . . Explain . . . Show me how . . .
Intermediate Level	
3. Application	**Teach learners how to apply the principles to their job.** Ask learners to explain how the information can be used. Introduce more complex principles.
4. Analysis	**Present basic problems for learners to solve.** At this level, trainers could present different scenarios to help trainees learn how to apply the principles. Introduce potential problems. Use scenarios, what-if exercises, or case studies.
Advanced Level	
5. Synthesis	**Increase the level of complexity** of problems presented in the intermediate level. Learners should be able to trouble shoot as well as make assessments and recommendations. Use more complex scenarios, what-if exercises, or case studies.
6. Evaluation	**Set up complex teaching situations.** At this level, learners should possess a strong grasp of the subject to be able to teach it to others or solve very complex problems. Train-the-trainer courses should be designed at this level. Ask learners to present challenging cases and show how they would solve the problem.

FIGURE 4. **Higher-level teaching strategies** (Adapted from Cantonwine 1999 and Bullard et al. 1994)

applicable to safety training. Praise, rather than threats, and constructive feedback are powerful reinforcers and motivators for longer-lasting behavior changes. Skinner's work also shows that, to be effective, positive praise (reinforcement) should be gien over different intervals, not just during the day of training (Elliott et al. 2000). When reinforcement is scheduled over periods of time and integrated into day-to-day operations, it has more sustainability. It is not enough to train workers once and hope they will use the principles taught. Rather than waiting until an accident happens to reapply reinforcement, positive reinforcement should continue on an ongoing basis—for example, during job observations, inspections, and safety meetings. Incentive programs and recognition are other examples of positive reinforcement that can be tied to training performance.

Skinner's research also demonstrated how the *environment* can act to either reinforce or hinder behaviors learned in training. In the case of safety, the environment can include the workplace, people, and job design. For example, Maria needs to train her employees on proper lifting techniques, but because heavy boxes are stored on shelves above shoulder level, the company's storage practices (the job design) will most likely promote unsafe lifting practices. To minimize these kinds of environmental barriers, instructors need to consider the impact of the environment on training performance and determine if the problem can be addressed during training or through the company's hazard-correction process. In Maria's case, because the hazard cannot be corrected immediately, she should incorporate interim solutions in her upcoming training and submit a hazard-correction recommendation to the department supervisor.

Bandura's concept of *modeling* is another behavioral technique that can be used to support safe work practices and principles learned during training. To use this method, trainers should model proper techniques during instruction and give participants adequate time to practice the skill themselves. Most importantly, trainers should elicit the help of supervisors and encourage them to consistently model safe work practices in their department during and after training, reminding them that they are in a position of influence and can be powerful role models for safety.

Motivation Theory

At some point during the training process, trainers will ask themselves, how can I motivate workers to want to learn about safety? To answer this question, instructors must first understand what motivation is, and that motivated people can often be recognized by their outward behavior. Researchers have defined motivation as:

- A person's tendency to find learning activities meaningful (Wlodkowski 1999).
- "An internal state that arouses action and keeps us engaged in certain activities" (Elliott et al. 2000, 332).

Motivation is so powerful that it influences how much people remember and the extent to which workers will participate in learning activities. Here lies one of the most challenging issues for trainers; if learners are not motivated, learning cannot occur, and injuries can result. For these reasons motivational strategies must be included in the instructional design process and not be left to chance.

It is important to recognize that motivation exists in everyone in varying degrees. The degree of effort learners will exert is influenced by a variety of *intrinsic* and *extrinsic* factors (Keller 1983).

Intrinsic Motivation

Intrinsic motivation comes from within the person, meaning the student wants to learn because of personal reasons, without external motivational influences such as praise and rewards (Elliott et al. 2000). Among the many factors that can greatly influence intrinsic motivation are the following: people's beliefs, attitudes, self-worth, and feelings about their job and health (Wlodkowski 1999). If, as a trainer, one can affect one or more of these dimensions, half the motivational battle has been won.

People's attitudes and beliefs can greatly influence their level of interest in safety. Some may believe safety is the company's responsibility, while others could believe that they have a role in safety and thus embrace training to avoid injury. To promote personal responsibility, a trainer should actively involve the employees in the training process.

Self-worth is how people feel about themselves and their abilities. When people feel confident, their desire to learn increases. Confidence can be negatively affected if people have experienced learning difficulties in the past or were in situations where they felt incompetent or embarrassed. One way trainers can promote self-worth is to help learners feel emotionally safe as well as confident in learning activities (e.g., create an environment where the participants are not worried about being embarrassed in front of a group).

The last intrinsic motivational factor of importance is how learners feel about their job and personal health. When people like their job (and supervisor) and they feel respected, their motivation to learn can be high. Furthermore, if well-being is a priority for learners, they will be receptive to injury-prevention information. Because intrinsic motivation factors vary from person to person, it is important for trainers to understand learners' motives. Even though these factors are primarily controlled by each individual, instructors can learn how to use extrinsic methods (those outside of the individual) to enhance intrinsic motivation.

Extrinsic Motivation

Whereas intrinsic motivation comes from within, extrinsic motivation comes from sources outside the individual. External factors that can enhance training motivation include the following (Wlodkowski 1999, ASTD 1997, Pike 1994):

- feedback and praise
- meaningful learning activities
- a comfortable learning environment
- free refreshments
- recognition and awards

An instructor can act as an external motivator and increase someone's desire to learn. Most people can recall an energetic teacher who sparked their curiosity for learning. Trainers can inspire by showing enthusiasm and creating pleasurable learning experiences.

Putting Theory into Practice: Motivation and Learning

The specific types of motivational strategies instructors should use will depend on both the characteristics and needs of the target audience. Therefore, it is important for trainers to know their audience and to identify and address potential motivational barriers.

Assessing Motivational Problems

Driscoll (2000) recommends that instructors take time before training to think about potential motivational problems. According to Keller (1987), motivational problems can be generated by the learner, the instructor, or the method of instruction. Trainers can identify and implement strategies to solve motivational problems using the ARCS model developed by Keller. The initials for this acronym stand for four conditions that must exist for learners to be motivated:

1. **A**ttention
2. **R**elevance
3. **C**onfidence (self-worth)
4. **S**atisfaction

ATTENTION

As discussed earlier in the cognitive section, the learner must pay attention in order for learning and mental processing to occur. In the ARCS model, attention refers to strategies trainers can use to gain the learners' interest and keep them motivated. Some trainers use an attention-gaining activity only at the beginning of instruction and then later notice a decline in learner interest and motivation. The important point to consider is that in order to sustain attention, varied strategies must be deployed throughout the training. In other words, trainers should vary the way the information is presented by changing the tone of voice, method of instruction, and learning activities (Smith and Ragan 1999). Other ways to sustain attention is to incorporate different modes of learning in a session, such as using interesting stories, visual aids, scenarios, discussions, and problem-solving activities that capitalize on students' interest.

RELEVANCE

Relevance strategies help learners see that what they are learning is meaningful and useful. This is often referred to as customized training. People are motivated when they feel training applies to their lives and their jobs, or that training can help them achieve a goal. If learners feel the training is a waste of time, they will not be motivated to learn. Researchers (McCown, Driscoll, and Roop 1996; Smith and Ragan 1999) suggest that trainers use the following techniques to establish relevance:

- Inform participants at the beginning of instruction how the information is useful and applies to them (e.g., state the course objectives).
- Give experienced workers an opportunity to be a co-trainer and share their knowledge with others.
- Use real examples, equipment, and challenges workers encounter in their job.
- If employees learn better in their native language, use a translator and provide materials in their language.
- Give employees a choice in the methods of instruction that matches their learning style; some may prefer Web-based learning, while others may like hands-on classroom training.
- Provide interesting, easy-to-read training materials that include color and familiar graphics.

CONFIDENCE

Confidence builds self-worth, and learners are motivated when they believe they can be successful or achieve a goal. Trainers can help build confidence in several ways (Gagne 1988):

- Provide learning opportunities where participants can experience success.
- Make sure the course difficulty level matches the students' abilities. Add challenging (not overwhelming) situations as trainees master basic concepts.
- Provide helpful feedback both during and after training and point out ways the trainees can further excel.

SATISFACTION

The last element required for motivation is learner satisfaction—meeting the learner's expectations. When people attend training, they usually have varied expectations. However, there are some needs participants have in common, which are to learn useful information, to have a pleasurable learning experience, and to have a comfortable learning environment. The following are examples of satisfaction strategies (ASTD 1997, Gagne 1988):

- Ask learners at the beginning of the course what they want to get out of the class.
- Survey employees to find out the best times to hold training. For example, having a class on a Friday at 3 P.M. may be demotivating to many employees because it is the end of the work week. Class length is also a motivating factor—find out the participants' preferred class length. Attending a class for a few hours versus all day can impact a person's satisfaction level.
- Inform learners when expected goals are achieved, such as providing answers to quizzes so learners can evaluate their performance; giving prizes or verbal praises for correct responses; or providing certificates of achievement for course completion.

Using the ARCS Model

John plans on conducting a one-hour refresher class on MSDS to teach employees about hazardous chemicals. Normally, he would only show a video and the employees would fall asleep. Figure 5 contains a list of strategies John can use to sustain employee motivation and attention throughout the session using the ARCS model.

Motivation Summary

To answer the question posed at the beginning of the chapter (How can I motivate workers to want to learn about safety?), instructors must first learn who their students are and understand what factors inspire or demotivate them. Because there is no definitive answer, Keller designed the ARCS model to help trainers

identify barriers that could negatively affect both intrinsic and extrinsic motivation. Strategies to address many motivational problems can be developed by answering the following ARCS questions before teaching or developing any safety-training class.

What strategies will I use to:

1. Gain students' attention and maintain it throughout the session?
2. Make training relevant to the learners?
3. Build learner confidence?
4. Ensure learner satisfaction and promote positive feelings about learners' successes?

Although the model does not cover all possible factors, it can help trainers reduce a number of potential barriers so employees are motivated to learn about safety.

ACTIVITY LENGTH	MOTIVATIONAL STRATEGIES
20 minutes	• First, explain how the training will help them prevent injuries. Also, ask employees if they encountered any challenges in reading an MSDS. Address their challenges during the lecture. These are examples of **relevance** and **satisfaction**.
	• To gain their **attention**, begin the session with a mock chemical accident that requires learners to find information using an actual MSDS, and then discuss their findings.
20 minutes	• Next, to make the training **relevant**, use real-life props, such as chemical containers and personal protective equipment, to lecture on how to read an MSDS of a commonly used chemical.
	• If possible, ask a knowledgeable employee to help give the lecture to build **confidence**.
15 minutes	• Then summarize what was learned by giving a group quiz where the participants use a different MSDS and work together to find the answers. This will also give employees additional practice on how to read an MSDS and help build confidence.
5 minutes	• Provide the answers to the quiz so employees can evaluate their performance. Give verbal praise for satisfactory performance on the quiz and for class participation. This is an example of a **satisfaction** strategy.

FIGURE 5. Motivational strategies

DEVELOPING TRAINING PROGRAMS

The goal of the first section was to provide insight on several learner-centered theories that affect learning: cognition, behavior, and motivation. Section two will focus on the actual training development process, which includes performance assessment, training assessment, audience analysis, learning styles, and setting goals and objectives. Each step builds upon theoretical principles discussed in section one and helps trainers gain a deeper understanding of learners' characteristics and needs.

The development process normally begins with an assessment. There are two types of assessments trainers need to become familiar with—a performance assessment and a training needs assessment. A *performance assessment* is designed to help trainers determine if training is needed to solve problems related to unsafe work practices and accidents. The information is used to improve workers' safety performance or prevent an accident from reoccurring. Conversely, a *training assessment* is used for curriculum development to determine which subjects should be taught. Each assessment produces different results, yet both are equally valuable in the development process.

Performance Assessment: Is Training the Solution?

When an unsafe work practice or accident is discovered, a common reaction is to immediately provide more training. This is like a doctor treating a patient without knowing the patient's symptoms. Before spending valuable time and money on training, managers and other decision makers, with help from the trainer, need to stop and assess the situation. *Finding out the cause of the problem should be the first course of action.* Assessing a performance problem is similar to investigating an accident. Both require problem-solving skills, identification of the root cause, and recommendation of corrective action.

Executing a Performance Assessment

According to Mager and Pipe (1997), trainers should first ask "Did the incident occur because of a knowl-

edge or skill deficiency?" and "Are there other factors that might be involved?" Other reasons could be related to motivation, lack of supervision, and job or equipment design. The problem could be the result of one or several of these factors. When a safety-performance problem occurs, the first step is to investigate its nature to determine if lack of knowledge was the cause or a contributing factor. To accomplish this investigation, interview supervisors and employees involved in the situation. If the incident was documented, review the report. During the interview, ask open-ended questions (described below) to promote two-way dialog, as opposed to questions that only require a yes-or-no response (Leshin, Pollock, and Reigeluth 1992).

Interview questions for supervisors. What type of feedback or coaching has the employee received and how often? How often does the problem occur? What task was the person trying to complete when the unsafe act occurred? What are the consequences of not solving the problem?

Interview questions for workers. Why was the job performed that way? Can you demonstrate how to . . . ? Can you describe how to . . . ? Why do people . . . (state the unsafe act)?

After collecting the facts, determine if training alone can solve the problem. If other problems are discovered or more information is needed, continue collecting information by observing employees and interviewing other workers if necessary (Gupta 1999).

Determining Solutions

Once the causes are identified, develop possible solutions that may or may not include training. When considering solutions, think about feasibility, cost factors, and the impact the solutions may have on other areas. Solutions to some common performance problems are described in Figure 6.

Training Needs Assessment

Determining What Should Be Taught

Whether a performance assessment calls for training that can solve the problem or is needed to fulfill

PERFORMANCE PROBLEMS	POSSIBLE SOLUTIONS
1. Lack of knowledge or a training design problem The worker does not know the information or forgets critical information when explaining safety procedures, such as how to lock out a machine.	• Provide training if there is a knowledge deficiency. • If someone cannot remember critical safety procedures that involve multiple steps, place job aids or posters in the work area. • Trainers may also need to look at the way training information is organized or use visual aids or other techniques that do not rely on memory.
2. Lack of motivation Workers feel training information is not practical and are not motivated to use it. Workers disregard company safety policies. The person feels safety is not his or her responsibility and wants to take short cuts.	• Ask employees to suggest ways training can be improved. • To make training relevant, complete an audience analysis. • In cases where policies are disregarded, ask the supervisor to conduct job-performance counseling. Make sure safety policies and enforcement standards are in writing and are clearly communicated to employees.
3. Lack of reinforcement Workers feel they are too busy and often forget to follow the safety procedures.	• Talk to the supervisor to see if there is work overload or a scheduling problem. • Ask supervisors to reinforce procedures on a daily basis.
4. Lack of leadership The organization or supervisor places greater emphasis on productivity, and safety is not a high priority.	• Safety should be addressed on a senior-management level. Accountability and responsibility standards should be developed and tied to performance evaluations for supervisors and employees. Incentive programs could be considered.
5. The way a job or equipment is designed Because the way a job is designed, an employee may bypass safety procedures to complete the task.	• Observe the job to see if something in the job process or the equipment is causing employees to work unsafely. For example, workers may bypass safety instructions to reduce defects, to achieve production quota, or to complete a deadline. • Talk openly with supervisors and employees to see what needs to be changed to make the job safer, or to make the environment more supportive of safe choices.
6. Language and cultural barriers Workers may perform an unsafe act because of cultural belief. Language barriers are discovered.	• Address cultural beliefs by explaining why safety procedures must be followed and the consequences if they are not. Supervisors may need to consider enforcement and feedback practices. • To overcome language barriers, provide training in languages that are understandable to employees. Check the accuracy of information being delivered by translators.

FIGURE 6. Solutions to performance problems (*Source:* Mager and Pipe 1997, Geller 1996)

regulatory requirements, instructors should complete a training assessment. According to Smith and Ragan (1999), an assessment can help trainers in any of the following ways:

- Identify the knowledge and skills that learners need to perform their job safely.
- Determine what subjects should be taught and aid in selecting appropriate learning activities.
- Find out what participants already know about the subject.
- Learn what to avoid.
- Plan reinforcement strategies to promote transfer of learning.
- Assess how much practice and training time is needed.

- Establish the level of difficulty for a course.

Once information is collected, it is accepted practice to use the results to develop companywide training programs, orientations, and single courses.

Executing a Training Assessment

Identifying potential hazards and reviewing past injuries are the most important elements of this particular assessment. The time needed to complete this process depends on the nature of the job and the types of hazards involved. A training needs assessment consists of three basic steps (Gupta 1999):

Step 1: Define the purpose of the assessment.
Step 2: Get prepared.

Step 3: Gather data and determine which subjects will be taught.

DEFINING THE PURPOSE

Having a purpose will make the process more efficient and help trainers determine what type of information is needed. For example, the purpose of the assessment is to design a safety-orientation training program, or to tailor a safety-training program for office employees.

GETTING PREPARED

The next step is to prepare a list of areas to review; this step will guide the data-collection process. Valuable information in developing training programs includes the following:

- specific knowledge and skills workers need to prevent injuries (obtain from job descriptions and supervisors)
- potential hazards of the job and the work environment
- types of personal protective equipment used or needed
- injuries related to the department
- OSHA-required topics and training frequency
- special department information, such as hours of operation, number of shifts, preferred training length, and days and times
- budget and record-keeping considerations
- existing safety documentation, such as accident reports, OSHA log of work-related injuries and illnesses, and current safety policies and training programs

GATHERING DATA AND DETERMINING THE SUBJECTS TO BE TAUGHT

Gathering data can involve several methods, such as interviews (with supervisors), job observations (if logistically possible), and safety documentation review. In cases where companies have different geographic locations, trainers may need to rely on telephone interviews in lieu of face-to-face discussions. One of the most useful documents for assessing training needs is a job safety analysis (JSA). This traditional tool is used to identify job hazards to help practitioners develop company safety policies. The methodology used to conduct a JSA is applicable to instructional design. Often, department supervisors and human resource managers can help trainers complete this task. To complete an assessment, use the following steps (National Safety Council 2009). An assessment worksheet can be found in Appendix A.

1. Identify potential job hazards using interviews, job observations, and information from safety documents.
2. Use the information in step 1 to identify the knowledge and skills needed.
3. Once the knowledge, skills, and hazards are known, the trainer can then identify the required safety-training topics for a particular department or job.

Figure 7 shows an example of a training needs assessment completed for Maria's office administration department, an assessment she can use to set up a training program.

LIST POTENTIAL HAZARDS	IDENTIFY THE KNOWLEDGE AND SKILLS NEEDED	LIST THE TRAINING TOPICS
Identify potential hazards or possible accidents that could occur.	Using the information in the first column, decide what knowledge and skills are needed to prevent injuries and also to fulfill OSHA training requirements.	Using the information in the second column, list the recommended safety-training topics.
Office Example:	*Office Example:*	*Office Example:*
1. Back injuries from lifting supplies	1. How to lift objects and use lifting equipment	1. Back-injury prevention and how to use lifting equipment
2. Repetitive-motion injuries using computers	2. How to prevent repetitive-motion injuries	2. Office ergonomics
3. Trips and falls	3. General office safety	3. General office safety
4. Workplace emergencies	4. What to do in emergency situations	4. Emergency action plan

FIGURE 7. Training assessment for office employees (Adapted from National Safety Council 2009)

Audience Analysis

An audience analysis is performed after the completion of a training assessment to specifically gather detailed information about learners; this process helps customize training according to the characteristics of learners. Skipping this step can result in wasted time and money; it can also lead to ineffective instruction, which can demotivate learners and create negative perceptions about future training sessions. Ultimately, the analysis can mean the difference between a poorly designed program and an effective one. Its importance cannot be overemphasized.

When completing an audience analysis, sensitive information should be kept confidential and used only by the trainer for course-development purposes. An audience description can vary in length from a few paragraphs to several pages, depending on how much detail the trainer needs. Information can be compiled in a number of ways (Gupta 1999, Mager 1988):

- Interview a representative sample of the audience in person or by telephone. This technique will also increase learner motivation because people feel valued when their opinions are considered and when they are shown a level of caring. Let people know how the information will be used and why it is needed.
- Observe the audience performing the job related to the subject.
- For a day, walk in their shoes. Shadow a person for a few hours to observe how to make the training relevant—when shadowing, follow the company's safety policies to avoid injury.
- Interview people who work with the target audience. Human Resources can be very helpful in providing audience information.
- Review past training evaluations and job descriptions.

Most importantly, when analyzing culturally and linguistically diverse audiences, avoid stereotyping—remember that no group is homogenous. Even though ethnic groups may share common experiences, there are differences within each ethnic group. Talk to different people within a cultural group to get broader viewpoints.

There are certain learner characteristics (e.g., learning styles and education level) that are important to know when developing programs. The information gathered will help the instructor develop course content that motivates participants. Trainers should spend a good portion of their development time on this step. The following five categories represent the critical characteristics to consider when assessing an audience: background information, general characteristics, education/prior knowledge, attitudes/interests, and preferred learning methods (Smith and Ragan 1999, Mager 1988). See Figure 8 for examples of important information that can be gathered for each category.

Depending on the subject that needs to be taught, certain information may be more critical. For example, physical characteristics such as height can be significant when training on proper lifting techniques because body dimensions are an integral part of the subject matter. Likewise, in chemical training, knowing the education range is valuable because the trainer may need to alter the vocabulary level accordingly.

IMPORTANCE OF LEARNING STYLES

Of the five characteristics just described, learning styles is being highlighted because it directly correlates to motivation and information processing. When learning activities are congruent with people's learning style, they are better able to cognitively process information and retain it in long-term memory (Sarasin 1999).

Everyone has a preference in how information is presented to him or her. Researchers (James and Galbraith 1985, Sarasin 1999) found that people learn best through one of the senses or a combination of senses. Some people process information *visually* (e.g., videos), others process it through *auditory means* (e.g., discussions), and still others process information *kinesthetically* (e.g., hands-on activities). Some researchers (Kolb 1981; Harb, Durrant, and Terry 1993) categorize learning styles by other modalities: concrete, reflective, abstract, or active. A *concrete learner* likes to learn through feelings and prefers activities that include other people. They also need concrete, real-life examples—as opposed to abstract concepts—to better understand things. *Reflective learners* like to learn by observing others, and they need time to ponder information. *Abstract*

CATEGORIES	EXAMPLES OF IMPORTANT INFORMATION
1. Background information	• Number of trainees • Tools and equipment used by the audience • Safety, operations, or supervisory barriers that might prevent the audience from successfully using the information on the job • Learning or physical disabilities that can impact training • Any injury information related to the audience • Think about ways the audience is similar and different
2. General characteristics	• Physical characteristics and cultural beliefs relating to safety and the subject matter • Age ranges • Job experience • Languages and dialects spoken
3. Education and prior knowledge	• Education levels, prior training experience, knowledge, and literacy levels
4. Attitudes and interests	• Attitude toward safety • Motivation to learn • Likes and dislikes about training • Hobbies and outside interests
5. Preferred learning styles	• Demonstrations, discussions, videos, scenarios, lectures, role playing, etc.

FIGURE 8. Target audience characteristics (*Source:* Smith and Ragan 1999)

learners, who are usually analytical thinkers, like information presented in a logical and organized manner. *Active learners* prefer action-oriented activities; they, like kinesthetic learners, learn through action.

What is important to know is that no one learning style is better than another. Both theories depict diverse ways people process and understand information.

Training an audience using the trainer's preferred learning style or only one learning style are common mistakes trainers make. Focusing on one learning style, for example, is a reason participants may become bored or demotivated during training—this approach lacks variety and relevance. As discussed earlier in the motivational theory section, variety and relevance are two required conditions in the ARCS model to gain attention and stimulate motivation. Because audiences have diverse learning styles, trainers should survey or interview employees not only to identify and incorporate different learning activities into the training, but also to ensure that each trainee's needs are met. Figure 9 provides a graphic overview of both learning theories to help trainers choose appropriate learning activities (Lawson 1997, Cantonwine 1999).

ADULT LEARNING STYLES	APPROPRIATE LEARNING ACTIVITIES
Visual Learners • Learn best by seeing the information	Diagrams, pictures, videos, handouts, charts, colorful visual aids
Auditory Learners • Learn best by hearing the information	Videos, lectures, discussions
Kinesthetic and Active Learners • Learn best through active participation	Demonstrations, role play, simulations, games, discussions
Reflective Learners • Like to assess their own knowledge and skills	Quizzes, tests, self-assessment exercises, what-if scenarios
Concrete Learners • Learn best by observing and when activities simulate their job	Real-life examples, scenarios, role play, simulations, use of actual job props when possible
Abstract Learners • Learn best when information is organized and requires mental processing	What-if scenarios, charts, statistical information, facts, problem-solving exercises

FIGURE 9. Learning styles and activities (Adapted from Lawson 1997 and Cantonwine 1999)

Putting Theory into Practice:
An Audience Analysis

The following example uses the audience-analysis principles described in this section to show how they would apply to a training situation at John's manufacturing company. It also includes a wide range of challenges that trainers may encounter, along with recommended training solutions. It is important to note that in this real-world example, the company employs minors (under the age of eighteen) during the summer. Every state has child labor laws that prohibit the use of dangerous equipment and machinery (U.S. Department of Labor 2006, NIOSH 2003, OSHA 2006). Trainers should become familiar with the child labor laws when minors are involved.

DESCRIPTION OF MANUFACTURING AUDIENCE CHARACTERISTICS

Course Title: Back-Injury–Prevention Training

Course Background Information

- Conduct a lifting training program for 50 employees in the Receiving Department.
- There are two shifts: 9 A.M.–5 P.M. and 5 P.M.–1 A.M.
- This is an initial training class for the audience.
- Manual lifting represents approximately 50% of the job (this information can be obtained from the job description or the supervisor).

- The audience also uses lifting devices such as dollies and carts.
- Back injury rates are low.
- Training is mandatory for all employees of the company.

General Characteristics of the Target Audience

- The audience is 90% male and 10% female.
- The audience age ranges from 15 to 40 (obtain from Human Resources).
- There is one worker who is hearing impaired but can read lips.
- Heights range from five to six feet.
- Lifting strength varies by person and gender.
- The languages needed for training are: English, Chinese, Spanish, and Tagalog; bilingual supervisors can assist in translation.

Education and Prior Knowledge

- Most of the audience completed high school and some completed community college.
- Even though this is a new training course, all participants have lifted objects in prior jobs or in their personal lives.
- Some are new employees while others have worked for fifteen years.
- Minors are employed during the summer (child labor laws apply).

Attitudes and Interests

- Attitudes toward using the correct techniques is fair because some feel they are strong enough

COMMON CHARACTERISTICS	TRAINING STRATEGIES TO USE
• Employees lift the same types of objects and use the same material-handling equipment.	• Use actual objects or equipment that employees use to establish relevance. Discuss the importance of using the material-handling equipment.
• All have some type of lifting experience. Employees either lift at home or work (prior knowledge).	• Ask the audience to share their prior lifting experience and have them discuss their lifting challenges at home and work.
• Everyone is from the same department.	• Use lifting examples that pertain to the department.
• Outside interests are similar in that they relate to physical activity.	• Discuss how the information benefits their personal activities, such as sports and fitness.
• Learning methods are similar; the audience likes active and visual learning activities.	• Use demonstrations with video feedback to provoke discussion on current techniques and props.
• Everyone has to complete the course.	• Bring refreshments. • Use relevant examples and ask knowledgeable workers to share their expertise with others; this process helps create a pleasurable learning experience.

FIGURE 10. Common audience characteristics and possible training strategies

to lift heavy objects rather than ask for help or use the carts—some feel asking for help is a sign of weaknesses.

- General audience interests include physical fitness, sports, and music.
- Supervisors have a positive attitude toward providing feedback after the training.

Preferred Learning Styles

- The audience prefers visual aids and active learning, that is, demonstrations and video with some discussion.

STEP 1: ANALYZE INFORMATION—LOOK FOR COMMON TRENDS

Once the audience description is completed, look for common audience characteristics to help make the training relevant to the participants (Smith and Ragan 1999, Jonassen and Grabowski 1993). Once the common characteristics are identified, list training strategies for each one using cognitive, behavioral, and motivational principles described in section one. Figure 10 describes the common characteristics and training strategies for John's audience analysis.

STEP 2: IDENTIFY AND ADDRESS POTENTIAL BARRIERS

It is not enough to simply identify commonalities; attention also needs to be given to addressing and finding solutions for potential barriers or unique challenges that can negatively affect motivation and learning. Figure 11 highlights potential training challenges for John and describes solutions that could be used to overcome each barrier.

STEP 3: HOW TO USE THE INFORMATION

Once the audience analysis is completed, the trainer should have enough knowledge about the participants to customize the training and make it relevant. Next, the trainer's job turns to developing goals and objectives before conducting the training.

Goals and Learning Objectives

Goals and objectives are developed after the needs assessment and audience analysis. In these two steps trainers will have determined what subjects should be taught, and what knowledge and skills trainees need in order to work safely. Next, through the writing of

BARRIERS OR CHALLENGES	SOLUTIONS TO BARRIERS AND CHALLENGES
• There are two work shifts.	• Conduct a class for each shift.
• The gender make-up of employees is mixed.	• Let the participants know that, regardless of gender, everyone needs to use proper lifting techniques.
• There is a gender and cultural stigma associated with asking for help or using a cart (actions perceived as signs of weakness).	• Discuss the perceived sign of weakness in an employee asking for help. Reinforce the company's policy on lifting. Use real-life cases of how back injuries have affected people's lives.
• The height of participants may affect lifting techniques.	• During demonstration exercises, use examples for taller and shorter people.
• One person is hearing impaired.	• Find out how the hearing-impaired person learns best. He or she can tell you about the special needs involved.
• Four training languages are needed.	• For multilingual training needs, find out how many workers need to have the class in their native language. Use bilingual supervisors or trainers.
• The length of employment varies from new to fifteen years.	• To address employment variations, include a review of basic principles for new employees and add demonstrations and problem-solving scenarios for more experienced workers.
• Minors sometimes work in the department.	• Review the state's child labor laws for prohibited equipment. During the training, reiterate to minors that they are not allowed to use forklifts or other prohibited equipment.

FIGURE 11. Training barriers and solutions at the manufacturing company

goals and objectives, trainers will learn how to describe the capacity of the trainees after training. *Goals* describe the overall intent of a course. They are broad statements describing the overall scope of the training and are generally not measurable (Mager 1988). For example, the goal of a workshop may be to teach supervisors how to conduct workstation evaluations for computer users. Notice that this statement does not describe how the trainer will accomplish the goal, nor does it describe the specific skills trainees will acquire. When developing goals, trainers should ask, what is the purpose of the course? Overall, what do I want learners to achieve? Once the goals are developed, the next step is to write the objectives, which are the key actions that are necessary to achieve the goals.

An objective is different from a goal. *Objectives* are statements that specifically describe what trainees will be able to do after training, the learning conditions under which they will be able to perform, and how learners will demonstrate competency (Dowling and McKinnon 2002). Objectives should not refer to the trainer. For example, an objective for an office ergonomics course reads as follows: provided with the tools and furniture, the trainee will be able to correctly set up computer workstations using the neutral-posture guidelines. Another distinct difference between a goal and an objective is that the latter, unlike the former, must be measurable, observable, and attainable (Lawson 1997). The office ergonomics example meets all three criteria. A trainer can see if a workstation is set up correctly (observable), and measure if a worker is sitting in neutral postures by using the ergonomics guidelines (measurable). And because all the necessary training tools would be provided to the learner, the objective is considered attainable. Courses can have more than one goal and usually have many

objectives; the number will depend on what a trainer wants learners to achieve—notice the number of objectives listed at the beginning of this chapter.

HOW OBJECTIVES ARE USED BY TRAINERS

Learning objectives are used for several purposes (Leshin, Pollock, and Reigeluth 1992):

1. To guide the instructor on what content, learning activities, and test items to include in the training. The information can serve as a reminder of items to include in a lesson plan.
2. To assess learners' knowledge and skills during and after instruction.
3. To help trainers plan how students will demonstrate competency.
4. To communicate to trainees what they will learn and the performance expectations.

The familiar phrase most frequently used to communicate course objectives is, "after the training, you will be able to . . . (*list what the trainees will be able to do—use action verbs*)." Objectives are also stated at the beginning of training sessions to initiate cognitive processing and stimulate learner motivation. By doing this, the audience will know what will be covered and what to expect.

WRITING OBJECTIVES

Keep in mind that objectives describe the trainee, not the instructor or course content. An effective objective has three components: condition(s), skill, and performance standard. A helpful way to remember the three components is through the acronym CSP. The following is an example of a learning objective that is typically worded in the order of that acronym (Mager 1988):

KNOWLEDGE, SKILLS, AND ATTITUDES NEEDED	CONDITIONS OR TOOLS TRAINEES NEED	SKILLS	PERFORMANCE STANDARDS
Knowledge needed: • Ergonomics principles • How to evaluate a workstation	• Ergonomics policy • Ergonomics principles • \Workstation • Neutral-posture checklist	Trainees will be able to set up a workstation	According to the neutral-posture guidelines

FIGURE 12. Developing learning objectives (*Source:* Mager 1988)

Condition: Given the ergonomics policy, a discussion on ergonomics principles, an actual computer workstation, and the neutral-posture checklist. . . .

Skill (action verb): The supervisors will be able to correctly set up workstations that promote neutral postures.

Performance Standards: The employee must be able to sit in neutral positions according to guidelines.

An easy way to write an objective is to break it down into four categories as shown in the ergonomics example (Figure 12). A goals-and-objectives worksheet is included in Appendix B.

Begin by writing down each knowledge, skill, or attitude trainees would need in order to work safely (column 1). Next, for each knowledge, skill, or attitude listed, describe the learning *conditions* (such as the tools, materials, activities, or equipment) that will be used to help learners achieve the desired performance (column 2). The condition part of an objective is typically worded as, given . . . (*then describe the learning conditions*)—for example, given the ergonomics policy, an actual computer workstation, and the neutral-posture checklist.

The third step describes the *skill* (column 3), which is the desired knowledge or abilities learners should possess after the training. An action verb is used to describe the skill. Some of the most common verbs used to describe safety skills are listed in Figure 13. For example, the supervisors will be able to correctly set up (*action verb*) the workstation.

Finally, *performance standards* (column 4) describe the acceptable levels of performance (meaning, when someone is determined to be proficient) and how competency will be measured. Standards can be stated in terms of speed, accuracy, quantity, quality, time, and frequency (Lawson 1997). After completing the work-

Analyze	Discuss	Practice
Approve	Instruct	List
Demonstrate	Conduct	Select
Describe	Investigate	Set up
Determine	Recommend	Solve

FIGURE 13. Common Verbs for Learning Objectives
(*Source:* Cantonwine 1999)

sheet, there should be one objective for each skill, knowledge, or attitude listed.

TESTING OBJECTIVES

Finally, to determine if an objective is effectively written, Mager (1988) suggests that trainers ask the following questions:

1. Does it say what the worker will be able to do after the training?
2. Does it describe testing conditions or real-world situations under which the desired performance would be achieved?
3. Does it explain how to recognize satisfactory performance?

It is important to remember that goals represent the overall desired result for a course and are stated in general terms; objectives, on the other hand, focus specifically on the learners' performance. Both goals and objectives are considered important elements in the training development process.

CONCLUSION

The focus of this chapter has been on learners: who they are, how they learn, and what motivates them. The goal of the first section was to stress the importance of learning theories and how they are the basis for instruction. In the second section, the emphasis was geared toward providing practical tools and strategies trainers could use to develop training programs. Although the principles in each section are different, the intent was to show that one cannot exist without the other. Throughout this chapter the stories of Maria and John were used to show the diverse worlds of safety training and how to apply the principles to real-life situations. And finally (as stated at the beginning of the chapter), if you know your audience, you will know what learners need and how to provide effective training to them, regardless of the work environment.

REFERENCES

American National Standards Institute (ANSI). Z490.1-2009. *Criteria for Accepted Practices in Safety, Health, and Environmental Training*. Des Plaines, IL: American Society of Safety Engineers.

American Society for Training and Development (ASTD). 1997. *How to Motivate Employees*. Info-line series. Alexandria, VA: ASTD.

Anderson, J. R. 1990. *Cognitive Psychology and Its Implications*. New York: W. H. Freeman.

_____. 1995. *Learning and Memory: An Integrated Approach*. New York: Wiley.

Atkinson, R. C., and R. M. Shiffrin. 1968. "Human Memory: A Proposed System and Its Control Processes." In K. Spence and J. Spence, eds., *The Psychology of Learning and Motivation*, vol. 2. New York: Academic Press.

Ausubel, D. P. 1977. "The Facilitation of Meaningful Verbal Learning in the Classroom." *Educational Psychologist* 12:162–178.

Bandura, A. 1986. *Social Foundations of Thought and Action: A Social-Cognitive Theory*. Englewood, NJ: Prentice Hall.

Bernstein, D. A., A. Clarke-Stewart, L. A. Penner, E. J. Roy, and C. D. Wickens. 2000. *Psychology*. Boston: Houghton Mifflin Company.

Bloom, B. S., M. B. Englehart, E. J. Furst, W. H. Hill, and O. R. Krathwohl. 1956. *Taxonomy of Educational Objectives: The Classification of Educational Goals. Handbook 1: The Cognitive Domain*. New York: Longman.

Bonner, J. 1988. "Implications of Cognitive Theory for Instructional Design: Revisited." *Educational Communication and Technology Journal* 36:3–14.

Bullard, R., M. J. Brewer, N. Gaubas, A. Gibson, K. Hyland, and E. Sample. 1994. *The Occasional Trainer's Handbook*. Englewood Cliffs, NJ: Educational Technology Publications.

Cantonwine, S. C. 1999. Safety *Training that Delivers: How to Design and Present Better Technical Training*. Des Plaines, IL: American Society of Safety Engineers.

Di Vista, F. J., and L. P. Rieber. 1987. "Characteristics of Cognitive Engineering: The Next Generation of Instructional Systems." *Educational Communications and Technology Journal* 35:213–230.

Dowling, N. L., and S. H. McKinnon. 2002. "Instructional Objectives: Improving the Success of Safety Training." *Professional Safety*, Journal of the American Society of Safety Engineers (47)9:41–44.

Driscoll, M. P. 2000. *Psychology of Learning for Instruction*. Needham Heights, MA: Allyn and Bacon.

Elliott, S., T. Kratochwill, J. Littlefield, and J. F. Travers. 2000. *Educational Psychology*. Boston: McGraw-Hill.

Gagne, E. D., C. W. Yekovich, and F. R. Yekovich. 1993. *The Cognitive Psychology School of Learning*. New York: Harper Collins.

Gagne, R. M. 1988. *Essentials of Learning Instruction*. Englewood Cliffs, NJ: Prentice Hall.

Geller, E. S. 1996. *The Psychology of Safety: How to Improve Behaviors and Attitudes on the Job*. Radnor, PA: Chilton Book Company.

Gredler, M. E. 1997. *Learning and Instruction: Theory into Practice*. Upper Saddle River, NJ: Merrill.

Gupta, K. 1999. *A Practical Guide to Needs Assessment*. San Francisco: Jossey-Bass Pfeiffer.

Harb, J. N., S. O. Durrant, and R. E. Terry. 1993. "Use of Kolb Learning Cycle and the 4MAT System in Engineering Education." *Journal of Engineering Education* (April) 82(2):70–77.

James, W. B., and M. W. Galbraith. 1985. "Perceptual Learning Styles, Implications and Techniques for the Practitioner." *Lifelong Learning* (January), pp. 20–23.

Jonassen, D. H., and B. L. Grabowski. 1993. *Handbook of Individual Differences*. Hillsdale, NJ: Erlbaum.

Keller, J. M. 1983. "Motivational Design of Instruction" in C. M. Reigeluth, ed., *Instructional-Design Theories and Models*, pp. 383–434. Hillsdale, NJ: Erlbaum.

_____. 1987. "Development and Use of the ARCS Model of Motivational Design." *Journal of Instructional Development* 10(3):2–11.

Knowles, M. 1988. *The Modern Practice of Adult Education: From Pedagogy to Andragogy*. Revised and updated. Englewood Cliffs NJ: Cambridge Books.

Kolb, D. 1981. *Learning Style Inventory*. Boston: McBer and Company.

Labor Occupational Health Program (LOHP). 2005. University of California, Berkeley. *Facts for Employers: Safer Jobs for Teens* (retrieved June 12, 2006). www.lohp.org

Lawlor, M., and P. Handley. 1996. *The Creative Trainer: Holistic Facilitation Skills for Accelerated Learning*. Berkshire: McGraw-Hill.

Lawson, K. 1997. *Improving On-the-Job Training and Coaching*. Alexandria, VA: American Society of Training and Development.

Leshin, C. B., J. Pollock, and C. M. Reigeluth. 1992. *Instructional Design Strategies and Tactics*. Englewood Cliffs, NJ: Educational Technology Publications.

Loftus, E. F., and G. R. Loftus. 1980. "On the Permanence of Stored Information in the Human Brain." *American Psychologist* 35:409–420.

Low, W. C. 1981. "Changes in Instructional Development: The Aftermath of an Information Process Takeover in Psychology." *Journal of Instructional Development* 4:10–18.

Mager, R. F. 1988. *Making Instruction Work*. Belmont, CA: Lake Publishing Company.

Mager R. F., and P. Pipe. 1997. *Analyzing Performance Problems*. Atlanta: CEP Press.

Maslow, A. 1987. *Motivation and Personality*. New York: Harper and Row.

Mayer, R. E. 1989. "Models for Understanding." *Review of Educational Research* 59:43–64.

McCown, R., M. Driscoll, and P. G. Roop. 1996. *Educational Psychology*. Boston: Allyn and Bacon.

Meier, D. 2000. *The Accelerated Learning Handbook*. New York: McGraw-Hill.

National Institute for Occupational Safety and Health (NIOSH Alert). 2003. Publication No. 2003-128. *Preventing Deaths, Injuries, and Illnesses of Young Workers* (retrieved October 22, 2006). www.cdc.gov/niosh/topics/youth

National Safety Council (NSC). 2009. *Supervisors' Safety Manual*. 10th ed. Itasca, IL: NSC.

Occupational Safety and Health Administration (OSHA). *Teen Worker Website* (retrieved October 22, 2006). www.osha.gov/SLTC/teenworkers

Ormrod, J. E. 1998. *Educational Psychology: Developing Learners*. Upper Saddle River, NJ: Merrill.

Pike, R. W. 1994. *Creative Training Techniques Handbook*. Minneapolis, MN: Lakewood Books.

Sarasin, L. C. 1999. *Learning Style Perspectives: Impact in the Classroom*. Madison, WI: Atwood Publishing.

Schunk, D. H. 2004. *Learning Theories: An Educational Perspective*. Upper Saddle River, NJ: Merrill.

Silberman, M. 1995. *Active Training: A Handbook of Techniques, Designs and Case Examples, and Tips*. Lexington, MA: Lexington Books.

Slavin, R. E. 2000. *Educational Psychology*. Boston: Allyn and Bacon.

Smith, P. L., and T. J. Ragan. 1999. *Instructional Design*. Upper Saddle River, NJ: Merrill.

U.S. Department of Labor. *Youth Rules Website!* (retrieved October 22, 2006). www.youthrules.dol.gov

Wildman, T. M. 1981. "Cognitive Theory and the Design of Instruction." *Educational Technology* 23:14–20.

Wlodkowski, R. J. 1999. *Enhancing Adult Motivation to Learn*. San Francisco: Jossey-Bass Publishers.

Woolfolk, A. E. 1998. *Educational Psychology*. Boston: Allyn and Bacon.

APPENDIX A: TRAINING ASSESSMENT WORKSHEET

Department / Job	Supervisor's Name	Date

Type of Training

Best Days and Times to Train	Number of Employees

Required Personal Protective Equipment

Accident Trends (if any)

List Potential Hazards	Identify the Knowledge and Skills Needed	List Training Topics

Source: National Safety Council 2009

APPENDIX B: GOALS AND OBJECTIVES WORKSHEET

Trainer: _____   **Date:** _____

Course Title: _____

Goals:

_____

_____

Guide to Developing Course Objectives

Knowledge, Skills & Attitudes Needed	Conditions (Tools, Materials, Activities, or Equipment Needed)	Skills	Performance Standards
List the knowledge, skills or attitudes trainees need to work safely.	Describe the learning conditions. Given a . . .	List the skills trainees will be able to do after the training (use action verbs). Trainees will be able to . . .	Describe when performance is good enough.

Write the Course Objective(s) in the CSP Format

_____

_____

_____

_____

Source: Mager 1988

PRESENTATION AND DOCUMENTATION OF SAFETY AND HEALTH TRAINING

5

Fred Fanning

LEARNING OBJECTIVES

▪ Become familiar with the basic applications of training in order to conduct safety training within an organization.

▪ Learn about various models and applications of training to make informed decisions about the best ways to present safety training.

▪ Learn how to document training to meet government standards and, in the process, gain ready access and understanding of the history of safety training conducted by an organization.

AS PEOPLE MOVE through life and interact with others, they assume roles as trainers and educators. People teach others through their words, actions, and deeds. That means that readers come to this chapter with real-life experience, and the key for them is to build on what they already know or perhaps change it into something that works better. If done right, this will allow employees and management to know what their roles and responsibilities are in preventing accidents. This is a skill that every safety, health, and environmental professional needs to have.

CONDUCTING THE TRAINING

This chapter is about adult learning, which is different from child or adolescent learning. The goal in providing safety training is to form an environment where adults want to learn, using hands-on learning techniques when possible.

Moran provides us with a model to follow prior to conducting training. He writes, "OSHA's training guidelines follow a model that consists of: determining if training is needed, identifying training needs, identifying goals and objectives, developing learning activities, conducting the training, evaluating program effectiveness, and improving the program" (Moran 2003, 151). This chapter will address the identification of training needs. Prior to developing a lesson plan, goals and objectives should have been established. "Instructional objectives, if clearly stated, will tell employers what they want their employees to do, to do better, or to stop doing" (Moran 2003, 153).

WRITING A LESSON PLAN

There are three documents that facilitate the transfer of learning from the instructor to the student: the syllabus, the course outline, and the lesson plan. The syllabus is a large, formal document. It is normally used in a school environment and is often approved by faculty administrators. The outline is also a formal document that breaks down the course of instruction into a list of elements. Instructor supervisors may also approve this document. The lesson plan is the deliberate process of documenting the breakdown of a course of instruction. The lesson plan is normally printed out and used to prepare for and conduct the lesson. This document is prepared by the instructor and does not require anyone's approval for use.

The lesson plan outlines the training and is used to break down a course of instruction into bite-size subjects or lessons that a student could learn in a concise and effective manner. The purpose of training "is to create change in learners that they consistently reproduce without variance" (Stolovich and Keeps 2002, 10). In this chapter training is further defined to include various formats that can be used in conducting training on the job through computers, through the Internet, in a workshop on equipment, or in groups located almost anywhere. The reason for this expansion of the definition is that "Learning, by contrast, is a much larger umbrella that covers all our efforts to absorb, understand, and respond to the world around us" (HRDC 1997, 11).

"The lesson plan is a must for all teachers because it acts as a reference and guide for each class meeting" (Grieve 2005, 67). There may be as many as eight lessons in a one-day course. For a course that requires several days to complete, the lesson plan may cover the extensive matter one day at a time. The flexibility and its use lie with the instructor. Foremost, the lesson plan provides instructors with a tool to develop the training based on the outcome of learning they want to achieve. Within the lesson plan the instructors identify points they want to stress. "The plan contains important questions and quotes from supplemental material" (Grieve 2005, 67).

An instructor will want to prepare for a lesson by going over the learning objectives, major points of learning, times for conducting training, and ways to conduct the training. The lesson plan provides him or her with all of that information. "An effective method of planning a course is to construct a plan

for each class meeting, number the lessons, place them in a loose leaf binder, and maintain them as a record and guide for activities" (Grieve 1996, 16). This method may be used to instruct everything from a one-day class to an eight-week college course. It is a very simple and effective way to provide an instructor with a plan for each lesson, a plan that is easy to follow and keeps the instructor on task.

Most instructors cannot keep an entire lesson in their heads. Instructors also need a way to document what was taught. Using a lesson plan allows them to document the content of the lesson. The material to be covered is placed in the lesson plan in a logical manner that will allow the instructor to provide a consistent and yet inclusive lesson to each class. The goal is to put pen to paper and develop a complete plan of how to conduct the lesson and then to use that document to present the training.

Once the goals and objectives of the training have been established, research will need to be conducted on the topic. In the past, instructors used the regulatory codes and standards, consensus standards, as well as books and periodicals from the local library, to research the topic. Notes were taken, and that information was integrated into the lesson plans and student handouts. Today instructors have the ability to conduct large amounts of research using the World Wide Web, where almost any subject for developing and conducting training can be found. Even some of the books and periodicals in the library can be accessed from a home computer. Identifying goals and objectives for the training and then conducting research to gather information needed for lesson plans and handouts will lead the instructor to identify an instructional method.

There are a number of methods that can be used to help an employee to learn. "Job rotations, special assignments, reflecting on experience, coaching and counseling, mentoring, manager as teacher, learning teams and self-development, and individual development plans are just a few available methods" (HRDC 1997, 16). Each of these methods has benefits and drawbacks. The most obvious method is to provide instruction in a classroom. However, it may not be the most effective method. Choose the method that best provides the environment for learning and then proceed with a format for the lesson plan.

There are a number of formats for the lesson plan. The instructor should choose one that is right for him or her. This normally includes identifying the course number and name, the date or dates of the presentation, and student and instructor activities that should take place during the lesson (Fanning, 2006).

The best way to organize the lesson plan is to put it in a format that allows for ease of instruction. This usually means laying out the plan in a linear fashion that focuses on the timeline of the class. This process allows the instructor to teach according to the plan and the timeline. The lesson plan should highlight major activities and identify videos, slide shows, and exercises to be used in class. Special instructions should be added for areas that require a unique activity or piece of equipment so that the instructor need not search for this information. It is also helpful to include notes that tell the instructor where to find the material. For example, the lesson plan may say the following (Fanning 2006):

Play video "Fall Protection" using video number 5115-0987 (NOTE: video is located at the factory engineering office. Video must be picked up and played forward to the starting point of video. After use, the tape must be rewound and returned to the engineering office.)

This type of instruction makes the training effective for students and easy for the instructor. The lesson plan should also periodically reference the timeline for conducting the course. For example, the lesson plan might say the following (Fanning 2006):

0900–0950: Brief slide show on "Slips, Trips, and Falls"

0950–1000: Break

This kind of detail will allow the instructor to remain on time and complete the lesson plan, covering all the material outlined for the student.

Supporting material comes in many forms. The task is to identify all the material available and then to determine which material will enhance learning. Supporting material might include articles in trade journals that demonstrate a teaching point or provide the student with an opportunity to think about a real-life application of the issue. Exercises also provide situations in which an individual or a group of students can think through real-world problems or issues and determine solutions to them. There are also talking points, information papers, OSHA guidelines, informational material from trade organizations, questionnaires, and newspaper articles, just to name a few. All this support material is used to emphasize points in class by bringing real-world application to the learning process.

Every lesson plan must have a beginning and an end. That sounds rather obvious, yet it is very easy to jump right into the middle of the teaching material or cut off the plan when time runs out. The beginning of the lesson plan helps identify the learning objectives and outcomes. It introduces the content of material and gives the student a reason to stay for the training. Like the beginning of a story, it sets the stage for the entire lesson plan. The beginning can include ice-breaking exercises to let the students relax and get to know each other. It can be used to set the stage for the class by checking the class materials and briefly telling the participants how each one contributes to learning. It is also a good time to refer to the timeline of the course and inform the students if videos, slide shows, or group exercises will be offered, or if analysis of articles will be conducted. In contrast, the ending provides a completion to the learning session and the lesson plan. The instructor can restate the learning objectives and outcomes and ask students if the objectives and outcomes were met. Instructors can allow students to wrap up what they have learned. The whole point is to bring the learning to a discrete close. The student may read articles, attend additional classes, read books, or attend lectures on the subject in the future, so the learning will probably go on, but each learning session must be brought to proper closure.

The final outline of a lesson plan is the result of simply putting the information into a format that identifies major points, supporting points, and general information. The outline allows the instructor to adjust for a better flow of information. The outline puts all the information into a neat package from which the instructor can develop the plan. Without a good and understandable outline, the lesson plan will not be effective or useful. The outline will help identify holes or weaknesses in the training material and provide research guidance to alleviate those problems; it will also help complete the process.

UNDERSTANDING GROUP DYNAMICS

Members of a class, course, or training program form teams. The same dynamics and development stages that affect teams in work situations also affect groups in training. The theory is that groups that are put together go through stages of development to form a team. Issues, hazards, and productive outcomes depend on the time and experience of group members. It is believed that all groups go through these stages. The amount of time and struggle a group has with each stage is dependent on the group. Some groups can go through the stages rather quickly, while others could get stuck at some point. The standard stages of group development taught in most, if not all, courses are commonly referred to as forming, storming, norming, and performing. Gardenswartz and Rowe developed a parallel theory for the stages of team development; their theory works along the same lines and is referred to as infancy, adolescence, middle age, and maturity (Gardenswartz and Rowe 2003, 194–195). Blanchard, Carew, and Parisis-Carew, authors of the *One Minute Manager Builds High Performing Teams*, tell us group interactions are broken down into two paths, which are content and process (Blanchard et al. 2009, 20). This theory was developed along with two branches of development. The content branch is made up of the *what* and the tasks, and the process branch consists of the *how* and the team functions (Blanchard et al. 2009, 20). These stages are important to an instructor because, as one can imagine, in several of the stages, learning will be difficult, if not impossible. The instructor can facilitate the development of the group through the various stages to the performing stage, where high-impact learning can take place with great retention.

People coming together, with all of the unknowns that surround the experience, represent the first stage. Gardenswartz and Rowe refer to the first part of their four-part stages of development as infancy. They tell us this stage focuses on the team members not knowing much. They state the basic unknowns are: "we keep asking what we are doing and why, team members don't know enough about each other, and are unclear about what we are supposed to do" (Gardenswartz and Rowe 2003, 195). During this stage the instructor can use ice-breaking techniques to end some of those unknowns.

Gardenswartz and Rowe tell us that their second developmental stage is known as adolescence. They tell us this stage focuses on the team members. "We're having trouble getting along, members are jockeying for power" (Gardenswartz and Rowe 2003, 195). Instructors, to facilitate an effective transition through this stage, can help students identify class norms or acceptable classroom behavior. They can also use group exercises to allow students to work with each other and become more familiar with each other's needs.

Gardenswartz and Rowe, on the other hand, inform us that the third part of their developmental stages is middle age. They tell us this stage focuses on the team members. "We're seeing the progress of work, team members are open and honest in asking questions and giving feedback, and as we get to know each other better, we are working more smoothly together" (Gardenswartz and Rowe 2003, 195). The instructor can facilitate this stage by again using group exercises when possible to get the students to work together.

Gardenswartz and Rowe inform us that the last part of their four-part stages of development is maturing. "We feel pride in our accomplishment, we're really cooking, and we all do what it takes to get the job done" (Gardenswartz and Rowe 2003, 195). The instructor takes advantage of this stage by challenging students with materials that stimulate learning and by allowing them to learn from each other.

Students, as members of a group, have distinct personalities, and they bring to class, for good or bad, their abilities to influence those around them. The instructor must identify each student's sphere of influence and use that to the class's advantage. For example, everyone remembers the class clowns, who acted out their skits in spite of the needs of the rest of the class. Often these class clowns influenced students through their antics. There are also other students who possess experience or knowledge that others look to for answers or ideas. In either case, the instructor should identify the influence of these members and determine the best way to use that influence for the good of the class and to further their learning.

Beside *influential* students, one also encounters over-achievers. These students excel and often arrive at the answers and solutions before other students. These overachievers can help others learn the lesson or see further applications of the knowledge. Unforunately they can also short-circuit learning by ending a lesson before the others have had an opportunity to learn the material. The instructor should thus use the strength of such overachievers to further group learning to the point where each student is ready to move forward.

There are many exercises that an instructor can use to open a presentation. The main goal of these is to prepare students to learn. Let us begin with the easiest method, introductions, which calls for each person to stand and tell the group about himself or herself. Normally people state their names, where they work, why they are taking this course, what they hope to get out of the course; they usually also share something personal with the group. Another way to use the introduction is to have the group split up into pairs. Each person in a pair should interview the other person. Questions that are asked during such interviews include the person's name, where they work, why they are taking this course, what they hope to get out of the course, and one thing personal to share with the group. When everyone is done, both people in a pair stand, and they introduce and tell the class a little about the other person. A third way to do the introductions is to give people 3-by-5-inch cards and have them write down their names, where they work, why they are taking this course, what they hope to get out of the course, and one thing personal to share with the group. Put all the 3-by-5-inch cards into a hat or box and have each person come forward and pull out a card. Each participant then stands and asks the person whose name is on the card to stand as well before introducing him or her. This provides some time for group members to relax, get to know each other, and begin to fit in with the group.

Group norms are rules that help maintain harmony and balance in the group. It is essential to identify these group norms and for each student to agree to abide by them. The instructor can help the group members to identify the norms or rules they feel are appropriate, and then also help them reach full agreement through a show of hands. This does not have to take a long time. The norms in a class are usually fairly straight-forward and often include letting everyone speak, not interrupting one another, raising hands and waiting to be called on to speak, being on time, turning off cell phones, agreeing to disagree, and so on. The instructor can expedite the process by providing the students with a standard set of norms to pick from. With this additional information, the process can take as little as ten minutes, but save hours of conflict in the long run.

Students in a class setting learn individual as well as group lessons. The group develops alternatives to the learning process, and through discussion and analysis determines solutions and their proper applications. This process is also used in the work environment where an organization or a team learns together. The group learning adds to the individual learning process; it may even provide individuals with applicable knowledge that the individual may not have otherwise received. The instructor can increase the possibility of group learning through group activities such as exercises, discussions, projects, presentations, and even group examinations.

COMPARING POPULAR TRAINING METHODS

In today's environment there is no one best way to learn material needed to be a productive and safe worker. For this reason, there are several ways in which an organization may want to provide training. Each method has its own positive and negative points. The primary means of providing training are the traditional classroom method, on-the-job training, and online training. Actually, the traditional method of training has been on the job. In the early years of our country, academic learning was restricted to the elite. Later, various movements obtained the right to a general education for everyone, and, at that stage, the country moved to the traditional classroom environment where a teacher told students what they needed to know and how best to interpret it. The method used by an organization depends on the organization, and there is no right or wrong choice.

The personnel of an organization need to look at the learning they want as an outcome and determine the best, most cost-effective, and supportable way to provide that learning. No organization should provide the traditional classroom method as the sole method. Instead, organizations should adopt a holistic approach to learning. It is beneficial to compare the above-mentioned primary methods of training.

When deciding on the training technique, an instructor could investigate whether on-the-job or classroom training will be a better fit for the lesson plan. At least three categories of on-the-job-training (OJT) expenses exist. Then there are costs associated with company equipment, which, because they are used for training, become *nonproductive*.

Of the many issues involved in the comparison between classroom-based training and on-the-job training, the two primary ones are cost and availability of actual learning. Other issues that one might consider are the cost of potential waste produced during on-the-job training or the cost of injury due to unsafe practices of workers. On-the-job training can produce variations in what is taught and learned because it requires more instructors and because of the variations that occur each day on the job. In addition, on-the-job training could pose a concern to the company insurance underwriter. A suitable classroom for training must also be located, a classroom in which audiovisual equipment could be required as part of the traditional classroom method.

Peer learning is essential if an employer is to get the most from a training opportunity. Each worker has information about the way work is done in the organization, information that could increase productivity were it known by all workers. In this age, where employers are asking their workers to think and improve their work processes, the natural extension of such a process is for workers to share their knowledge with their colleagues. This can happen in the classroom. However, because the instructor drives the learning process and the lesson, the amount of peer learning is small. However, in on-the-job training, the student is out among his or her peers and will normally be privy to information about how things work, short cuts, and lessons learned at work. The main concern at this stage is making sure that peers are not teaching the new employee bad habits. However, if the organization is open to workers having ideas and expressing ways of doing their jobs better, the bad effects of peer sharing can be greatly reduced.

It is much cheaper to put workers in a classroom and tell them what they need to know. In addition, learning on the job, because it keeps employees from *productive* work, can be quite expensive. This learning process requires the supervisor or trainer to focus on teaching instead of *working*. In a classroom, the instructor can deal with 25 to 30 students effectively. However, for on-the-job training, the ratio of trainer to students needs to be closer to 1 to 1 or 1 to 3 trainers to students, thereby significantly increasing its cost. However, that is but one measurement available. The actual learning should also be measured. Putting those 25 to 30 students in a classroom may yield a 25 to 50 percent knowledge retention rate. On-the-job training, on the other hand, may provide a 45 to 70 percent retention rate of the work students practice each day. That would make on-the-job training the most effective.

The second comparison that can be made is between classroom and online training. When comparing classroom training with online training, one should first consider the hardware and software they have or need, as well as the need for fast internet connections and perhaps even a company intranet setup. When considering classroom training, the company must have access to a classroom and the automation equipment needed to run slide shows, videos, and audio presentations.

Most online training comes *canned*, which means that it is produced with a specific topic in mind, and thus is primarily able to teach that particular topic. An organization can purchase a customized course, but that will normally cost more money. In most cases the canned presentation will meet the organization's needs and can be purchased on a per-student basis or for a period of time. Courses of instruction may also be purchased for downloading onto company intranets and used at the company's convenience. The automation that the company is currently using is also a major consideration. The automation required for online training is fairly sophisticated and requires the most modern software with the newest hardware. If the organization does not meet this format, it may have to purchase computer hardware and software and even install an intranet.

As noted above, peer learning is essential if an employer is to get the most from a training opportunity. Peer learning can happen in the classroom, but the drawback is that the instructor drives the lessons and the learning process, potentially stifling peer learning. However, online peer learning is high if the learning is connected to chat rooms or online conferences; if it is not, then there is virtually no peer learning.

Let us return to some of the beneficial points of classroom training. It is much cheaper to put workers in a classroom and tell them what they need to know than to provide computers, modems, and other automated equipment for online training. However, if a company already has access to the automated equipment needed for online training, a large classroom or audiovisual equipment would be unnecessary. In a classroom the instructor can deal with 25 to 30 students, with little time spent on each of them. However, in online training, the student-trainer ratio is normally 15 students to 1 trainer, and the training provides the student with a self-contained training package. The actual learning should also be measured. Putting those 25 to 30 students in a classroom may yield a 25 to 50 percent retention rate on the training provided. Online training may provide 85 to 90 percent retention because students can work at their own pace and even go back to previous lessons. These reasons make online training the most effective. "Classroom training, although normally more expensive because of the classroom, provides a better learning environment that supports the student and allows for the security to ensure the student actually takes the training" (Fanning 2009, 1).

The third and final comparison is between on-the-job training and online training. This is a more modern comparison that completely eliminates classroom training. Online training has a student ratio closer to 1 to 15 and provides the students with the ability to move through the training at a variety of locations. This training ratio is a little misleading because each student receives one-on-one time with the instructor. This method of training is online, with the contact between instructor and student over an internet connection. The class can be active, with an instructor and additional students, or it can be passive, with a computer program conducting the class, with the student responding to the computer replaying information. An active online class is conducted at specific periods of time that accommodate a variety of time zones and locations. Work is completed and submitted online. Instructors use e-mail, blogs, and social networking accounts to create a common environment where students can discuss the issues presented in the course. The passive classes are built and launched on a Web site. The student can register, review, and complete online examinations, interacting with the online program. Companies must consider the need for hardware and software as well as the need for fast modem connection and perhaps even a company intranet setup.

The issue of canned online training has already been addressed, but the topic is worth raising here because on-the-job training is the most tailored way to provide training. What can be more tailored than a person learning to do the job by actually doing it? However, an organization can purchase a customized course that meets the organization's needs; the purchase can be made on a per-student basis or for a period of time. Courses of instruction may also be purchased for downloading onto company intranets and used at the company's convenience. The automation that the organization is currently using is also a major consideration. The automation required for online training is fairly sophisticated and requires the most modern software with the newest hardware. Of the many issues involved in this comparison, the primary two are cost and availability of actual learning. Other issues or costs that one might consider are waste produced during on-the-job training or unsafe acts leading to worker injuries. On-the-job training can produce variations in what is taught and, obviously, what is learned, due to the limited instructor-to-student ratio; it can also produce variations that occur each day on the job. In addition, the company insurance underwriter might voice concerns were training provided on the job. With on-the-job learning, the student normally has ready access to a live mentor in the form of his or her supervisor. This situation not only facilitates the learning process for the present course of instruction, but also for all training in the future.

In contrast, the online courses can connect the student to an online instructor who can provide mentoring similar to that of the on-location supervisor. So even though the course may be without an instructor, there are ways instructors can be part of the process.

A value judgment is hard to make in this comparison because of the variables involved in both training methods. On-the-job training can be quite costly because the supervisor or trainer is not doing *work* while training, and because waste is produced by the student and there is a potential for student accidents. However, learning by doing has been an effective method of training through the ages. There are a lot of benefits to this type of training. The students learn hands-on in the environment where they will work. They actually do the work, which allows them to form a connection between the learning and the work. This method works best for training needed on machinery or processes. However, if the work involves automated equipment or decision-making or thinking skills, the use of online training can be just as effective because the actual use of automation is built into the course. Retention is also greater with online courses because the students can repeat the training again or access information they might have forgotten.

MEDIA AND TECHNIQUES

"Engagement is what it's all about today in education, and technology promises unique ways to engage students in learning. In particular, educational technology enthusiasts tout Web 2.0 as the silver bullet for motivating even recalcitrant students to get with the program" (Simkins and Schultz 2010).

Web 2.0 refers to the wide range of easy-to-use online tools that foster interaction, collaboration, and group productivity. Examples include (Simkins and Schultz 2010):

- social and professional networking sites
- blogs
- wikis
- file-sharing and collaboration sites
- collaborative resource tagging
- user-submitted reviews and ratings

One Web 2.0 application is the digital music player. The more famous of these players is the iPod® and the MP3 player. These players have significantly changed the way we listen to music in this country, and have the potential to do the same for the way we give and receive training.

The iPod® is a small media player from Apple Computer. There are other products on the market, but the name iPod® is most recognizable, and many people use this name to refer to MP3 players from other companies. From this device comes the term PodCast. This is short for iPod® Broadcast, which is an audio broadcast that can be played on the iPod® or similar small device. The PodCast is becoming commonplace when listening to lectures. Today's instructor can record and send PodCasts via email to students with assignments or lectures to be listened to before class starts. This can level the playing field by providing students with basic information. This allows the instructor to get the students to the same level of knowledge before starting class.

There is a great deal of written material that workers can read to learn the information they need. The primary sources are books, periodicals, and workbooks. Many students have used these sources and have a great deal of experience with them. In some cases, students may have already formed opinions about the usefulness of printed material; these opinions, depending on whether they are positive or negative, may support or hinder the learning process.

Books are something we are familiar with. They are the mainstay of public education in this country and are used by many to enjoy free time. However, books have their pros and cons. "Pros are that they are cheap, the reader can access worldwide experts, there is more opportunity to go into depth, the reader does not have to be certain of the application, it is self paced, they can be read practically anywhere, and serve as a constant reminder" (Clegg 2000, 91–92). Cons include ". . . the reader can't learn from a book, they won't actually read it, there isn't a book that meets our specific needs, it's the instructor shooting him or herself in the foot, we've got a library, and the student gets to keep something we've paid for" (Clegg 2000, 92–93). Books are a great way to disseminate information to the workforce that can read and be counted on to read the book. Literacy is a great concern in this country and must be considered when providing reading assignments to workers. An adjunct to that issue is the large numbers of workers who speak English as a second language. This situation leaves the company with the possibility of having to purchase books in more than one language, if that is possible, or not purchasing books at all. Books can be used as lessons in themselves, or they can be used to supplement a course as source material. Books can be reread by the student and even kept as a resource for future use, should questions arise.

Periodicals are known as magazines or newsletters that are printed periodically. They have some of the pros and cons of books. Many Americans enjoy reading magazines and spend a great deal of money on them each year. However, they normally do not purchase educational periodicals. There is a distinct difference in the quality of periodicals. A safety article in a magazine such as *Professional Safety* has more credibility than a safety article in *Time*. The former is an industry periodical that focuses on safety and peer reviews its articles, while the second is an entertainment magazine that uses reporters to develop stories. Periodicals are a great source of training if the suitable ones are identified and used properly; some research may be needed to identify a peer-reviewed academic or industry periodical. Periodicals are normally not used alone to teach a subject, but rather they are used as source material to develop the lesson plans and for group exercises on a specific topic.

Workbooks are another throwback to public education and a great source of information. They have many of the shortcomings as books and periodicals that must be overcome before they are used. Workbooks enable students to apply lessons learned through application. An instructor can even grade this work. As with other materials, workbooks can be kept for future reference by the student or serve as proof of course completion.

In addition to printed material, there is also nonprinted material. This is material that is not normally provided in hard copy in a readable format, or it supplements a hard copy in an alternate format. The newer-generation workers are familiar with these nonprint applications and prefer them to books.

The first example of the nonprint material is the e-book, which is in an electronic format and can be used on a personal computer, laptop, or a personal digital assistant. The e-book is normally read from the electronic device in much the same way that the book is read. The electronic book can also add hot links to Web sites for further information and allows the user to bookmark special sections for rereading or to mark one's place. The e-book saves physical space. Because the books are electronic, they reside in cyberspace and not on a bookshelf. They do have to be read and, in that sense, they have a great deal in common with the printed book. Some e-books are simply the electronic versions of printed books; in other cases, an e-book can be unique in that there is no printed version.

Distance learning replaces the old method of teleconferencing where students in a classroom listen to lectures from a trainer over the telephone while viewing slides operated by a facilitator:

> Distance learning, also known as interactive videoconferencing (IVC), occurs when two or more people at different locations see and hear each other at the same time (two way interactive video). Participants can see the remote instructor on the monitor, which can be projected for larger classes. (*Media and Methods Magazine* 2010)

> Video streaming technology allows schools that do not have videoconferencing capabilities to participate in these educational experiences and ask questions via email, instead of face-to-face interaction like a point-to-point call. (*Media and Methods Magazine* 2010)

> Cisco is delivering its own take on videoconferencing over 3G/4G networks with the Cisco Cius tablet. (*The Buzz* 2010)

This tablet is a small, hand-held device, about the size of a book, using the cell phone network for access. In addition,

> AVI-SPL [Audio Visual Innovations (AVI)] and Signal Perfection Ltd [(SPL)] announced the launch of Caméléon, a first-of-its-kind multifunction telepresence

solution designed to adapt to a customer's environment while providing the highest quality meeting experience. (*The Buzz* 2010)

The Caméléon is an interactive system of devices, PCs, and monitors that create the telepresence. These new tools are designed to enhance the usefulness of videoconferencing, making it available to almost anyone anywhere.

Video is normally operated through a digital videodisk. Most organizations have the equipment necessary to play this form of material. In most cases, employees have the same ability to play the material. Video is a popular teacher at small firms.

Digital recordings can be a useful way to train the target audience, and they can also be reused to train a wider group of employees.

Today students are open to experience-sharing. This method allows students to share lessons they have learned or ways to apply those lessons. This method is especially important for adult students who have a great deal of life experiences. They can share these life experiences with others to prove a point, share learning, or adapt learning to new situations.

Every individual has life experiences, which are normally unique and forged through trial and error. This makes each person an instructor. If there were a way they could share all that information, it would benefit the entire organization. Experience-sharing is how an employee can communicate that information. Lesson plans should facilitate this type of learning through opportunities to share. Instructors should allow and encourage students to speak about their experiences and demonstrate how those experiences apply to the subject under study. This can be done through group exercises, individual presentations, individual papers, debates, or through open discussions between pairs of students. The key is to get the valuable experience of each person out in the open for all to share and learn from. Individual sharing can be used to supplement an ongoing training program such as classroom, on-the-job, or online training.

Roundtable discussions are also a good way for students to get together and share information. The instructor acts as a group facilitator, keeping the discussion going and on track. The students take turns adding information to the discussion, analyzing the points made, determining the validity of the points, and discussing ways in which the material discussed could be used to solve a problem in the workplace. These discussions can be formal or informal. An instructor who keeps the discussion on track usually facilitates formal roundtable discussions. The process is in the format of a lesson plan and is intended to develop solutions to problems or to share information to facilitate learning. However, the roundtable discussion can be informal and run by students. They determine the structure or lack of it to be used and take the discussion where they want. They can use the session to supplement class learning or just to share experiences with each other. Roundtable discussions can be used to supplement a class or training program.

There is a great deal of publicity about the chat room these days. It is considered by many to be a bad thing that distracts people from their work, lives, and, in some cases, reality. However, the cyberspace chat rooms and discussion boards can be a great place for students to share information, discuss alternatives, opine about each other's information, analyze the data, and develop solutions for problems. The chat room and discussion board are basically the same thing. They occupy a site in cyberspace where e-mail or live messages are posted for all to see and comment on. Some sites are live while others have some delay. The cyberspace discussion can be considered the same as a roundtable discussion in the way it is applied. One occurs in cyberspace and the other in physical space and time. This method can be a stand-alone learning device or used to supplement an on-going training program, such as classroom or on-the-job training.

The value of experience-sharing lies in its importance to the student. The student can share and receive information, learning for free. In most cases there is not even a personal cost of embarrassment, fear, or reprisal connected to the learning process. Experience-sharing can add to any training program and offers the instructor another approach to provide information to students from other students. With the exception of connecting to cyberspace, there is little cost involved in experience-sharing. However, many homes are now connected to cyberspace and most people know how to use it and feel comfortable with it. The cyberspace option also provides anonymity if students need to pursue a thought or idea that otherwise might embarrass them. Students retain a great deal of information learned through experience-sharing because it is done at the student level. They often find more meaning in it and thus more of a reason to remember it. Some of the material learned through this method is not usable and a little may even be counterproductive to the learning objectives. However, these normally do not detract from the ease and the low-cost option of using experience-sharing.

There is a large audience across the nation for self-improvement. Millions of dollars are spent each year on books to help one diet, speak another language, live a stress-free life, love one's children or spouse more, make more money, or handle personal problems better. "Self-development is a collection of techniques and approaches for an individual to manage their own process of learning. These include self-analysis of competencies and interests, personal development plans, learning contracts, learning logs, reading lists, involvement in professional organizations, networks, attending demonstrations at other organizations, and participating on interagency committees" (HRDC 1997, 17). Because of the popularity of this method, students are probably more open to using it. Instructors can use the self-improvement approach to develop lesson plans and identify methods of instruction that help employees improve. Instructors can point out to the worker the benefits of training and also encourage students to apply themselves in learning to improve themselves.

COLLABORATIVE AND ACTIVE LEARNING

Today more than ever society is moving away from telling people what to think and allowing them to think for themselves. This is causing a major shift in how we learn. Many organizations are adapting to this new style of collaborative or active learning. The Motorcycle Safety Foundation has made a giant leap in providing training to motorcycle riders that uses the instructor as a coach rather than as a teacher and requires the students to lead their own learning through classroom discussions and hands-on riding of the motorcycle. It is a shift to think that an instructor—who provides the conditions for students to learn and the material to learn—can stand back and coach the students through learning the objectives of the lesson. It may seem even harder when one realizes it takes this organization sixteen hours to turn a person who has never ridden a motorcycle into one who can ride a motorcycle with basic proficiency and complete a skills test.

Students taking responsibility for their own learning have obvious links to other students as members of the class or perhaps as employees of the same organization. There are also deeper links that each student may have to the other students. One student may share previous learning experiences or work experiences with one or more students, giving that student links to the class as a whole. Some students may also share beliefs and values with other students, which will link them to those students and the group as a whole. The instructor should identify links and make use of them to facilitate learning within the group. Students accept ideas more easily when they share links with other members of the group who accept those ideas.

"In reality, teachers are on a stage; they are actors or actresses whether or not they recognize and admit it" (Grieve 2005, 17). One role that instructors play is that of facilitating. This role is difficult for instructors because it puts them in a position of not directing the learning but establishing the conditions under which it occurs among the students—with the materials provided or from completely new sources identified and provided by students. To do this effectively, instructors must be able to consider that adult students know a great deal about the world, and perhaps even the subject being taught. With a little help, the students might be able to figure the material out on their own with more retention and better understanding than an instructor could ever provide.

Groups might use interactive videoconferencing, video-streaming, interactive systems such as Caméléon, or tablets that achieve access via cell phone networks. *Peer-to-peer networking* is another way to actively engage in the learning process.

The evolution of the World Wide Web from Web 1.0 to Web 2.0 is creating subtle but profound changes in the ways human beings locate and access information, communicate with, and learn from each other. The paradigms for learning have already evolved beyond traditional classroom models to synchronous and asynchronous, interactive, and collaborative learning, which is further extended by Web 2.0 tools and social networking approaches (Gunawardena, et al. 2009).

As Burgess (2003) points out:

By incorporating social networking into the online course curriculum, instructors help women increase their social capital. . . . Instructors can include a number of activities to introduce learners to a social networking framework (Burgess, 2009).

She recommends that trainers do the following to encourage students to participate in social networking to improve learning (Burgess 2009):

- Create a profile, and encourage students to follow.
- Define community early in the course.
- Create a class network.
- Blog to reflect.

The group has a lot of work to do in a collaborative or active learning environment. This is due to the group ownership of the learning environment. In this method of learning, the students cannot just sit back and expect the instructor to spoon-feed them the information they need. In this method each student is hungry and ready to learn because of the environment and freedom to take the learning as it comes and move it in any direction to further explore thoughts and concepts. There are three types of roles that students take: task roles, maintenance roles, and blocker roles. Task roles include initiator, contributor, information seeker, information giver, evaluator, and summarizer. Maintenance roles include harmonizer, encourager, gatekeeper, and compromiser. Finally there are blocking roles, including dominator, blocker, aggressor, and disrupter.

Students can also serve as instructors in almost all methods of training. In collaborative learning the student may lead a discussion on the subject or ways to implement the subject. The student may serve as a facilitator of a session used by other students to discuss, analyze, and implement ideas. Students may also be called upon to develop and conduct lessons for the entire class as part of the grade for completing the course. In general, all students bring life lessons to the training. Each student can provide feedback to class activities, relating lessons learned to life experiences they have had. This way each student is an instructor and a student for the group. Each student can learn from his or her fellow students if the group is open to learning from each other.

In collaborative or active learning students take responsibility for their learning. They identify themselves with thoughts and ideas they want to know. They put forth the effort necessary to expand those thoughts and ideas while sharing them with fellow students to explore new ways of learning and applying what they learn. This puts the student squarely in charge of his or her learning. Instructors must facilitate this role and make sure they do not take it from the students or allow the students to give it to them.

In a collaborative or active learning environment, fellow students may record the proceedings of a learning session in the role of recorder. The recording is also used as minutes of the proceedings for each student to use in the future and to provide applied lessons for grading by the instructor. Each student who documented his or her own work traditionally played this role. Today, with learning in groups, there is often a group product that is documented and graded rather than individual products. This role also allows the student to learn from the process. The role is not one of passively taking notes but of actively viewing and trying to make sense of the process and how others participate in it.

If possible each student should step back from the proceedings and watch the process, rather than work on the problem, in the role of observer. This rare experience can teach a student more about process than a lecture or book on the subject. The student stands back from the group, listening to, watching, and feeling what is taking place. He or she notes the body language used as well as the words; determines if group norms are followed or changed; and is prepared to brief the group on what he or she observed. This provides a learning experience not just for the observing student but also for all the students who participated.

Great insights can be gained from the information shared by the observer. Instructors should include the use of observers whenever they engage in group work where the process is as important as the product.

When conducting safety training, one is normally providing training for adults who are in the workforce. These adults learn differently than children do; they should be given credit for the life experiences they bring to the training. The instructor must take advantage of the adult's experience by providing them opportunities to engage in the learning process. This can be done through group exercises, presentations, hands-on exercises, student-led training, or allowing students to determine answers or solutions to problems rather than being told the textbook answer. By engaging learners, the instructor can increase retention and understanding of the material.

Active learning is a buzz word for many. Some instructors use it to describe almost any kind of learning. This is unfortunate because it tends to confuse students about what active learning really is. Most of us can remember sitting in an auditorium or classroom and listening to someone speak about a particular topic. In this situation there is no effort given by the learner to participate in the learning. Lecturing is often done because it is the easiest way to teach or instruct for the person doing the speaking, it has been modeled for years so it must work, and it is the fastest way to put out a lot of information (Bowman 2003, 11). However, Sharon Bowman, in *Preventing Death by Lecture*, tells us that people normally remember only 20 percent of what they hear (Bowman 2003, 2). To increase how much a student remembers, the trainer must provide learning opportunities for more than one sense. By providing material for the student to see and hear, retention is improved.

Passive learners are *not* active in the learning process. Their role in a passive learning environment does not require them to perform any action. Many learners become bored and tired, begin to daydream, or let their minds drift to other subjects. When learners are active in the learning process, they are more awake, focused, and interested in the learning that is taking place. Learners should also be interacting with each other, the environment, the instructor, and training

materials. Learning environments should be interactive and not passive. Interactive learning environments facilitate the learning process for the opposite reasons that passive environments degrade learning. "*Interactive* means that listeners are talking to each other, participating in activities with each other, and learning from each other" (Bowman 2003, 14).

Now it is important to take a look at what active learning is. Students have always sat in classrooms listening to others speak and learning information from that speaking. This is the model of teaching that has been used for centuries. This model, on occasion, required the student to write notes, work problems, speak to the group, and do homework in an effort to increase the learning that took place—all of which added to the learning. "The best way to make sure our listeners learn, remember, and use what we teach them is to involve them in the learning" (Bowman 2003, 82).

"Hands-on means that listeners are doing something, as opposed to just sitting and listening" (Bowman 2003, 14). This can be anything that includes movement and action. Things like reading, writing, standing, moving parts of the body, and asking or answering questions are just a few examples. This takes a little more work on the part of the instructor because activities must be planned and prepared for. It also takes more time than standing in front of the class and lecturing.

We have all done the obligatory reading of endless paragraphs for homework throughout our school years. That type of reading is important, but reading can also be done as the class is in session. Reading a short passage can add to most students' retention of the material. This reading can be done aloud by an individual learner to the group from a page or slide. It may also be done as a group reading aloud. The option also exists that each student reads a passage to him or herself, followed by group discussion.

In addition to reading, we have all done the necessary written homework assignments. That type of writing is as important as reading for homework. However, writing can also be done as the class is in session. Writing a bullet, sentence, or even a short passage can add to most students' retention of the material. This writing can be done on butcher paper, white boards, or even chalkboards by an individual learner in front of the group. It may also be done as a group telling a recorder what to write. The option also exists that each student writes a passage to him or herself then shares that writing with a group of students.

Each person is accustomed to speaking in small, informal groups. Instructors should take advantage of this experience and put students into small groups that facilitate a discussion of the class topics. This discussion allows each student to share with his or her fellow students experiences that relate to the learning objective, and then the other members of the group can discuss the relevance and applicability of each other's ideas. New ideas are thus shared and evaluated. In most instances a group can generate more ideas than a single instructor, making the small group method more productive.

Work in the classroom should require students to work through to solutions, not just to learn ideas and concepts. This focus on problem solving will teach work skills that employees can use for preventing accidents as well as performing other job duties. By focusing training on problem solving, the instructor ties classroom lessons to real-world life experiences.

Higher-order thinking involves taking a problem apart, looking at the pieces, determining what allowed it to occur, seeing how the environment affected it, and then putting it all back together in a new form that can be understood and to which a solution can be applied. The real difference lies in the application of synthesis, or putting the pieces back together to determine a usable solution.

"We must first assume we are educating adults who have had years of experience that brings richness to the learning situation—both for themselves and for their students in the classroom" (Ryder 2002, 1). The employees in the workplace are capable of taking problems apart and putting pieces back together to identify solutions. Listing pieces and steps or reciting directions will not help an employee to think for himself or herself. Building higher-order thinking skills into training provides employees with the experience of thinking for themselves to determine the best course of action. Employees who can think for themselves usually have a better understanding of hazards in the

workplace and are better able to translate the information about that hazard into a solution to reduce or eliminate the hazard and are able to decide which solutions will produce the best results. Linda Ryder tells us that synthesis looks like "proposing a plan for an experiment" or "formulating a new scheme for classifying objects, events, or ideas" (2002, 5). According to Ryder (2002), a person using higher-order thinking also uses evaluation skills such as reasonableness, validity, reliability, appropriateness, and correctness.

To determine if the solution to a problem works, the individual or group that develops the solution must simultaneously develop a method of evaluation. As the instructor develops lesson objectives, a way to evaluate the learning is also developed. This evaluation should be short and long term. The evaluation plan must contain a methodology to check the learning when the student returns to work.

The instructor must work to bring meaning to the learning. If meaning can be found, then the students will retain more of the information and want to use the information in their work. The topic of using discussion to facilitate learning has already been addressed. However, there is another aspect to this that helps a student develop meaning. Each student has self-talk going on in his or her head at all times. This talk can support or detract from the meaning of the learning. The thoughts and ideas that a student thinks must integrate the learning to bring meaning to the subject. Students also speak to each other about ideas and concepts that may at first seem unrelated to the subject being taught. However, in hindsight the ideas and concepts being discussed may directly relate to each other, and the dialogue between students may bring meaning to the learning. The instructor can identify what students say in the form of questions and comments in class and determine what those statements and questions mean to the learning. Students also find meaning in watching what other students and instructors do. Their actions may identify a meaning to the learning that the student alone does not identify, yet can share once he or she sees action to support the learning. Finally, students find meaning in doing. Students can be told how to carry out a particular duty and may know the material, but if students actually perform the duty, they not only learn through hearing, but also through seeing, feeling, and smelling. Through these additional attachments to the learning, the student finds meaning.

A good example of active learning is to teach a student the process of speaking to a coworker about an unsafe practice. To make that learning point interactive, the instructor lets a student pretend to perform an unsafe act and then lets a second student speak to the first about the hazards and potential outcomes. The students get more out of the interactive nature of the method. This method also applies to computer and automated training. Many organizations like the idea of buying videotapes and playing them to teach their workers about safety. The video could, to promote active learning, have areas where it is stopped while students perform a task. The same method may be used for computer-based training: requiring a student to do something to react to points made by the software provides the basis for interaction for the student. There are many ways an instructor can use interactive learning, and each time it is used, the learning is reinforced.

Case studies and role-playing are effective methods that allow a student to look at a real-world situation and determine the facts that occurred, identify relevant causes and contributing factors, and then determine courses of action that could eliminate or control the problem. The fact that these learning situations are born of real-world cases provides the students with applicable learning that they can find meaningful.

The first step to any successful learning from the case-study method is to design a case that provides for the learning of the material identified for the class. There are canned studies that can be used. However, they are less effective than studies that are directly tied to a particular learning point. The case study must also be interesting to the student. A boring case study, no matter how effectively written, will not make the student want to participate with passion.

After the case study has been written, it must be conducted. The instructor must make sure that all material necessary for the study is provided. This includes physical material as well as time. A great case study that is executed badly disrupts the learning process, and the students may lose interest and not learn the lesson. The students in the class must analyze the evidence contained in the case study carefully and with an eye for detail. This will allow them to see the pattern of events that occurred and how each point was related to the next. A careful and detailed examination or analysis of the evidence is followed by a synthesis of the information, and from that synthesis the students form conclusions, recommendations, and implications for courses of action.

There are many things a case study offers the instructor. Case studies teach integrated ideas to the students that directly apply to the way life works.

The case study provides the students with an opportunity to work through an organized problem. This facilitates the learning process and allows learning points to be raised as the students moves through the case study. This helps the students not only to learn the material but also to place the learning in perspective with the problems they will face in real work. This leads the students to an opportunity to demonstrate what they have learned to the instructor, as well as to themselves. Demonstrating the learning to themselves is the more important of the two. By demonstrating learning, a student has the opportunity to participate in the lessons and learn from the practice as well as the lesson that is intentionally designed into the class.

Role-playing is another very powerful technique. Role-playing can be spontaneous. Everyone should be given a role, even it is only to observe.

All learners are assigned a role, and the validity and effectiveness of the learning is based on their enthusiasm in playing their role. The real learning is based on the believability of the role-play and how that role-play forces the other participants to respond in their roles. Another strength of role-play is that it simulates complex interpersonal interaction that in itself creates a valuable lesson, not just about the topic, but about how it can be used and how others will respond to it.

In addition to the identified learning objectives, the students who participate in role-playing learn some valuable life skills that will help them to use the learning objectives in the workplace. Role players will learn and practice subtle interpersonal skills as they work through the role and interact with other role players. The students will also learn that there are hidden complexities to each situation that may not be clear or taught in the lesson. This ancillary learning helps the students to use the learning in their lives. This provides a great deal of benefit to the employer.

DOCUMENTING SAFETY AND HEALTH TRAINING

Many training requirements state or imply that the employer shall document that training.

Employers should maintain an office file on each employee. This file, which should include a record of training completed by the employee, provides a historical document that shows what training the employee has received and the frequency of training.

As the leader of an organization, the employer must determine the minimum qualifications of the trainers they will use. An evaluation of the instructor's academic training, background, and experiences can provide the employer with the information needed to determine if an instructor is qualified and competent to present the courses needed by the employees. If the trainer is from outside the organization, the employer should locate and speak to others who can provide the employer with adequate information from which to make an informed decision as to the qualifications and competencies of a trainer. An employer who has identified trainers should develop a list of the trainers and the courses they are qualified and competent to present.

Documenting training provides both a means for the employer to document employee training and provide employees with a document that not only shows their completion of training but also allows them to take pride in their accomplishment. A certificate, letter, memorandum, or other written document can do this. The length of the training, what the employees desire, and reasonable cost should determine the method the employer uses. Obviously, a certificate can be expensive, whereas a short letter or card could be much cheaper. However, what do they mean to the workers? If one provides them with a document they do not value, they may not experience pride in their accomplishment.

The format for documenting training must include the full name of the person receiving the training. The title of the training should be included along with the date the training was conducted. The length of training should also be included. The method used to conduct the training should be included so that it is clear which version was used and what that version included. Some choices discussed in this chapter include the use of classroom with lectures, computer-based Web training, and on-the-job training. The employer will also want to include the method of evaluation used to test the knowledge or skill learned by the employee. The choices that are most commonly used are written examinations, including quizzes and tests, oral examinations, and hands-on examinations. The name of the person or company conducting the training should be noted on the record. It is also very important to note whether the training is a refresher or initial training. The next logical question is how long to keep the record. The Occupational Safety and Health Administration requires that training records for the *Hazard Communication Standard* be kept for the length of employment plus 30 years. For most purposes, five years is long enough to keep training records. This will allow the training records to be kept for the same period of time as some OSHA forms (Fanning 2003, 50). However, the employer must meet any specific requirements in OSHA standards that require they be kept longer.

SUMMARY

The organization cannot expect employees to perform their jobs safely if they have never been trained to do so. The amount of training and its corresponding cost determine what an organization can afford. However, even 5-minute toolbox talks can provide training if a company is strapped for money. This chapter has addressed the methods and procedures of presenting and documenting training. There are a variety of methods that can be used by organization personnel. The key is to identify the training need and the best method to deliver it, develop a lesson plan for what will be presented, present it, and finally document it properly to make sure there is an adequate record. Training must be built into the organization's processes. The tragedy is that, if it is not, it becomes an add-on, and little thought is given to it.

REFERENCES

Alexander, Brian. 2006. "Web 2.0: a new wave of innovation for teaching and learning?" *Educause,* March/April 2006.

Bixby, Daniel W. 2010. "To Be Continued: Using Social Media for Training Conversations." *T+D, American Society of Training and Development.*

Bises, Stephen D., and Daniel J. Fabian. 2004."Sophomore Men: The Forgotten Class, the Forgotten Gender, Recruitment and Retention in Higher Education." *Magna Publications,* Volume 20 Number 3.

Blanchard, Kenneth, Donald Carew, and Eunice Parisis-Carew. 2009. *The One Minute Manager Builds High Performing Teams.* 3rd ed. New York: William Morrow.

Bowman, Sharon. 2003. *Preventing Death by Lecture.* Glenbrook, NV: Bowperson Publishing Company.

Bradley, Paul. 2009. "Special Report: Distance Learning, Whither Twitter." *Community College Week.*

Burgess, Kimberly R. 2009. "Social Networking Technologies as Vehicles of Support for Women in Learning Communities." *New Directions for Adult and Continuing Education,* Issue 122, pp. 63–71.

Clegg, Brian. 2000. *Training Plus: Revitalizing Your Training.* Sterling, VA: Kogan Page.

Fanning, Fred. 2003. *Basic Safety Administration: A Handbook for the Safety Professional.* Des Plaines, IL: American Society of Safety Engineers.

———. 2009."Classroom vs. Computer Based Training." *The Communicator,* volume 2, number 2, Winter 2009. American Society of Safety Engineers.

Gardenswartz, Lee, and Anita Rowe. 2003. *Diverse Teams at Work: Capitalizing on the Power of Diversity.* Alexandria, VA: Society for Human Resources Management.

Grieve, Donald. 2005. *A Handbook for Adjunct/Part-Time Faculty and Teachers of Adults.* 6th ed. Ann Arbor, MI: Adjunct Advocate Inc.

Gunawardena, Charlotte N., Mary Beth Hermans, Damien Sanchez, Carol Richmond, Maribeth Bohley, and Rebekah Tuttle. "A Theoretical Framework for Building Online Communities of Practice with Social Networking Tools." *Educational Media International,* Volume 46, Number 1, pp. 3–16.

Miner, Zach. 2009. "Twitter Takes a Trip to College." *U.S. News & World Report,* Vol. 146, Issue 8, pp. 56–57.

Moran, Mark. 2003. *Construction Safety Handbook.* 2d ed. Rockville, MD: Government Institutes Inc.

Ryder, Linda B. 2002. *Higher-Order Thinking Skills* (retrieved August 1, 2002). www.amsc.belvoir.army. mil/ecampus/sblmp-nr/readings/Higher-level_ thinking_skills/Higher_Order_Thinking/html

Schneier, Craig, Craig Russell, Richard Beatty, and Lloyd Baird. 1994. *The Training Development Source Book* 2d ed. Amherst, MA: Human Resource Development Press.

Simkins, Michael, and Randy Schultz. 2010. "Using Web 2.0 Tools at School." *Leadership Association of California School Administrators,* Jan/Feb 2010, Volume 39.

Stolovich, Harold, and Erica Keeps. 2002. *Telling Ain't Training.* Alexandria, VA: ASTD Press.

"Video Conferencing." *The Buzz.* Service Online, 09/2010 (retrieved October 20, 2011). blog.svconline.com/ thebuzz/2010/09/17/videoconferencing-watch-avi-spl-cameleon/

"Video Conferencing and Video Streaming." 2010. *Media and Methods Magazine,* January/February 2010.

Young, Jeffrey. 2009. "Teaching with Twitter Not for the Faint of Heart." *The Chronicle of Higher Education,* Volume A1, Number 10.

APPENDIX: ADDITIONAL READING

Cantonwine, Sheila Cullen. 1999. *Safety Training That Delivers.* Des Plaines, IL: American Society of Safety Engineers.

Fanning, Fred. 2003. *Basic Safety Administration: A Handbook for the New Safety Specialist.* Des Plaines, IL: American Society of Safety Engineers.

COST ANALYSIS AND BUDGETING OF SAFETY AND HEALTH TRAINING

6

Brent Altemose

LEARNING OBJECTIVES

▮ Understand the factors that contribute to the costs and financial benefits of safety, health, and environmental (SH&E) training.

▮ Perform a comparison of the costs and benefits of training alternatives.

▮ Be able to estimate the return on investment (ROI) and break-even point for a training class or program.

▮ Acquire the tools to plan a training budget.

IN MOST ORGANIZATIONS, particularly large organizations, significant resources are dedicated to training. Nearly $60 billion is spent each year in the United States on workplace training programs (Phillips 2002). Despite this large sum, the true cost of training programs is often not evaluated or recognized (Phillips 2003). Furthermore, safety risks are typically not adequately incorporated into economic planning and decision making (Asche 2004). Safety, Health, and Environmental (SH&E) and training professionals may be intimidated by financial concepts, or, worse yet, they may be worried that their programs or jobs may be jeopardized depending on the outcome of the analysis. But it would be difficult to imagine making a large capital expenditure, such as a new ventilation system, without considering the costs and benefits, or the most cost-effective way to implement the system. Careful utilization of cost analysis and budgeting techniques is just as important for a training program.

This chapter discusses how to leverage training dollars through effective budgeting, accurate cost estimates, and utilization of cost-benefit analysis techniques. Proper application of these techniques will not only identify where training money is being spent, but it will also aid in projecting the costs of proposed programs and comparing the costs of alternatives. Furthermore, business and accounting terms, besides being more credible to management, are better understood by them than is safety jargon (Bird, 1996).

The advent of computer-based training and other technology-driven training techniques has made cost analysis more critical, because the cost of such programs varies widely (Devaney 2001). These technologies have resulted in great savings in some cases; for example, where training has been provided to large numbers of people in a cost- and time-effective manner. In other cases, however, instructor-led training may actually be more cost effective, particularly when the total number of people to be trained is relatively small, and they can easily be brought together in one location.

COSTS OF TRAINING

An accurate estimate of the cost of training depends on an evaluation of many factors, but one should not be intimidated by the scope of information that needs to be collected. Even though detailed and thorough data lead to more accurate estimates, in many cases precise estimates are not available. If the estimate is reasonable, and it is based on experience and the best available data, then it will have great value in making training-program decisions. Sometimes, industry benchmarks are the best data available. The American Society for Training and Development (ASTD) Benchmarking Forum is one source of training-cost data (Waagen 2000, 4).

The method for collecting data is described in detail in this section and supplemented by the following realistic example that will be revisited throughout this chapter. Say, a mid-size telecommunication company, XYZ Telecom, is considering a new computer-based training program for hazard communication (HazCom). The program will be used to provide both initial and refresher training to employees located in three states at twenty different locations. Approximately 500 employees will complete the 2-hour initial training for new and transferred employees. Every year about 4000 employees will take an hour-long, mandatory refresher training. An *off-the-shelf* program, with some customized company-specific designs, will be purchased for the above purposes.

Table 1 shows a worksheet for collecting data to estimate the cost of safety training, including data filled in for the XYZ Telecom example. The cost data, as well as the expected timing of the expenditure, which is important for both budgeting and cost-benefit analysis purposes, are recorded. *Note:* This example is not intended to demonstrate the entire breadth and depth of costs that may need to be considered. It is not feasible to describe all of the possible costs of training with a single example. However, this section and the accompanying example will demonstrate the types of costs that will need to be considered.

Development Costs

A significant contributor to the cost of a training program, particularly a new program, is the cost to develop the program. Development costs include the time spent by subject-matter experts, training professionals, computer programmers, or others, depending on the course. It is worth noting that even off-the-shelf programs may present development costs for reviewing their content, customizing them to the organization's needs, or even simply integrating them into the existing training program. When estimating the time required to develop a traditional, instructor-led course, it is best to assume twenty hours of development time for each hour of class time; for self-instructional print media such as workbooks, the development time is typically 80 hours per hour of class time; for computer-based training, the time varies widely, but may reach or exceed 300 hours per hour of class time, depending on the level of complexity of the training (Head 1994, 64). The addition of video and audio to computer-based training can be particularly time-consuming. However, as the example will show, if the cost of this time is amortized across a large number of students, it very well may be the most cost-effective option.

Either internal personnel or external consultants could be involved in course development. For internal personnel, the cost of development time is based on the *loaded cost* of the internal salaries. The loaded cost includes base salary, fringe benefits, and, in some cases, opportunity costs, which are discussed later (Phillips 2003, Nathan 2009). Fringe benefits generally amount to 25–75 percent above the employee's base salary, and include costs to the organization such as health benefits, matching retirement contributions, vacation pay, bonuses, and so on. (Head 1994, 35). To calculate the total cost to the organization, multiply the average loaded-salary rate by the number of hours worked specific to the project. For external consultants, multiply the expected hourly rate by the number of hours worked. Do not forget to include any travel costs associated with the course development.

Not all courses are customized; there are also many off-the-shelf safety training programs available. For these programs, be sure to include the cost to review the content to ensure applicability and suitability for the target audience and target workplace.

The cost of materials during course development might include money spent on presentation materials such as videos. For computer-based training, evaluate whether upgrades to technology infrastructure will be necessary. Also be sure to factor in the cost of computer workstations if new workstations will be required to deliver the training for a particular group. For instance, if the target audience is a group of manufacturing employees who do not have their own computer workstations, computer labs, shared computers, or kiosks may need to be provided. Of course, the cost to purchase software must also be included. Other types of equipment may need to be purchased as well, such as disposable gloves and suits for a course on emergency response.

For XYZ Telecom's computer-based HazCom program, it was estimated that 150 hours would be spent by internal personnel to learn the software and to customize the course content. The average salary of these personnel is $45 per hour, and the estimated loaded-salary rate, including fringe benefits, is $70 per hour. Multiplying 150 hours by the loaded-salary rate of $70 per hour, the total organizational cost is $10,500. External consultants and travel were not needed because the vendor included training in the cost to purchase the software, which was $8000. No other significant development costs were expected.

Implementation Costs

When internal personnel are used as instructors, their salary cost should be computed as a loaded cost in the manner previously described (average loaded-salary rate times the number of hours worked). In addition, if training is not their primary job function, there may be an additional cost to the organization, which can be recorded in the table as "Other business impacts." Other business impacts are described in more detail in the student-costs discussion. For external consultants, again use the going rate for their services. Finally, include expenses the instructor will incur while traveling to and from the training sessions, expenses such as the cost of their time, their meals and lodging, the airfare, and so on.

The cost of time spent by employees attending training cannot be ignored in training-cost analysis. In fact, student costs often represent more than 80 percent of the overall cost of a training program (Head 1994, 36). *Student costs* include the loaded salaries paid to employees for their time in training, incidental expenses (such as travel costs, if applicable), and *lost-opportunity costs*, which are described later. Due to the significance of these costs, the choice between two equally effective programs—one which is appreciably shorter in duration—quickly becomes apparent, because the shorter program dramatically reduces salary and lost-opportunity costs.

Considering salaries and lost-opportunity costs also can highlight the importance of offering training at a time and place that is most convenient to the employees and the organization. For instance, offering computer-based training (CBT) or a training class near the employees' work site can eliminate significant time lost travelling to and from training. Offering training outside of normal business hours can reduce lost production time; however, the cost analysis must also consider overtime pay for off hours. In order to accurately assess all of these costs, the SHE professional should actively engage knowledgeable individuals from the organization, such as production management and human resources professionals.

To compute the cost of student salaries, multiply the average loaded-salary rate by the number of hours of training (including travel time) and by the total number of students. Also include their incidental expenses. Finally, it may be important to consider the other business impacts such as lost-opportunity costs. In this context, lost-opportunity costs refer to productivity that may be lost in manufacturing, or sales opportunities that may be missed while employees are attending training. In a more generic sense, opportunity costs refer to an engineering economics concept that says whenever funds (or time) are invested elsewhere, the opportunity to obtain a return on investment is lost (Grant et al. 1990).

TABLE 1

Training Cost Data Worksheet—Computer-Based Training Example

TYPE OF COST	Estimated Unit Cost	Unit Multipliers	Total Cost	Timing of Expense
DEVELOPMENT COSTS				
Curriculum Development				
Internal salaries—loaded cost	$70/hour	150 hours	$10,500	Year 1
External consultants				
Meals, travel, and incidentals				
Materials				
Presentation materials (videos, etc.)				
Computer hardware				
Computer software	$8000	n/a	$8000	Year 1
Equipment purchases				
Marketing materials (flyers, etc.)				
IMPLEMENTATION COSTS				
Instructor Cost				
Internal salaries—loaded cost	$35/hour/ coach	20 × 24 hrs. 20 × 5 hrs.	$16,800 $3,500/yr.	Year 1 Year 2 to 5
External consultants				
Meals, travel, and incidentals	$100/coach	20 coaches	$2000	Year 1
Other business impacts				
Student cost				
Internal salaries—loaded cost	$35/hour/ employee	500 × 2 hrs. 4000 × 1 hr.	$35,000 + $140,000 = $175,000/yr.	Year 1 to 5
Meals, travel, and incidentals				
Other business impacts	$20/hour/ employee	50 × 2 hrs 500 × 1 hr	$2000 + $10,000 = $12,000/yr.	Year 1 to 5
Materials				
Student materials (manuals, etc.)				
Equipment rental				
Facilities cost				
Lease or rental of facilities				
Catering				
Cost of new construction				
Telecommunication charges				
Facilities overhead				
OTHER LIFE CYCLE COSTS				
Recordkeeping, evaluation of training,	$35/hour/	3 × 20 hrs.	$2100	Year 1
revisions to training	employee	3 × 15 hrs.	$1575	Year 2 to 5
Software licensing or maintenance fees	$1000/yr.	n/a	$1000/yr.	Year 1 to 5
Information technology support—	$52.50/hr.	100 hours	$5250	Year 1
internal salaries—loaded cost		40 hours	$2100	Year 2 to 5
		YEAR 1 COST	$232,650	
		YEARLY COST, YEARS 2 TO 5	$194,175	
		TOTAL PROGRAM COST, 5 YEARS	$1,009,350	

To obtain these lost-opportunity costs, SHE professionals typically need to rely on production or sales departments to estimate them. It is important to understand the basis for these estimates, so that there is no double-counting of certain costs and benefits (for instance, employee salaries will likely already be factored into the cost of producing a product).

Sometimes, the costs of temporary or reassigned personnel are included in a training-cost analysis. This is not necessary, however, when the internal salaries of those involved with the training are included in the cost analysis, because the inclusion presumes that employees will be away from their standard job and, therefore, not involved in productive work. If replacements fill in for these employees, it is reasonable to assume that the cost would be similar to the loaded-salary cost of the absent employees. Even though temporary personnel are typically paid less, they may also be less productive. If the costs of lost productivity, decreased work quality, or lost sales are above and beyond the loaded-salary cost of the absent employee, those costs should be included in the analysis. If someone does not fill in for employees while they are attending training, their salary should still be included in the cost analysis because of their reduced total productive hours for the week, month, or year.

A discussion of the cost entries in Table 1 will produce a better understanding of the reasons for including them in the overall cost analysis. In Table 1, under "Materials" in the section on "Implementation Costs," the costs of all materials provided to students should be included, such as handbooks, binders, training aids, and so on. This is also the place to include the cost of equipment rented for the training, such as audio-visual or training-aid equipment (if purchased, they should be included in development costs). A driving simulator for a defensive driving course or entry equipment for a confined space course are examples of training-aid equipment that might be rented.

Overhead costs for training may include the cost of corporate management, office space, conference rooms, and utilities. These costs are typically low or insignificant (2 percent or less of the total cost) if existing, suitable training facilities are available within the organization (Phillips 2003, Phillips et al. 2007). However, if these fixed overhead costs are actually increased—for instance, if facilities must be obtained, refurnished, or remodeled to accommodate training, then these associated costs should be identified and included in the analysis. If necessary, assistance from accounting, operations, or engineering departments may be required for an accurate estimate of these costs.

For technology-driven training, such as computer-based training, employees may need coaching on the use of the technology. Also, be sure to account for the cost of ongoing information-management support, whether internal or external.

The cost of compiling and tracking training records is another consideration. In some organizations, a validated tracking system may be required. Such a system could increase both the time and cost of the tracking system.

Finally, include the cost of at least one cycle to review, test, and revise the training program. This might include having a pilot program with a small class, for instance, or sending a selected group of employees through a computer-based program.

The estimated implementation costs for XYZ Telecom's HazCom training are shown in Table 1. Because the program is completely computer-based, one might expect instructor costs to be zero. However, in this example, a "coach" was to be trained at each of the company's twenty locations to provide instruction for employees who needed extra help getting started, a need created by the fact that many employees do not spend significant time on a computer. The coaches were expected to spend four hours being trained (including travel time) and twenty hours coaching employees the first year, followed by five hours for every subsequent year thereafter (program life was estimated to be five years). The loaded average salary rate used in the table for both coaches and students was $35 per hour, which was obtained from the human resources department, which indicated that the average company salary was $20 per hour and the cost of fringe benefits an additional $15 per hour. For the sake of simplicity, salary increases over the 5-year life of the program were neglected. However, this may be an important consideration, because average salaries typically increase every year, due to factors such as cost-of-living increases and general inflation. An assumption about the rate of inflation can be applied to estimate the amount of salary increases. The student costs in the example include the time employees spend in training, at $35 per hour, with 500 employees per year taking the initial 2-hour training and 4000 employees per year taking the 1-hour refresher. Because the training is delivered on computers at each employee's work site, the travel time and the incidental expenses are zero.

For one group of critical employees, additional lost-opportunity costs were identified. This group was the service department, whose employees, because of their level of training, could not be replaced by temporary personnel or reassigned internal personnel. When someone in this department is absent, a lesser volume of work is completed, including fewer installations of equipment for new customers. The absence of these employees also increases the average amount of out-of-service time for existing customers when problems arise. Previous estimates have shown the cost to the company to be at least $20 per hour when service department personnel are absent; the cost is due not only to lost business in the form of customers who are not charged for the days the services are out of order, but also due to customers who decide to use another service provider because the time required for repair or for establishing new service is unacceptable. The additional $20-per-hour cost for service department personnel is included. Approximately 50 new service department personnel will be required to take the initial 2-hour HazCom training, and 500 personnel will be required to take the 1-hour refresher course. Note that the above is, of course, a fictional example. These costs are difficult to estimate, but they should be kept in mind because they may be significant.

In the above example, all necessary instruction and student materials were electronic, so no cost was included. Also, all facilities and equipment necessary for the training were already available.

Other Life-Cycle Costs

Costs for the entire anticipated life cycle for a training class or program should be considered. Life-cycle costs may include costs for record keeping, for training evaluation, for reviewing and revising training content, and so on. Life-cycle assessment methods are discussed further in the introductory chapter, "Basic Economic Analysis and Engineering Economics."

In our example, the cost of record keeping is minimized due to the electronic nature of the training records. However, three human resources employees will each spend approximately fifteen hours per year running reports, at a loaded salary rate of $35 per

hour. In the first year, each of these employees will spend an additional five hours being trained to run the reports.

All costs of revisions and updates to the software were included in a 5-year service contract with the software vendor. For $1000 per year, the vendor provides technical support and any necessary updates to the material based on changes and regulations. However, additional internal information-technology support was expected for networking issues and for calls to a centralized help desk. It was estimated, based on past experience with similar software, that 100 hours of support would be necessary in the first year, and 40 hours each year thereafter. The loaded salary rate for information-technology support personnel is $52.50 per hour ($30-per-hour base salary plus $22.50 fringe benefits).

Based on these estimates, the total cost to implement this program at XYZ Telecom for five years is over $1,000,000! Why even go through all this analysis! Is it not easier just to sell the $8000 software purchase to management than it is to explain why the total cost of the program is over a million dollars? Well, if this is where the analysis stopped, it would mostly likely be better to avoid presenting these intimidating numbers to management. But understanding the true cost of training is the first and most critical step to an effective cost-benefit analysis, which is the best way to reveal cost-saving opportunities within the organization.

COST-BENEFIT ANALYSIS IN SH&E TRAINING

At first glance, a cost-benefit analysis for SH&E training may appear bleak. As discussed in the introductory chapter, "Basic Economic Analysis and Engineering Economics," SH&E investments are not generally seen as making money for the organization. Worse yet, SH&E training often may have a lower benefit-to-cost ratio than other SH&E investments, such as hazard prevention and control or management leadership and employee involvement (Jervis and Collins 2001). However, recent studies have demonstrated that SH&E training can reduce injury rates, which consequently has financial benefits. In one study, safety-trained construction laborers were 12 percent less likely to file for workers' compensation, and this percentage increased to 42 percent for construction workers between 16 to 24 years old (Dong et al. 2004). In another study of workers in the plumbing and pipefitting industries, 3.4 percent of workers who received safety orientation were injured, compared to 11 percent of workers who did not receive the orientation (Kinn et al. 2000). Effectiveness of the training is a key consideration. Typically, only 10 to 15 percent of training is retained after one year, making training-program design for effective knowledge transfer critical (Machles 2002). Furthermore, we know that simply transferring knowledge will not change behaviors (Geller 2005), making frequent on-the-job reinforcement of SH&E training objectives even more critical than the training content.

Many of the benefits of training are intangible and difficult to quantify, making cost optimization and justification all the more critical. When an effective SH&E training program is implemented, and all of the benefits of the training are carefully considered, including the financial ones, the case for training becomes much stronger.

A well-executed cost-benefit analysis is the best tool available to both secure and manage available training funds. This type of analysis not only demonstrates the value of training to the organization, but it also identifies opportunities to improve the training process and to modify or eliminate ineffective programs. Furthermore, credibility with management is gained by using financial language that they are familiar with; this practice helps demonstrate to them the need to fund training initiatives (Phillips et al. 2007).

Unfortunately, such an analysis is rarely performed, at least on a formal basis. Too often, alternatives such as computer-based training or outsourcing of training are ruled out-of-hand as being too expensive, even though they might actually save the organization money. Worse yet, expensive, trendy programs are often implemented without an adequate analysis of their true benefit.

It is also important to recognize that cost-benefit analyses can be time-consuming. However, although the task may appear daunting, cost-benefit analysis of training has been successfully applied even at small-and medium-sized businesses (Devaney 2001). Be sure to identify in advance how the data will be used. Make sure the organization's management is willing to consider alternatives to existing training programs. If improvements will not even be considered, the cost-benefit analysis will be a waste of time.

Eventually, in order to secure funds for a new training initiative (or even to continue the existing budget), the costs must be justified. Whether this justification is a formal proposal to the board of directors or an informal presentation to the boss, it must be well thought out.

Benefits of an Effective SH&E Training Program

While reduced costs of training certainly may be one of the benefits of a new program, other benefits of training also must be evaluated and included, particularly for new programs or to justify programs that do not address regulatory requirements. For SH&E professionals, the benefits of training are typically cost-avoidance benefits, such as reduced injuries or fines that have been averted. However, some training may have other benefits, both tangible and intangible, such as increased productivity or improved organizational reputation. Some of the benefits to consider are:

- reduced workers' compensation costs
- reduced absenteeism and/or time away from work due to injury
- avoiding indirect costs of injuries and accidents (e.g., investigation costs, retraining of personnel, decreased productivity)
- avoiding fines due to regulatory noncompliance
- decreased legal liabilities (lawsuit settlements, etc.)
- avoiding property damage caused by incidents and accidents
- improved attendance and increased productivity
- improved public image as a responsible organization
- increased job satisfaction of employees

As discussed earlier, many of the benefits shown in the list above are intangible or are difficult to estimate. Still, it is appropriate and often necessary to include estimates of these benefits in a complete cost-benefit analysis. The estimates used should be realistic and conservative (i.e., not overstated) so that valid, credible conclusions are reached. Uncertainty in the data is best dealt with through a sensitivity analysis, as described later in this chapter. It is also reasonable to include in the analysis arguments such as "If we avoid one lost-time injury as a result of this training, it will pay for itself," as long as this outcome is a realistic possibility if employees are not trained. Some of these variables can also be analyzed after the fact; for instance, by comparing workers' compensation costs before and after training. Note that analyzing injury costs is a complex task, and further discussion of the costs of accidents is provided in other sections of this handbook, including the "Cost Analysis and Budgeting" chapter by Michael Toole in Section 1, "Management of Safety Engineering Work." When analyzing injury costs, it is particularly important to include indirect costs, which can range anywhere from 2 to 20 times the direct medical costs of an injury (Brady et al. 1997, Brandt 1999, Hinze 2000, Kinn et al. 2000, Miller 1995, OSHA 2010). The wide range of indirect costs cited in these references depends largely on what type of indirect costs are included and whether only costs to the employer are included, or whether societal costs are also considered. When deciding which factor to apply, it is important to consider the objectives of the analysis and the assumptions made in the reference used.

Investment Analysis Methods

As discussed in the introductory chapter, "Basic Economic Analysis and Engineering Economics," by James Ramsey and Anthony Veltri and the "Cost Analysis and Budgeting" chapter by Michael Toole in Section 1, there are many different ways to analyze and express cost data. Three concepts are used in this chapter to illustrate how to apply engineering economics to an SH&E training program: the return on investment (ROI), the break-even point, and net present worth (NPW). The ROI concept is particularly useful in communicating the costs and benefits of training to the organization because it is a simple but powerful concept, and it is a term that is frequently used and easily understood by management. However, the SH&E department should work with the finance department of the organization to learn and understand the terminology used there.

ROI and the break-even point are closely related terms. ROI is expressed as a percentage, and is equal to the net program benefits (savings and profits minus costs) divided by the total program cost (Phillips 2002, 17). The break-even point is the time required to recoup the initial or incremental investment and is equal to the program cost divided by the yearly benefits (Grant et al. 1990). For instance, consider a request to spend $20,000 to implement a new training program that will save the company $10,000 per year. In this simple example, the ROI per year is 50 percent ($10,000 ÷ $20,000) and the break-even point is two years ($20,000 ÷ $10,000 per year).

There are several ways financial planners use ROI information. First, alternatives may be compared, with the greatest percent return or shortest break-even point being, of course, the preferred choice from a financial perspective. A second way to use ROI is to determine whether to initiate a program at all. For instance, if the $20,000 investment example was for an office safety-training program that is not required by regulation, the organization would need to decide if a 50 percent ROI or a 2-year break-even point is acceptable. The ROI a given organization expects varies greatly, and depends on many factors, including the availability of capital, the company's profit margin, and so on. The finance department of an organization should be able to help determine how to present cost-benefit analysis information and also to determine what management might typically be looking for in terms of a return on investment.

As also discussed in the "Cost Analysis and Budgeting" chapter in Section 1, the ROI and break-even point, while powerful and easily understood, are both limited since they ignore the time value of money as well as all cash flows after the return on investment or break-even point is reached. Therefore, an even more powerful concept is net present worth. The power of this concept lies in its explication that all cash flows can be converted to one value and therefore accurately compared. Unfortunately, it is less widely understood and therefore not as commonly used in training cost analysis. However, if it is difficult to express the cost-benefit analysis in terms of ROI, or if it is necessary to compare many different options or more complex patterns of cash flow, one should consider using this or similar techniques, such as equivalent annual cost. An example of both techniques is presented at the end of this cost-benefit analysis discussion.

Now consider the example of XYZ Telecom's new HazCom training program. As seen in Table 1, the estimated cost to the organization is $232,650 in the first year, and $194,175 each year thereafter. Additional information is needed for the cost-benefit analysis. It is important to first analyze whether this option is preferable to others. In this example, only one alternative is considered. A separate cost analysis of the existing stand-up training revealed an estimated cost to the organization of $215,000 per year. So, in the first year, the additional cost to the organization to implement the program is $17,650 ($232,650 − $215,000). In subsequent years, $20,825 per year will be saved ($215,000 − $194,175). So the ROI = $20,825 per year ÷ $17,650 = 118 percent per year. The break-even point (beginning at the end of the first year) = $17,650 ÷ $20,825 = 0.85 years, or about ten months. In the view of most organizations, this is a relatively short period to recoup the investment. Please note that these calculations are simplified for demonstration purposes, and therefore assume linear and constant cost and benefit streams over time, and do not amortize the costs of benefits over a period of time. A more precise consideration of cash flow is described in a forthcoming example using the NPW concept.

In comparing the two training alternatives, consider what happens if a new piece of information is presented. XYZ Telecom instituted the new instructor-led HazCom training program two years ago. The cost to develop the new program and train the instructors via train-the-trainer courses was over $100,000. Should the fact that this cost will now be wasted deter the organization from pursuing the computer-based training program? The answer is no, it should not. The money spent previously cannot be recovered, and therefore the cost analysis is

TABLE 2

Example Analysis of Two Training Alternatives Using Net Present Worth

Conversion of Yearly Costs (A) to Net Present Worth (NPW) at Year 1

	Computer-based training	Instructor-led training
Year 1	NPW = $232,650	NPW = $215,000
Year 2–Year 5	A = $194,175; NPW = $643,360	A = $215,000; NPW = $712,360
NPW	NPW = $876,010	NPW = $927,360

A = Yearly Cost; NPW = Net Present Worth = A $\{[(1 + i)^n - 1] \div [i^*(1 + i)^n]\}$; n = number of years; i = rate of return = 8% or 0.08 for this example.

Assumes costs incurred at the beginning of each year. Equation for Net Present Worth based on Future Costs (NPW = $F(1 + i)^{-n}$) for Years 2–5 could also be used and is the appropriate choice if the annual yearly costs are not equal.

not affected by this information; the new computer-based program is still more cost effective. One way to look at it is that there is only one past, and it affects all future alternatives equally. It is the difference between alternatives that is relevant in the comparison (Grant et al. 1990). Of course, depending on the objectives of the analysis, the sunk costs (money that has already been spent) may be relevant. For instance, if the objective is to retrospectively perform a cost-benefit analysis on a training program, the historical costs must be included. Furthermore, sunk costs may bias the organization's view of past choices, for better or for worse.

Another way to compare two alternatives is by using net present worth (also known as net present value in economics textbooks). The calculations of the NPW for the two alternatives in the XYZ Telecom example are shown in Table 2.

As shown in Table 2, the NPW (i.e., cost, in this case) of the computer-based training alternative is less than the NPW (cost) of the instructor-led training, and therefore the computer-based training should be chosen. A critical value in this analysis is the rate of return (i) chosen for the calculation, which should be based on the norms of the organization. In this example, a rate of return of 8 percent per year was used. Notably, organizations that expect high rates of return are not willing to accept long periods of time to achieve a return on investment.

Because HazCom training is required in the United States, as is similar training in many other countries, there is no alternative for XYZ Telecom but to provide and complete this training. However, if the training were not required, it would still be reasonable for management to request a cost-benefit analysis to determine if the training should be held, in which case the cost-benefit comparison is conducted between the training program and a *do-nothing* alternative. For the sake of argument, what if HazCom training were not a regulatory requirement? The cost-benefit analysis would need to compare the program costs ($232,650 in the first year and $194,175 each year thereafter) to the benefits and savings realized by the organization. Assume that HazCom training reduces costs for XYZ Telecom by $200,000 per year, in the form of reduced injury or accident rates. Based on this, during the first year, the organization incurs a net cost of $32,650 but has a net gain of $5825 per year thereafter. This translates to an ROI = $5825 per year ÷ $32,650 = 18 percent per year. The break-even point = $32,650 ÷ $5825 = 5.6 years. Although an 18 percent ROI may sound attractive, five years is a long waiting period for most organizations to reach the break-even point for an investment.

Sensitivity Analysis

One problem with many cost-benefit analyses is that they omit uncertainty as a consideration (Myers et al. 2008, Phillips et al. 2007). As discussed in the "Cost Analysis and Budgeting" chapter in Section 1, if a different set of assumptions were made in the cost-benefit analysis, a different conclusion might be drawn. Using techniques discussed in that chapter, a range of values should be considered for each variable, and the impact on the analysis should be considered. Spreadsheets and even more sophisticated software that utilize Monte Carlo analysis techniques may be necessary; however, even a simple substitution and recalculation, changing a few critical variables, can be very revealing.

For instance, as presented in the example in Table 1, consider the impact on the cost-benefit analysis if the number of hours spent by employees in training was 10 percent higher (internal salaries–loaded cost), or $192,500 instead of $175,000. Then, the annual cost (A)

shown in Table 2 would be $211,675 for computer-based training, with a total NPW of $933,993. This is more than the NPW for instructor-led training, and, unlike the first case, leads us to the conclusion that instructor-led training is the more cost-effective option—or, more accurately, that the true outcome is more uncertain than our initial analysis might imply.

More advanced techniques, such as a *Monte Carlo analysis*, may be necessary if there is a fairly wide range of uncertainty for multiple cost and benefit estimates in the analysis. In these cases, a random variable can be assigned to each cost and benefit across the expected possible range of outcomes. Then, a large number of iterations (100, 1000, or more) to calculate the ROI, NPW, or other outcome variable would be applied by using a random number generated for each cost and benefit.

Selling SH&E Training to Management

An SH&E training program is only one aspect of a comprehensive injury- or accident-prevention program. Furthermore, in the real world, organizations do not have unlimited funds and usually do not have sufficient funds for all of their desired programs. Theoretically, an optimal equilibrium point exists where total prevention and detection costs of SH&E programs equal the potential failure costs, including injuries and accidents (Behm et al. 2004, 23). Therefore, it is necessary to prioritize and optimize training programs based on the overall impact each program has on the organization's training goals and, of course, on the bottom line. Still, it is important to recognize that a more cost-efficient alternative is not always the best choice either, because training effectiveness must also be considered. An in-depth cost-benefit analysis should consider training effectiveness as a variable as well. As previously discussed, more effective training may provide greater benefits in terms of injury avoidance.

Sometimes, when the cost-benefit analysis of an existing training program reveals little or no ROI, those who implemented the program may feel threatened or insulted. Despite this situation, it is important to take an impartial view and to see the results of the analysis as an opportunity to make positive changes that management could ultimately view as a victory.

There are many reasons why a program may not have an attractive ROI. Sometimes, these reasons are due to suboptimal program design and are thus avoidable. For instance, an inadequate needs assessment may have been performed, and therefore injury rates were not impacted as expected. Or, perhaps a popular trend in the training industry was chosen, such as computer-based training, but it was not appropriate for the situation or application.

On the other hand, SH&E training will not always be financially beneficial. Even the likelihood and magnitude of potential fines by regulatory agencies and the potential costs of injuries and illnesses may not outweigh the costs of training. Less scrupulous organizations might use a cost-benefit analysis to justify discontinuing a training course, even if regulations require it. However, often the legal and moral obligations to provide training are paramount to the financial analysis. For instance, even if the potential for an injury due to the unexpected energization of machinery is extremely low in a particular organization, lockout/tagout training should be provided to employees, where applicable, because the potential severity of an injury is so great, and because there are regulations requiring such a program.

If a cost-benefit analysis is performed, at some point a presentation of the findings will likely be necessary. When preparing a presentation, first examine the cost-benefit analysis and establish a position. Identify the goals of the presentation. Is the goal to secure a budget? Or is it to gain management's support for the goals of the training program? Focus the message specifically to achieve these goals.

Be prepared to make specific requests or recommendations and be able to back them up. Also be sure to consider how and whether the recommendations fall in line with the organization's overall culture, strategies, goals, and metrics; be sure to highlight any areas where there is a direct, positive impact. This might include not only organizational goals around SH&E, such as incident rates, but also organizational financial goals, such as profitability through reduced operating costs.

Assess the attitudes that the target audience is likely to have. Will they be supportive? Resentful? Threatened? Tailor the message accordingly. For in-

stance, if the audience is likely to be skeptical of the findings, devote a little extra time to providing background on the evaluation process; this step should help build credibility for the results.

The exact message depends on the culture of the organization and the anticipated level of support by management. In a highly regulated industry, such as pharmaceuticals, making the case based on regulatory obligations may be very effective. In other organizations, an appeal based on humanitarian values (saving lives and avoiding injuries) may be the best approach. However, management will pay more attention to the message when it is expressed in financial terms (Bird 1996). In general, the most effective way to convince management to invest in SH&E is first to convince them of the inherent worth in reducing the risk of harm (i.e., tug at their heart strings) and then to clinch the argument with the supportive economic analysis (i.e., appeal to their purse strings) (Myers et al. 2008). If the SH&E program recommendation is based on legal or moral issues, but the cost-benefit analysis is not overly supportive of the recommendation, the presentation obviously should not focus on the financials.

Finally, if the cost-benefit analysis reflects negatively on an existing training program, be sure to present a plan for improvement. Do not be afraid to suggest *cutting your losses* and scrapping a program in favor of a new approach.

MANAGING A TRAINING BUDGET
Getting the Most Out of the Training Dollars

As professionals, SH&E practitioners are asked to perform a function that many of them are ill prepared for: managing a budget. Even though this section is not intended to provide a comprehensive discussion of the subject, it does provide some helpful tips for training budget management as well as some time- and cost-saving ideas for a training program. For more information on budgeting for SH&E, see both the introductory chapter, "Basic Economic Analysis and Engineering Economics," and the "Cost Analysis and Budgeting" chapter in Section 1.

A needs analysis is critical to establishing the scope of the training program. First, determine what courses will be offered, including regulatory requirements (e.g., HazCom), courses aimed at addressing a specific hazard or source of injuries (e.g., ergonomics), and courses that are situation- or process-specific (e.g., training on grounding and bonding for employees who work with flammable liquids). In order to facilitate the rest of the budgeting process, consider prioritizing courses based on whether they are "must haves," such as regulatory requirements, or whether they are expected to have a significant impact, or whether they are "nice to haves," which might include classes that are not required by any regulation or have more uncertain and less significant benefits. Also consider conducting a cost-benefit analysis of each course before prioritizing.

Note that when working within an existing budget or with limited resources, it may be necessary to cut some courses from the budget, or to offer certain courses in a more cost-effective manner. If a larger budget is required, though, do not be afraid to request an increase if justified.

Table 3 shows an example of a budget-planning worksheet. Internal costs, such as the cost of employee time, while important when performing a cost-benefit analysis, are not considered in this budget. Examples of both capital (assets that can depreciate over time) and expense items (ongoing costs) are included.

One word of caution—do not assume an organization's existing list of training courses to accurately reflect what is really needed. Often, training is conducted year after year without adequate consideration to its relevance and, in fact, its appropriateness; furthermore, the frequency of the required refresher courses may not have been adequately considered when the class was established. So define the scope of the training program based not on what currently exists, but rather on a careful needs analysis. Section I of this volume provides more detail on regulatory issues in SH&E training. At times, tough decisions will need to be made. For some courses, new training materials may have to wait until another year. Other courses may need to be cut out completely.

Consider the example presented in Table 3. After submitting this request, the SH&E manager was told that she had to trim $18,000 from the expense budget. What courses should she cut? One approach is to jus-

TABLE 3

Sample SH&E Training Budget–Planning Worksheet

Budget Line Item	Capital	Expense
New Employee Orientation		
Materials		$1000
Hazard Communication		
New computer-based program	$8000	
Excavation Safety		
External consultants		$12,000
Employee meals, travel, etc.		$24,000
Lockout/Tagout		
Employee meals, travel, etc.		$3000
Electrical Safety		
External train-the-trainer course		$3000
Employee meals, travel, etc.		$4000
Emergency Response Teams		
External consultants		$3000
Course materials (suits, gloves, etc.)		$500
Employee meals, travel, etc.		$1000
Emergency Action Plan		
Course materials		$500
Laboratory Safety		
Annual fee, existing software		$1000
Ergonomics		
External consultants		$15,000
Office Safety		
Course materials		$500
Defensive Driving		
External train-the-trainer course		$2000
Employee meals, travel, etc.		$5000
Fire Safety		
External consultants		$6500
Fall Protection		
External consultants		$10,000
Other		
New electronic records database	$18,000	
TOTALS	$26,000	$92,000
TOTAL ANNUAL TRAINING BUDGET = $118,000		

tify why funds cannot be cut from the budget, and this may work, given the right data or persuasive arguments. Those arguments may not suffice in every situation, though. So which courses can be sacrificed?

Cutting ergonomics training might be a tempting choice if regulations do not require it, but in this case the SH&E manager was expecting the program to reap great benefits in terms of injury reduction. So she looked elsewhere. The excavation safety course was contracted with a reputable national firm and included hands-on demonstrations using backhoes to slope the sides of a trench and to construct shoring.

Employees were brought in from multiple locations to attend the training. Utilizing a cost-benefit analysis, a much more cost-effective alternative was indentified: to purchase the training materials and deliver the course in-house, forgoing the hands-on demonstration. The SH&E manager was concerned, though, that the course may not have the same impact without the hands-on practice. But she realized this: the target audience digs trenches and constructs shoring nearly every day. The training objective at this point was really to influence behavior, because all but the newest employees were familiar with the regulations and techniques of excavation safety. So, in the end, the organization was able to save most of the requested $18,000 budget cut by using the new approach to this training class.

When making a request to spend capital or expense money from the budget, consider what policies or thresholds the organization has for these requests. For instance, capital expenditures for items such as new computer equipment may have a different process than an expense expenditure, which might include items such as paying for an instructor or training materials. Also, the number and level of approvals necessary often depends on the total dollars spent.

When submitting a yearly budget request, carefully consider how budgets are managed in the organization. Some common budgeting techniques are zero-based budgeting and baseline budgeting (Shim 2009). If an organization uses baseline budgeting, it needs to look at the previous year's budget and justify why maintaining or increasing the budget is necessary, or, more commonly, where costs can be cut. On the other hand, with zero-based budgeting, the entire budget must be justified *from the ground up* each year, in which case the concepts in this chapter are even more critical.

Another important concept in budgeting is opportunity costs. When money is budgeted for a certain program or purpose and left unspent, there is a cost to the organization in terms of missed opportunity (Shim 2009). For instance, the money could have been invested elsewhere to grow a business or to earn interest. Thus, one must not fall into the trap of requesting more money than one really needs or can spend.

Effective budget execution includes continuous record keeping, tracking, and monitoring. And even though the actual tracking and record keeping may be performed by the accounting or finance departments, do not rely solely on these departments to accurately reflect where the budget stands. Lag time in debiting accounts may cause financial reports to overestimate the amount of funds that is truly still available. Therefore, use a log to track expenses as they occur, similar to using a check register for personal expenses.

Continuous Improvement

All training programs and courses are candidates for continuous improvement. Some ideas for saving time and money for SH&E training are as follows:

- Shorten training times by focusing course content on the training objectives.
- Provide training materials, such as bulky handouts, electronically to save printing costs.
- For geographically dispersed audiences, save on travel costs by using computer-based training, teleconferences, or a train-the-trainer approach.
- Do not use highly experienced, highly paid trainers to teach basic topics if other qualified trainers are available (or could be trained to deliver the material).
- Save on development costs by purchasing off-the-shelf training programs.
- Where travel time is not an issue, consider providing long courses in shorter segments. It may be possible to offer shorter segments at more convenient times or outside of core business hours.
- When multiple topics are covered in one course, switching to several modules may allow more flexibility for employees in terms of attending only the specific segments they need.

Consider coaching, on-the-job training, or other alternatives to traditional training that may save significantly on the cost of instructors, development, materials, and travel.

Another source of ideas for continuous improvement of training costs may come from course attendees. If feedback consistently indicates that the course is too long, a shorter class might accomplish the same learning goals in a more efficient manner. Or, if many employees indicate that they would prefer computer-based training over the current instructor-led course, then perhaps computer-based training would allow for easier scheduling and impact less on employee productivity.

Cost-benefit analyses must be periodically reviewed or redone to determine if the current program is still the most cost efficient (Grant et al. 1990). If, ten years ago, computer-based training was considered too expensive, it may be that technological developments in the ensuing years have made that alternative more attractive for the present. Furthermore, assumptions made in the original analysis may no longer be valid, or they may have been proved wrong through experience. Perhaps the initial cost-benefit analysis for outsourcing respiratory-protection training and fit-testing was based on a much smaller number of employees than are currently in the program. Outsourcing may now be justified, so it may be time to crunch the numbers again. The frequency with which the analysis should be redone depends on how rapidly the content and available delivery alternatives are changing. At least once per year, when reviewing the SH&E training program, ask the following questions:

1. Are improved alternatives available?
2. Are substantial changes to the content required?
3. Is the program no longer meeting its objectives?

If the answer to any of these questions is yes, a cost-benefit analysis to compare alternatives should be considered.

In conclusion, the concepts described in this chapter, including cost accounting, cost-benefit analysis, and budgeting, are all critical tools in the ongoing efforts to improve training. By employing these concepts, SH&E professionals are likely to not only save their organizations time and money, but also to improve their own status and image with management.

REFERENCES

Asche, F., and Terje Aven. 2004. "On the Economic Value of Safety." *Risk, Decision and Policy* 9(3):263–367.

Behm, M., A. Veltri, and I. K. Kleinsorge. 2004. "The Cost of Safety." *Professional Safety* (April) 49:22–29.

Bird, F. E. 1996. *Safety and the Bottom Line*. Logansville, GA: Febco.

Brady, W., J. Bass, R. Moser, Jr., G. W. Anstadt, R. R. Loeppke, and R. Leopold. 1997. "Defining Total Corporate Health and Safety Costs—Significance and Impact." *Journal of Occupational and Environmental Medicine* 39(3):224–231.

Brandt, J. 1999. "Hitting the Injury Iceberg." *Ergonomics Supplement*, pp. 160–165.

Devaney, M. 2001. "Measuring ROI of Computer Training in a Small- to Medium-Sized Enterprise." In *In Action: Measuring Return on Investment*, vol. 3, pp. 185–196. Edited by J. Phillips. Alexandria, VA: American Society for Training and Development.

Dong, X., P. Entzel, Y. Men, R. Chowdhury, and S. Schneider. 2004. "Effects of Safety and Health Training on Work-Related Injury Among Construction Laborers." *Journal of Occupational & Environmental Medicine* 46(12):1222–1228.

Geller E. S. 2005. *People-Based Safety: The Source*. Virginia Beach, VA: Coastal Training Technologies Corp.

Grant, E. L., W. G. Ireson, and R. Leavenworth. 1990. *Principles of Engineering Economy*. 8th ed. New York: John Wiley & Sons.

Head, G. E. 1994. *Training Cost Analysis: A How-To Guide for Trainers and Managers*. Alexandria, VA: American Society for Training and Development.

Hinze, J. 2000. "Incurring the Costs of Injuries Versus Investing in Safety." In *Construction Safety and Health Management*. Edited by R. J. Coble et al. New York: Prentice-Hall.

Jervis, S., and T. R. Collins. 2001. "Measuring Safety's Return on Investment." *Professional Safety* 46(9):18–23.

Kinn, S., S. A. Khuder, M. S. Besesi, and S. Woolley. 2000. "Evaluation of Safety Orientation and Training Programs for Reducing Injuries in the Plumbing and Pipefitting Industries. *Journal of Occupational and Environmental Medicine* 42:1142–1147.

Machles, D. 2002. "Training Transfer Strategies for the Safety Professional." *Professional Safety*, February 2002.

Miller, T. R., and M. Galbraith. 1995. "Estimating the Costs of Occupational Injury in the United States." *Accident Analysis and Prevention* 27(6):741–747.

Myers, M., H. Cole, J. Mazur, and S. Isaacs. 2008. "Economics & Safety: Understanding the Cost of Injuries and Their Prevention." *Professional Safety*, April 2008.

Nathan, E. P. "Determining the ROI of an Online English as a Second Language Program." *Performance Improvement* 48(6):39–48.

Occupational Safety and Health Adminstration (OSHA). 2010. *OSHA $afety Pays Program* (retrieved October 2, 2010). www.osha.gov/ dcsp/ smallbusiness/safety pays/index.html.

Phillips, J. 2003. *Return on Investment in Training and Performance Improvement Programs*. 2d ed. Burlington, MA: Butterworth-Heinemann.

Phillips, P. P. 2002. *The Bottom Line on ROI; Basics, Benefits and Barriers to Measuring Training and Performance Improvement*. Atlanta, GA: CEP Press.

Phillips, P., J. Phillips, R. Stone, and H. Burkett. 2007. *The ROI Field Book: Strategies for Implementing ROI in HR and Training*. Burlington, MA: Butterworth-Heinemann.

Shim, J. K., and J. G. Siegel. 2009. *Budgeting Basics and Beyond*. Hoboken, NJ: John Wiley & Sons Inc.

Waagen, Alice K. 2000. *How to Budget Training*. Alexandria, VA: American Society for Training and Development.

ADDITIONAL RESOURCES

Adams, S. 2003. "Costs Drive Safety Training Needs." *HR Magazine*, January 2003.

Kilgore, C., and P .L. Clemens. 2008. "Economy-Based Countermeasure Decisions: A Tutorial for SH&E Professionals." *Professional Safety*, April 2008.

Purcell, A. 2000. "20/20 ROI." *Training & Development*, July 2000.

Snyder, M. 2004. "The Time-Cost-Quality Triangle." *Training & Development*, April 2004.

SAFETY AND HEALTH TRAINING BENCHMARKING AND PERFORMANCE CRITERIA

7

Richard A. Stempniak and Linda Tapp

LEARNING OBJECTIVES

■ Understand the concepts of assessment for safety and health training.

■ Be able to discuss the benefits of assessment and their use in improving safety and health training.

■ Apply the concepts of assessment to safety and health training.

■ Be able to discuss the assessment criteria provided in ANSI Z490.1.

■ Understand benchmarking basics and be able to apply them to safety and health training.

ANY COMPANY THAT regularly provides safety and health training for its employees is making a considerable investment of money and staff time. A good investment will yield a good return on investment (ROI). Because the principal value of employee safety and health training is in what employees *learn*, evaluation or assessment of a program's value should concentrate on "doing assessment as if learning matters most" (Angelo 1999).

Assessment is the process of collecting "the best possible data about . . . learning and the factors that affect it" (Walvoord 2004).

Breaking the definition down, "best possible data" are generally those indicators available to the person(s) doing the assessment during and after instruction. These indicators can include:

- questions answered by employees about the subject being taught during the instruction session
- instructors' judgment on whether the employees they are training understand and retain the information presented to them
- questions answered by employees after a training session regarding their perception of the effectiveness of the instruction
- employee performance on the job after training
- formal grades or quiz results
- impact on company operations

KIRKPATRICK'S FOUR LEVELS OF EVALUATION

Donald Kirkpatrick set the standards for training effectiveness metrics when he identified four distinct categories of measurement. These are commonly known as the four levels of evaluation. These four levels are:

- Level 1: The nature of employees' reactions

- Level 2: The extent of employees' learning
- Level 3: The extent to which employees' learning is reflected in their on-the-job behavior
- Level 4: The extent to which employees' changed behavior affects the organization (Kirkpatrick 1998)

The first two levels are relatively simple to evaluate. Employees' reactions to a training class can be determined by means of a simple questionnaire or by what is often known in the training industry as a "smile sheet," which usually asks participants to rank the instructor and instruction on a scale of 1–5. One way to measure the extent of employees' learning is by using both pre-test and post-test evaluations. The improvement, evident in increasing percentages of correct responses, helps to demonstrate how much trainees have learned as a result of their training. Levels 3 and 4, however, are much harder to evaluate, because the data involved can require either subjective or objective measurement (Cheney 2001). If employees have been trained in the safe handling of chemicals, it may be difficult to measure how they apply this knowledge once back on the job. Who should do the observations depends on the particular program in place. It could be the supervisor but it could also be a safety trainer or line worker trained in observation techniques. One method that can be used is making workplace observations that are then recorded and tracked—but, again, it is important to have taken baseline measurements by making pre-training observations. Even when results of the training are known, fully understanding their effects on an organization can be even more difficult. Training may affect many unknown areas within the organization—or even have external effects. Decreases in worker compensation costs or reduced employee turnover can provide partial methods of measurement, but any such forms of evaluation should insist on tying the data as directly as possible to the training given. Still other effects may never be known—an employee may use safe chemical handling techniques at home as well as at work because of the training presented, thereby avoiding a serious chemical burn at home.

WHY ASSESS?

Assessment has several purposes:

- determining the ROI the program yields the company because of lower accident and injury rates.
- continuously improving employee safety and health training (We are assuming this is one of the company's regular business goals. If not, and the company has set no goals whatsoever for its safety and health program, it will be nearly impossible to complete a valid assessment. As the saying goes, "If you don't know where you're going, how will you know when you get there?")
- continuously locating and evaluating factors affecting safety and health training (whether positively or negatively), including the physical environment during training, the trainer's knowledge of the subject and ability to teach, class size, individual employees' ability to learn (particularly as affected by interest in learning the subject), the training's format and content, including length of class, and the existence of language barriers
- discovering what employees are learning from the program and what their reactions to it are: for example, are employees applying their training on the job; is such application achieving results—a better safety record with fewer accidents and injuries, less lost work time, increased productivity, and more employees taking personal responsibility for following safety procedures (Kirkpatrick 1998)
- identifying topics or themes that are missing in the training (Are expected improvements in behavior or knowledge not seen after the training has concluded? A topic or tangential topic may have been subconsciously excluded from the class content.)

Assessment is intended to have a local, fairly rapid (evident within months) effect on the safety and health training program in order to help the company more rapidly attain its goals. Assessment focuses on continuous improvement by following a cycle of evaluation, planning, and implementation of change as necessary. To be as effective as possible, assessment results should take their appropriate place in the company's annual planning and budgeting process. A review of incidents and accident investigations that have occurred at the facility can also be used to identify gaps in existing training.

The Benefits of Assessment

The greatest benefit assessment can give a company is in its role as a catalyst for change. Done properly, assessment can provide a basis for wiser planning, budgeting, and revision of procedures, preventing the wasting of resources in response to vague notions about what might (or should) be effective (Walvoord 2004).

Continuously assessing safety training effectiveness and rapidly instituting changes in that training can save lives and reduce levels of injury and property damage, allowing the company to redirect funds from insurance and compensation budget lines to even more productive uses.

Types of Assessment: Summative, Formative, and Systematic

The Occupational Safety and Health Administration (OSHA) includes three methods of evaluating training effectiveness in its informational booklet on training requirements (OSHA Pub. 2254). These include student opinion, supervisor observations, and workplace improvements, which can be further divided into five commonly accepted types of training evaluation: participant satisfaction, learning outcomes, attitude changes, behavior/job performance changes, and productivity/accomplishment of goals (Dinardi 2003). These five areas of evaluation can be considered formative assessments, summative assessments, systemic assessments, or some combination of them.

Summative assessment occurs after training has been completed and is used to evaluate the overall effectiveness of a fully developed training course, informing decisions about whether to continue, expand, modify, or drop particular training in response to its results. Summative assessment measures outcomes. In its simplest

form it answers the question: Did the training cause the company to achieve its stated goal? The primary audience of summative assessment is management.

Assume that the company has established "the elimination of all preventable motor-vehicle accidents" as a goal for a safety training course it commissioned. The course is to be taught over six weeks, and classes will be held every Monday morning from 10:00 A.M. to noon. A summative assessment of that course would issue a report containing the number of preventable motor-vehicle accidents during the quarter *prior* to the completion of the training course and the number of preventable motor accidents in the quarter *after* the completion of the course. If the second number dropped to zero, the course would be judged a success.

A more complex summative assessment would not only answer the above question but also document the course's processes, including how the selection of students for this course was made and what measurements of their learning were taken during the course. The assessment would also report on any unplanned outcomes, such as the reduction in miles driven by employees in company vehicles during the quarter (the assessment process would have to continue to discover the cause of such an occurrence; perhaps the employees stopped driving company vehicles for personal errands). A summative assessment would help to determine actions and conditions that affected training outcomes such as these.

Formative assessment takes place while the training program is under development. Though the trainer may be using a particular training outline or manual, it is not written in stone and may be changed in response to the formative assessment conducted. The conclusions drawn from formative assessment are used to modify and improve the processes of the training while the course is still being developed or is underway.

When assessing the training during the development phase, it is important to ask three things: (1) Is the training understandable? Can the trainees easily understand the material being presented and the instructions for interactive activities? (2) Is the training content accurate—for example, is the material that is presented indeed correct? (3) Is the training functional—do all parts work? Do the handouts match the slides?

Do prepared quizzes adequately cover the content of the class? Does the training match the current course objectives? It is essential to consider understandability, accuracy, and functionality during the development phase (Carliner 2003).

Formative assessment observes training activities, anticipates potential problems, and monitors employees' current job conduct for positive or negative changes that may have been brought about by training (Boulmetis and Dutwin 2000).

In the example above, the formative assessor may monitor the job performance of those being trained. Here are some typical questions: Did the accident reports of one employee, or certain employees, suddenly increase or decrease as a result of training? Did those whose preventable accident count increased misunderstand something the trainer said? Did the awareness level of an employee or employees increase regarding a particular situation or activity? What about those employees whose preventable accident count decreased? Did a particular point made by the trainer hit home? Should that particular point be repeated and emphasized again in training? Are most of the employees consistently late to class or late in returning to work?

The formative assessor should report these data to the trainer, allowing him or her to make changes in the course that will eliminate misunderstandings, place more emphasis on key concepts or ideas, and (if necessary) adjust training dates and times to increase employee attendance.

This type of assessment is detailed, diagnostic, and informal. It asks why negative results suddenly occurred and what trainers can do right now—before the next class session, even—to prevent those results from occurring again.

Systematic assessment examines a training program systematically by studying the input, throughput, and output associated with it. *Input* includes the trainer, the employees, the location of instruction, the outlines of topics or subjects the trainer will cover at each training session, and training materials and equipment such as printed handouts, projectors, and viewing screens. The room where the training will take place should be large enough for each trainee to feel comfortable and able to comfortably participate in class activities and see all visual aids, such as slides

or flipcharts. The benefits of good training will be diminished if overcrowding distracts students (Dinardi 2003). In addition to supplying adequate space, the training location should also be climate controlled, well lit and ventilated, and free of outside distractions. Unfavorable physical factors can make it difficult for trainees to pay attention to instruction (Hutchinson 2003). All elements of input, including the trainer and the employees in training, should be planned for before the first training session. *Throughput* refers to those events or actions that occur as the training is conducted, as well as to the adequacy of resources, including teaching aids, handouts, and facilities. *Output* is the results of the training and includes the number of employees trained, the total cost of the training both in dollars and staff time, and (of course) the safety performance of the employees after training. The efficiency of the training process is assessed in this state (Boulmetis and Dutwin 2000).

Systematic assessment is essential to understanding whether an organization met its goals and what amount of measurable improvement followed the training. These improvements are not limited to improvements in safety records, but also include an organization's overall increase in performance and productivity.

Systematic assessment is a *before, during, and after* progression. Before training, define the goals of the training. During training, collect and organize evidence about the employees' learning process. After training, ask, "Did the training help meet the training goals?" All three steps must be performed to complete a systematic assessment.

WHO ASSESSES, AND WHEN?

Assessment may be carried out internally or externally—that is, by an employee or by an outside consultant. Whoever assesses should ideally be part of the planning process that organizes the training and should stay involved, participating in the formative assessment process while the training is developed and conducted, and perform the summative assessment after the training is completed.

Ideally, the assessor involves all the stakeholders in assessment, just as all of them should be involved in planning. The *stakeholders* are everyone involved in the training program, including the management; external sources of funding, if they exist; training staff; employees to be trained; and the supervisors of those employees. Frequently these last two groups of stakeholders are left out of both planning and assessment during and after the completion of training—especially when the training is driven by an urgent need (such as when management perceives a need for training because accident frequency and associated costs have recently increased dramatically). In a case like this, management orders the training of employees. The company's training staff (or a person who is designated) sets up training through an internal employee or external consultant, and training is then conducted. The accident record may improve, but it may not. Lack of improvement after training may be caused by the exclusion of the recipients of the training—the employees and their supervisors—from the assessment process (Boulmetis and Dutwin 2000).

Except in cases where there is an emergency need to train employees about a particular hazard that has just injured another employee, a company should use of a formal training planning cycle that includes a standing committee, a formal group of employees, or a training department that makes recommendations to management about the nature of the company's training needs: What subjects should be taught, and by whom? Who should receive the training? What assessment process should be used? This group may even be able to suggest possible external sources of funding to underwrite the cost of training.

Methods of Assessment and Data Collection

Within the several types of assessment discussed above are two methods by which data can be collected; one is direct and the other is indirect.

Direct assessment attempts to evaluate trainees by examining empirical data such as that provided by exams, quizzes, projects, and future on-the-job behaviors and attitudes. The *one-minute paper* technique elicits prompt but (because of its brevity) limited employee answers to one or two specific questions about the course in general or a specific class session. Cross and Angelo (1998) explain the technique by stating that a trainer should stop the class session a

few minutes early, posing one or two questions to which trainees are asked to react. The trainees write their answers anonymously on half-sheets of paper. The instructor simply tabulates the answers and makes note of any useful comments.

Pros: This method can provide valuable self-correcting feedback, enabling more effective teaching and learning. It allows a quick response to the trainees and demonstrates respect for and interest in student reactions, encouraging active engagement in the class process. It also allows individual students to compare their responses with the class as a whole.

Cons: If one-minute papers are overused or poorly used, the technique can degenerate into a gimmick or an exercise in polling, obtaining feedback that neither the trainer nor the rest of the class want to hear or act upon. Preparing a question that can be immediately and clearly comprehended and quickly answered can be harder than it sounds (Cross and Angelo 1998).

The most direct method of assessment is collecting data on the accident records of trainees after they return to the job (if the intent of the training was to change behaviors that caused accidents or to provide new safety information to be used in the prevention of accidents). This is part of summative assessment and is probably the major piece of data at which management will look. Similarly, direct observations of behavior can be made. If safe forklift-driving training was given, the safe forklift-driving skills of the trainees could be observed and evaluated. If training was provided on company-specific energy control procedures, the correct applications of these procedures can be observed and recorded.

Indirect assessment measures include asking employees (and their supervisors) how well they thought they learned. This is qualitative (rather than quantitative) evidence, but if employees are asked a week or two after the training has been completed, they will have a better perspective on their own retention of the training material, and their supervisors will have had a better opportunity to observe their employees' on-the-job behavior (Walvoord 2004).

Cohen and Colligan, in their study *Assessing Occupational Safety and Health Training* (1998), cited numerous examples of successful training programs that were designed to reduce specific accidents or injuries (see

Table 1). Table 2 provides extracts from the Bureau of Labor Statistics's work-injury reports that indicate real or possible gaps in job safety and health training. This study is an example of a systematic assessment.

As the above examples demonstrate, health and safety training requires continual assessment conducted as if *learning matters most*. By monitoring, and by using feedback indicators, instructors can continue to improve the quality of training by changing and adjusting the training course outline and instructional methods.

BENCHMARKING

Benchmarking is about comparing and measuring performance against other similar organizations and then using lessons learned from the best ones to introduce breakthrough improvements (Koskela 1992). Benchmarking can and should be used in goal-setting, especially if the organization's goals are to perform at the highest level. One example can be found in the United States' attempt to lower traffic fatalities by comparing the U.S. rates to other nations and then using this data to set goals (TRB 2010).

Benchmarking is a type of assessment based on comparison to external activities and sources. These external activities and sources can be external to the department being benchmarked (such as another department conducting safety and health training), external to the company, or even external to the industry. The idea of benchmarking started in 1979 when the Xerox Corporation decided to be a leader in their industry. Businesses have used benchmarking to improve in all areas, from financial controls to employee compensation packages. Benchmarking can also be applied to health and safety training—with dramatic results. Benchmarking is easier to implement in areas involving easily measurable outputs, such as production. In areas that are more difficult to measure— such as training—it proves to be more of a challenge.

Benchmarking is best treated as a continuous process whereby the effectiveness of the safety training is continuously monitored and measured so that the quality and desired outcomes continue to increase.

What is benchmarking in relation to safety and health training? Benchmarking is the process of learning from the best in order to make a program or process stronger. Its three steps are (1) evaluation of the training program intended to be improved, enabling the (2) identification of weaknesses or other areas for improvement, and, finally, (3) identification of other companies with strong safety and health training programs to look at for best practices and leadership.

One of the main benefits of benchmarking is its ability to rapidly help a program improve. Without benchmarking, changes to a training process or program may occur only by trial-and-error. Needed improvements may take longer to identify and make as issues are more clearly seen. Benchmarking can help identify what has already been proven to work at other companies by comparing safety and health training programs, allowing personnel to make the changes necessary to bring their programs closer to the *benchmark* or the level of excellence set by the identified leader. This can rapidly improve the quality of a safety and health training program.

Types of Benchmarking

Benchmarking can be either internal or external. External benchmarking can further be broken down into three types: competitive, cooperative, and collaborative.

Internal benchmarking occurs when different parts of a company are compared to each other, or when one part is compared to itself over time. The number of hours employees attend training from year to year is one type of safety training benchmark used by some companies. *External benchmarking* involves looking outside the company. *Competitive* benchmarking looks at what competitors are doing; although this information may be difficult to discover, informal research can help. *Cooperative* benchmarking targets an unrelated industry against which to benchmark, so long as the other industry has the same practices in the area of safety and health training. *Collaborative* benchmarking occurs when similar companies voluntarily share information (sometimes anonymously) for the purpose of benchmarking.

TABLE 1

Training Intervention Studies as Found in the Literature Addressing Various Types of Occupational Hazards

			Safety/Injury Hazard Control			
Work Setting Operation (Ref)	**Training Objective**	**Training Plan**	**Evaluation Method**	**Extra-Training Factors**	**Results**	**Comments**
96 operators of industrial lift trucks at two warehouse sites. (Cohen & Jensen 1984).	To promote operator awareness and adoption of 14 specific actions critical to safer operator/vehicle use.	Focus was on 14 worker behaviors that could be observed, measured, and related to accident occurrences as defined by a task-hazard analysis, 5 training sessions (20–45 minutes long) were given on 5 successive days; 1 introductory, 3 instructional, and 1 practice/exercises. Slides were used to show incorrect/correct behaviors; Practice sessions had group grade performance of each trainee on a practice run.	3 observers counted frequencies of the correct/incorrect 14 behaviors as noted at 8 locations at each warehouse on a daily basis. At Warehouse 1, operators were divided into 3 groups: training only, training + feedback, and a control group that was trained only after 1st post-training evaluation. Study plan had monthly pre-training and post-training 1 & 2 phases, plus a retention phase that was 3 months after post-training 2. At Warehouse 2, all workers trained at same time and all received feedback.	All levels of management had input into the program and supported its development. Feedback supplied daily through verbal and posted summaries of group performance. All groups subjected to training set at 80% goal attainment level.	For Warehouse 1, at end of retention phase and after all workers trained, overall decrease in incorrect acts was 44%. Training + feedback group showed best scores in post-training 1. At Warehouse 2, overall improvement in 14 behaviors was 70%. 12 of 12 target behaviors indicated clear improvements; 2 were resisted because they involved an uncomfortable posture, and exposure to exhaust fumes.	The effect of training to achieve safer work behaviors is clear. Question: Will it reduce accident/injury rate in lift truck operations?
55 workers in 4 sections of the vehicle maintenance division of a city public works department showing one of the highest injury rates as compared with other divisions (Komaki, Heinzman & Lawson 1980).	To effect changes in worker behavior with regards to proper equipment/tool use, wearing personal protective/safety equipment, improving housekeeping procedures, and other actions aimed at upgrading general safety performance.	Accident logs for past 5 years reviewed and weaknesses in current safety program used to frame behavioral targets specific to each of the 4 sections. After baseline observations directed to existent behaviors, workers attended session to view/discuss slides of unsafe acts and ways to prevent them, which became formulated into safety rules. Copies of these rules issued to workers.	Checklist of pre-scribed safety behaviors was used by trained observers who monitored workers' actions in each section 3–5 times per week. Study plan had 5 phases where these observations were taken to show the effects of training alone, training plus feedback, withdrawing and then reinstituting feedback as compared with baseline data. Total study span was 45 weeks; phases varied from 5–11 weeks.	Upon completion of training phase, supervisors of each section indicated goals to be met in complying with safety rules and observed and provided feedback on level of adherence through graphic displays. In subsequent phases, this graphic feedback was withdrawn and then reinstituted to define its effect in enhancing safe behaviors as prescribed in the original training.	Comparing % safe acts against the pre-training baseline data for the various phases showed the following gains: Training alone = 9%; Training + feedback = 26%; Feedback withdrawn = 17% (reduced the previous gain by 9%); Reinstituting feedback = 21% (regained 4% of the previous loss). During the 8 month period of the program, lost-time injuries dropped to 0.4 per month; before program the rate was 3.0/month; after program the rate was 1.8/month.	Results show feedback as important motivator in realizing benefits of workers training and increased worker knowledge. Authors comment that management gave verbal support to program but was inconsistent in actions such as attending safety sessions or recognizing persons for their program efforts. Frequency of feedback notices by supervisors also dropped off in the last phase, which could account for less than the full recovery of the earlier gain.

(*Source:* Cohen and Colligan 1998)

TABLE 2

Extracts from Bureau of Labor Statistics (BLS) Work Injury Report or Discerning Real/Possible Gaps in Job Safety/Health Training

Database Sample Surveyed (period of survey)	Limitations in Extent/Nature of Training					Follow-up Actions/Needs
	Form/Source of Training	Training Content	Workforce Coverage	Date of Last Training	Age/Job Experience	
1400 respondents to survey of 2000 workers with reportable injuries from ladder mishaps (Winter 1978).	73% not provided written instructions on safe use of ladders. 78% trained on-the-job.	66% lacked training in how to inspect ladders.	59% lacked training of use of ladders.	Of those noting training, 50% indicated it took place over 1 year ago.	Most injuries in 25–34 year old group (25%).	
803 respondents to survey of 1230 workers with reportable injuries from scaffold mishaps. (July–November 1978).	On-the-job training noted by 62%–71% in learning different safety requirements; over 50% by just watching others.	Safety requirements covered for scaffold assembly, planking, inspection, weight limits, guard rails; no more than 71% noted training in any topic.	26%–35% of respondents indicated no training in any of the topics noted in the content column.	71% indicated training received more than 1 year ago (71% from other than the current employer).	Highest % of injured in 25–34 year old group (24%); next was 20–24 year olds group (18%).	
1364 respondents to survey of 2300 workers with injures from welding/cutting operations (July–November 1978).	Both on-the-job and classroom training noted but not more than 37% received either form of such training.	81% believed subject coverage adequate but coverage of different topics ranged from 40% to 83%.	30% indicated they learned welding/cutting safety on their own through job experience. 11% never had any safety training.	69% of those receiving training noted the date of more than 1 year ago.	26% had less than 1 year of work experience; 16% less than 6 months. 2–34 year old group had greatest % of injuries (32%).	
1746 respondents to survey of 2300 workers with reportable injuries from power saw use. (September–November 1978).	On-the-job and classroom instruction were main forms of training but each noted for no more than 39% of the worker respondents.	For those receiving training, coverage of various topics drew response rates varying from 32% to 59%.	89% learned power-saw safety through their own job experience. 17% never had any safety training.		44% working with saw less than 1 year, 19% less than 1 month. 20–24 year old group and 25–34 year old group tied for highest % of injuries (25%).	
1033 respondents to survey of 1881 workers with reportable head injuries at work (July–September 1979).	Information on "hard hat" protection mainly from supervisor or safety officer (81%), but co-worker (19%) and printed material (25%) also noted.	Instruction emphasized when and where to use (61%); Other topics such as how to adjust, maintain and types available drew less than a 35% response.	32% received no information or instruction on "hard hats".		20–24 year old group had highest % of head injuries (32%).	In head injury cases 41% of the respondents did not know of any action employers took to prevent recurrence. Where noted, accident investigation and issuance of warnings were main (33%) follow-up actions, training noted at 1%.

(Continued)

TABLE 2

Database Sample Surveyed (period of survey)	Limitations in Extent/Nature of Training					
	Form/Source of Training	Training Content	Workforce Coverage	Date of Last Training	Age/Job Experience	Follow-up Actions/Needs
1251 respondents to survey of 2005 workers with reportable foot injuries at work (July–August 1979).	Given information on safety shoes from supervisor or safety officer (92%).	Information stresses where/when to wear (41%); coverage of features available, maintenance, and advantages ranged from 6% to 17%.			Most foot injuries in 25–34 year old group (25%) followed by 20–24 year old group (23%).	Fewer than 25% wearing safety shoes at time of accident though 72% aware of company policy on wearing shoes in specific areas and jobs. 21% indicated employer took no follow-up actions after injury. 28% did not know of any.
1052 respondents to survey of 2118 workers with reportable eye injuries at work (July–.August 1979)	Main instruction on eye protection from supervisor or safety officer (91%); co-workers (15%0 and classroom session (14%) also noted.	Subjects of where and when to wear drew a 72% response; followed by type to wear (39%). Care and limitations had a 16% response.	20% of respondents had no instruction in use of protective eye wear.		25–34 year old group had highest % of eye injuries (32%). Next was 20–24 year old group (25%).	Though over 70% of workers indicated company policy on wearing eye protection, more than 20% noted enforcement came after injury. Common response to nonuse was impractical or not required.

* The shaded entries in the tables are meant to suggest major training deficits for sizeable percentages of the afflicted workers.

(*Source*: Cohen and Colligan 1998)

Benchmarking can be broken down into ten steps (Camp 1989). When benchmarking any area, the first step is to determine specifically what you want to benchmark. When deciding what to measure as part of a benchmarking project, first establish what the key performance measures are and what activities are going to improve the overall safety program. Benchmarking efforts will not be effective without the right metrics. In areas of health and safety training, it might be a good idea to benchmark how many hours employees attend training in comparison to employees of other companies—as well as the type of training delivered and the nature of the delivery method itself, whether classroom, on-the-job, or online. A little more difficult, though still useful, is benchmarking the ROI of health and safety training.

The second step of benchmarking is to identify certain leaders in the areas against which the company will be benchmarking. This will likely be the most difficult step.

The third step is to collect data that can be used to benchmark against the top performer, collecting data from industry leaders as well as the company to be benchmarked. Steps two and three both require the identification of industry leaders and the collection of their best practices, information that can be found in many places, including the following, which were included in the *Department of the Navy Benchmarking Handbook* (Kraft n.d.):

- newspaper articles
- internal publications
- magazine articles
- trade and industry publications
- journals
- seminars
- professional associations
- industry experts
- press releases
- software and hardware vendors
- literature searches
- consulting firms
- plant tours
- newsletters

- interviews
- focus groups
- commercial services

Company safety and health data is continuously updated on the Internet by many organizations and is freely available. Government Web sites, such as those provided by the Occupational Safety and Health Administration (OSHA) and the Bureau of Labor Statistics (BLS), can be relied on to provide free and accurate information. Accident and injury statistics provided by these groups can be one asset in benchmarking efforts.

It is important only to evaluate and collect information that relates specifically to the health and safety benchmarking project in question. How much better or more successful are their best practices than the procedures and programs currently in place?

The fourth step is to identify gaps between the company's performance and that of the leaders. What do they do that is successful that can be emulated? The size of the gap should also be considered both at the current time and in the future. The size of the gap could have implications for the safety and health training program.

The fifth step is to extrapolate the data from the leaders, evaluating where they will be in 3–5 years. That should be the benchmark for the company's health and safety training program.

The sixth step is communicating the findings of benchmarking efforts to gain support for improvement plans from every level in the company. This step cannot be overlooked. Improvement plans often require additional funding. Thorough explanation and excellent communications are often necessary to achieve this.

The seventh step is to develop goals to present to senior management. Based on the results of benchmarking, goals can be set that are aligned with where the leaders will be in 3–5 years (the goals identified in step 5). The goals should be in the form of operational statements that will enable specific action plans to be developed.

The eighth step is to develop action plans based on the goals submitted to senior management. A goal to increase the percentage of employees attending safety training on a particular topic needs a step-by-step plan to ensure that the goal in this area is met.

The ninth step is to put the action plans into place and monitor and report on progress. If the goal is to provide eight hours of safety awareness training to all new hires—and two hours are currently provided—a detailed plan to expand the current class needs to be in place that has measurable goals and a timeline.

Finally, the tenth step is to recalibrate the benchmarks. Benchmark levels change over time, making benchmarking like aiming at a moving target. Set a schedule for recalibrating benchmarks and *follow through.*

Considerations When Benchmarking Safety and Health Training

Benchmarking safety and health training can be an important tool in emphasizing the impact of a sound safety and health program to senior management (and throughout the organization). The information collected during a benchmarking study will help provide objective data about the results of safety and health training. The return on investment for safety training can be difficult to measure, but benchmarking can help to determine this. Benchmarking also serves to improve safety and health training programs and, in doing so, improves the safety program as a whole. The financial benefits of a successful safety and health program were discussed in the chapter, "Cost Analysis and Budgeting" by Brent Altemose in this section of the Handbook.

Benchmarking is most valuable when results, not just activities, are measured. Measuring training results can be the most difficult task of all. In safety training, the real measures of training effectiveness are whether or not trainees have gained new skills and whether or not they apply these skills in the workplace in ways that support the overall safety program.

In any safety program's benchmarking efforts, the existence of various methods of computing metrics may affect the benchmark. Some companies calculate injury rates by different methods, according to where they are located or using parent companies' guidelines. When collecting benchmarking data, make sure to compare like with like.

There are common difficulties in carrying out benchmarking. These include: (1) a lack of suitable partners for comparing data; (2) constraints on resources

SIDEBAR

ANSI Z490.1-2009 Criteria for Accepted Practices in Safety, Health and Environmental Training

Training Program Management

When ASSE developed this Standard, the right-hand column, designated "Explanatory Information" (*not* a part of the ANSI Z490.1-2009 Standard), suggested that "[w]hen evaluating training program management, some of the functions to review include, but are not limited to: accountability, responsibility, development, delivery and evaluation processes." ASSE also went on to state: "When evaluating the training organization and administration, some of the elements to review include, but are not limited to: staffing, budgets, facilities, equipment, documentation and record keeping."

In terms of safety training program evaluation, ANSI Z490.1-2009 states (ANSI Z490.1-2009 [9–10]):

3.4.1 The training provider shall periodically evaluate the training program.

3.4.2 The elements to be evaluated shall, at a minimum, include:

- training program management
- training process
- training results

Training Process

ASSE explained in ANSI Z490.1-2009 (10), "When evaluating the training process, some elements to review include, but are not limited to, the:

- clarity and appropriateness of training goals;
- relevance of training goals to trainees;
- learning objectives;
- content and methods that support the learning objectives;
- adequacy of learning environment
- training effectiveness."

Training Results

In addition, as part of ANSI Z490.1-2009, ASSE suggests the following: "Training results should be used to improve the training program. When analyzing training results, some of the elements to review include, but are not limited to: a definite plan of action for training employees; a plan for conducting regular needs assessments; support for lifelong learning; adequate funding; program manager competence; links among training program elements; the provision for training program long-term and strategic planning; a system for identifying competing demands, and the ability to set priorities."

such as time, money, and expertise; (3) staff resistance; and (4) confidentiality of data (Holloway 1997).

In addition to what has already been reviewed from the ASSE interpretation of ANSI Z490.1-2001, Section 6, which deals with training evaluation, will now be discussed.

6. TRAINING EVALUATION IN ACCORDANCE WITH ANSI Z490.1-2009

Training evaluation tools may measure performance of trainees, trainers, training events, or training programs. Training providers must incorporate appropriate evaluation tools into each training event. This section provides acceptable criteria for the different evaluation approaches.

"There are a wide range of outcomes that can be evaluated such as: the trainee's possession of some knowledge, skill ability, and/or attitude; the trainer's ability to effectively transfer knowledge, skills, abilities, or attitudes to the trainees; the trainee's satisfaction with the training experience; the ability of the training to contribute to the organizational goals." (ANSI Z490.1-2009 [15])

6.1 GENERAL CRITERIA

6.1.1 The evaluation approaches for each training event and the tools for implementing them shall be established during training development.

ASSE states: "Different evaluation approaches may be selected to evaluate each specific outcome mentioned above."

6.1.2 An evaluation shall be made of the trainee's achievement of each learning objective, considering the performance, conditions, and criteria specified in the learning objective.

ASSE states: "In some instances, trainees may be allowed to *test out:* i.e., demonstrate achievement of the learning objective(s) without attending or participating in the training event. The criteria for *testing out* should be specified during training development. Special care should be taken to ensure regulatory compliance."

6.1.2.1 The evaluation tools used shall be reliable and valid measures of the trainee's achievement of the learning objective.

ASSE states: "A *reliable measure* is one that gives consistent results over time. A *valid measure* is one that reflects the knowledge, skills, abilities, or attitudes specified in the learning objective."

6.1.2.2 Successful completion of each evaluation shall be specified during training development.

ASSE states: "Successful completion of an evaluation will depend on a number of factors, including the evaluation approach and the importance of the learning objective(s). For example: successful completion of a test may be specified in terms of percent correct; successful completion of an observation may require the trainee [to] perform the steps of a task in the proper sequence; successful completion of a project may require that all key elements be included as per instructions."

6.1.2.3 Training providers shall furnish trainees with the results of any test or task observation included as part of the evaluation.

ASSE states: "The trainees may use feedback for seeking more information or practice, and to contribute to a plan for future training. Supervisors, managers, and trainees may use the information for individual performance support, for job design issues, or other job-related issues."

6.1.2.4 Training development shall include procedures for assisting or retraining trainees who do not achieve the learning objective(s).

6.1.3 Each trainee or trainer being evaluated shall be properly identified.

6.1.4 Evaluation shall comply with all applicable regulations.

ASSE states: "Regulatory requirements often reflect the minimum acceptable level of training. The training may exceed required regulatory levels."

6.1.5 The training program shall include periodic evaluation of trainees in relation to learning objectives and determining the effectiveness of the program.

ASSE states: "Periodic reevaluation should also be part of training development and general requirements, including regulations mandating refresher training to occur at certain and specific cycle times."

6.2 EVALUATION APPROACHES

An evaluation shall be conducted using one or more of the following techniques.

ASSE states: "The selection of the type of evaluation is based on the particular learning objective(s), audience, and desired outcome(s). The training program should attempt to incorporate all four types of evaluation as appropriate."

6.2.1 Reaction Survey

A reaction survey shall be designed to be easily administered, tabulated, and summarized, with space for written comments.

ASSE states: "A reaction survey is a subjective evaluation of the training course by the trainees. Questions about trainer presentation skills, accommodations, pace, and difficulty and usefulness of content may be included in a reaction survey. Results from a reaction survey may be used by trainees to assess and report their learning, or by trainers to assess and improve the course design and delivery."

6.2.2 Evaluation of Knowledge, Skills, and Abilities

An evaluation of knowledge, skills, and abilities shall take place while the trainee is in the learning environment.

ASSE states: "Tools used to evaluate knowledge, skills and abilities may take many forms, depending on the focus of the learning objective(s). These include: written test; oral examination; completion of an assigned project; demonstration of the skill in a simulated work setting; on-the-job demonstration of the skill in the trainer's presence.

Note—Evaluation of knowledge, skills, or abilities may be administered as pre- and post-tests only, or self-administered evaluations. They may be automated, as technology permits."

6.2.3 Observation of Performance

Observation of performance shall be used when it is necessary to verify that the trainee can demonstrate the targeted skills or abilities under actual work conditions.

ASSE states: "This approach may include pre- and post-test measurement to link performance of training. Performance information may be collected from supervisors, coworkers, or customers, or from indirect measurement such as those found in production records or safety reports.

When observation of performance reveals a gap between the desired performance and actual performance, the factors that prevented the desired performance should be identified. These may include nontraining issues, such as the availability of equipment on the job, conflicting information from a supervisor, or other indication of lack of organizational support for implementing the targeted skills."

6.2.4 *Organizational Results*

Measures of organizational results shall be used to link training to overall organization performance.

ASSE states: "To measure organizational results, training factors must be isolated from nontraining factors. To do this, there is often a control group of workers who have not received the training.

"Fundamental to this type of evaluation is an agreement on key business measures before the training takes place. These may include, but are not limited to: increase in safe behavior(s) by all trainees; increase in implemented preventive measures and controls; reduction in near hits, injuries and illnesses; reduction in worker's compensation claims; improved environmental compliance; or higher return on investment (ROI)."

6.2.5 *Rubrics*

Rubrics are a set of criteria used for the assessment of a trainee's achievement. Rubrics judge the quality of services, products, or performances (Popham 2003). In addition, rubrics are "descriptive scoring schemes" used for analysis (Moskal, 2000). Rubrics have been widely used in the K–12 education communities for

years; however, rubrics are now being introduced into the world of industrial (safety) training programs as a means of plotting the trainee's success rate. Generally, rubrics are performance-based, leading to the evaluation of the trainee's performance to a given set of tasks. It is therefore the responsibility of the trainer to specify the criteria that he/she will use to evaluate the trainee. Figure 1 shows a sample evaluation form. According to the Web site, TeAch-nology.com (rubrics), "Rating scales can be either holistic or analytical. Holistic scales offer several dimensions together while analytical scales offer a separate scale for various dimensions."

How do we develop a rubric?

According to TeAch-nology.com, there is a four-step process for developing a rubric:

1. Define the learning outcome/objective that students (trainees) are expected to achieve.
2. Determine how to describe each level of the activity.
3. Define scores (numerical or qualitative) that can be assigned for each activity.
4. Once the level is determined with rating scales assigned, share the description with the students (trainees) and ask for feedback, so that each level is clearly understood by the students (trainees).

6.3 COMMITMENT TO CONTINUOUS IMPROVEMENT

6.3.1 The information from training evaluations shall be used for continuous improvement of the course content, delivery methods, collateral materials, and learning environment.

ASSE states: "Management may use the information to assess the effectiveness of the training program

Subject	0 No Understanding	1 Minimal Understanding	2 Majority Understanding	3 Full Understanding
X				
Y				
Z				
Notes				

FIGURE 1. A typical rating scale

in meeting organizational goals and to determine the level of investment in training."

CONCLUSION

In any good organizational safety environment, assessment is essential for the continuing improvement of the organization's safety program. Without a valid assessment program in place (and the tools to do it), the organization's long-term goal of an improved safety program is merely a dream. Return on investment cannot be measured with respect to the success of an organization's safety program unless an assessment program is in place. Benchmarking is one way to continuously strive to improve health and safety training, and thus the entire safety and health program. Continuous improvement of the organization's safety and health program (training) is paramount in today's health and safety environment and is truly vital to its success.

REFERENCES

Ahmed, Ishfaq et al. 2010. "How Organizations Evaluate their Trainings? An Evidence from Pakistani Organizations." *Interdisciplinary Journal of Contemporary Research In Business* 2(5) (accessed August 29, 2011). ijcrb.webs.com

American National Standards Institute (ANSI), Committee Z490 on Criteria for Accepted Practices in Safety, Health and Environmental Training. 2009. *American National Standard Z490.1-2009*. Des Plaines, IL: American Society of Safety Engineers.

Angelo, Thomas A. 1999. "Doing Assessment as if Learning Matters Most." *AAHE Bulletin* 51(9):3–6.

Boulmetis, John, and Phyllis Dutwin. 2000. *The ABCs of Evaluation: Timeless Techniques for Program and Project Managers*. San Francisco: Jossey-Bass.

Boxwell, Jr., Robert J. 1994. *Benchmarking for Competitive Advantage*. New York: McGraw-Hill.

Burke, Lisa, and Holly Hutchins. 2008. "A Study of Best Practices in Training Transfer and Proposed Model of Transfer." *Human Resource Development Quarterly* 19(2):107–128.

Camp, Robert C. 1989. *Benchmarking: The Search for Industry Best Practices that Lead to Superior Performance*. Milwaukee: Quality Press.

_____. 1995. *Business Process Benchmarking: Finding and Implementing Best Practices*. Milwaukee: Quality Press.

Carliner, Saul. 2003. *Training Design Basics*. Alexandria, VA: ASTD Press.

Cheney, Scott. 2001. "Benchmarking: Evaluation and Research." *American Society for Training and Development, Info-line* 9801.

Cohen, Alexander, and Michael J. Colligan. 1998. *Assessing Occupational Safety and Health Training: A Literature Review*. Cincinnati: National Institute for Occupational Safety and Health.

Cole, Nina 2008. "How Long Should a Training Program Be? A Field Study of 'Rules-of-Thumb'." *Journal of Workplace Learning* 20(1):54–70.

Cross, K. Patricia, and Thomas A. Angelo. 1998. *Classroom Assessment Techniques: A Handbook for Faculty*. Ann Arbor, MI: National Center for Research to Improve Postsecondary Teaching and Learning.

Dinardi, Salvatore (ed.). 2003. "Worker Education and Training." In *The Occupational Environment: Its Evaluation, Control, and Measurement*, 2d ed. Des Plaines, IL: American Society of Safety Engineers.

Galbraith, Diane, and Sandra E. Fouch. 2007. "Principles of Adult Learning Application to Safety Training." *Professional Safety* 52:(9):35–40.

Herman, Aguinis, and Kurt Kraiger. 2009. "Benefits of Training and Development for Individuals and Teams, Organizations, and Society." *Annual Review of Psychology* 60:451–474.

Holloway, J. A., C. M. Hinton, D. T. Mayle, and G. A. J. Francis.1997. "Why benchmark? Understanding the processes of best practice benchmarking." Proceedings of Business Track, British Academy of Management Conference, London, pp. 271–291.

Hutchinson, Linda. 2003. "ABC of learning and teaching: Educational environment." *BMJ* 326:810–812.

Kirkpatrick, Donald L. 1998. *Evaluating Training Programs: The Four Levels*, 2d ed. San Francisco: Berrett-Koehler Publishers.

Koskela, L. 1992. *CIFE Technical Report: 72*. "Application of the New Production Philosophy to Construction." Palo Alto, CA: Stanford University.

Kraft, Joan. n.d. *The Department of the Navy Benchmarking Handbook: A Systems View*. unpan1.un.org/intradoc/groups/public/documents/aspa/unpan002509.pdf

Moskal, B. M. 2000. "Scoring Rubrics: What When, and How?" *Practical Assessment, Research and Evaluation*, 7(3).

Occupational Safety and Health Administration (OSHA). 1998. *OSHA Standards and Training Guidelines, OSHA 2254*. www.osha.gov/Publications/2254.html

Popham, J. W. 2003. *Test Better, Teach Better: The Instructional Role of Assessment*. Alexandria, VA: Virginia Association for Supervision and Curriculum Development.

Transportation Research Board (TRB). 2010. *Special Report 300: Achieving Traffic Safety Goals in the United States:*

Lessons from Other Nations (accessed August 29, 2011). www.onlinw.trb.org/onlinepubs/sr/sr300.pdf

Walvoord, Barbara E. 2004. *Assessment Clear and Simple: A Practical Guide for Institutions, Departments, and General Education.* San Francisco: Jossey-Bass.

Ya Hui Lien, Richard Bella, Yu Yuan Hung, and Gary N. McLean. 2007. "Training evaluation based on cases of Taiwanese benchmarked high-tech companies." *International Journal of Training Development* 11(1): 35–48.

APPENDIX: RECOMMENDED READINGS

Boston, Carol. 2002. "The Concept of Formative Assessment." *Practical Assessment, Research & Evaluation* 8(9) (retrieved October 30, 2004). PAREonline.net/getvn.asp?v=8&n=9

Diamond, Robert M. 1998. *Designing and Assessing Courses and Curricula: A Practical Guide,* rev. ed. San Francisco: Jossey-Bass.

Fitz-Gibbons, Carol Taylor, and Lynn Lyons Morris. 1987. *How to Design a Program Evaluation.* Newbury Park, CA: SAGE Publications.

Hill, Daryl C. (ed.). 2004. *Construction Safety Management and Engineering.* Des Plaines, IL: American Society of Safety Engineers.

Maki, Peggy L. 2002. "Moving from Paperwork to Pedagogy: 'Channeling Intellectual Curiosity into a Commitment to Assessment.'" *American Association for Higher Education, AAHE Bulletin* May: 3–5.

Massachusetts Institute of Technology Teaching and Learning Laboratory Staff. 2004. *Assessment and Evaluation Electronic Forum* (retrieved October 30, 2004). www.mit.edu/tll/assessment.htm

Stark, Joan S., and Alice Thomas (eds.). 1994. *Assessment and Program Evaluation.* New York: Simon and Schuster.

Best Practices in Safety and Health Training

8

Michael Behm and C. Keith Stalnaker

LEARNING OBJECTIVES

▮ Specify indicators of an effective safety and health training program.

▮ Explain the limitations of training as a solution in OHS problem solving.

▮ Explain the role training plays in a company's overall safety and health program.

▮ Describe the six key principles when designing and delivering training to adult learners.

▮ Describe the training requirements of widely used safety and health standards, including ISO 14000, ANSI Z-10, and OHSAS 18000.

▮ Explain the difference between education and training.

▮ Define the desirable characteristics of a safety and health trainer.

▮ Identify several organizations that are involved with safety and health training research.

IN READING THE CHAPTERS from this section of the handbook, several safety and health training best practices clearly emerge. The purpose of this chapter is to offer additional considerations for strategy development in the area of occupational safety and health training.

A goal of most companies is for employees and managers to have the required aptitude, skill, and knowledge to successfully and safely carry out their jobs. Training is one means that leads to a skilled, knowledgeable, and collaborative workforce. When effectively integrated with personnel resources, management development, and technical procedures, training can help provide a workforce that achieves reliable operations and drives performance improvement.

Training should *not* be utilized as the primary method for solving occupational health and safety issues. It is one of the simplest solutions, but is usually the most ineffective (Petersen 1999). Too often, an organization will seek to train employees if it views occupational health and safety (OHS) solely as a people problem rather than as a systems problem. As this handbook demonstrates, the hierarchy of controls should be followed in solving OHS problems, and training falls into the category of administrative controls. Elimination, substation, and engineering controls should be considered *before* training and other administrative controls. While training does not remove hazardous conditions, it can help people recognize hazardous conditions so they can be removed or controlled (Brauer 2006). Moreover, effective training will usually supplement the higher-order controls to ensure they are and remain effective. An adequately designed employee training and education program can assist the organization in considering and utilizing higher-order controls to solve OHS problems. Workers typically have excellent process knowledge. Combining this knowledge with OHS education can drive organizational creative thinking in OHS. Of course, the organization needs adequate communication channels and a high level of trust within its culture for this to occur freely.

Training is a challenge in even the most diligent organizations. When the difficulties of designing and implementing an effective training program are overcome, the challenge then becomes keeping the program that way. The Institute of Nuclear Power Operations (INPO 2002) analyzed the twenty most significant events in nuclear power since 1974 to identify common event causes. Operator knowledge and training weaknesses were identified as causes in seven (35 percent) and were contributors to most others. Training-related deficiencies included improper operator responses to abnormal conditions and making erroneous assumptions during operations. The National Academy for Nuclear Training (NANT 2003) cited examples of training-related problems in the nuclear industry that are likely to exist in many industries. The problems NANT identified include the following:

- field work being performed by unqualified persons
- knowledge and skill weaknesses that lead to field performance issues
- deficient training content
- inadequate evaluation of trainees

Examining the training practices of others and learning from their successes and failures are ways for the safety professional to improve safety training. The materials presented in this section are intended to help the safety professional identify training methods that add value and contribute to safety performance. The practices described may not be appropriate for every training situation. Establishing the appropriate training practice for a specific situation requires careful analysis and evaluation that may reflect competing objectives and priorities.

ADULT LEARNERS

Safety and health professionals design and deliver training to adult learners. This presents challenges but also opportunities to enhance overall organizational learning. Milano and Ullius (1998, pp. 24–27) devised six key principles for designing and delivering training to adults. They are highlighted below.

1. *Personal experience is the key learning tool.* Adults come to training with vast personal experiences that they want to use and share. They learn quickly when things fit well into their experience and need more time to process those that do not. They want to be involved in the learning process.

2. *Motivation for learning is driven by needs, problem solving or personal satisfaction.* Adults are most driven to learn about things that directly relate to their needs. This assumes the learners recognize the need for safety training. A needs assessment is important not only for the trainer and the organization, but the learners must also recognize the need for training.

3. *Adults are independent learners.* While adult learners may value the trainer's opinions and message, the ultimate test of the training is whether they apply it in their work lives. The applicability will depend on whether they judge the training to be valuable. This reinforces the importance of assessing the training, as discussed in other chapters.

4. *Protecting the learners' self-esteem is critical.* Adult learners need to feel that they can question what is being taught and discuss their personal experiences without threat. Safety management systems, safety culture, and organizational trust are essential foundations for this environment and are critical components of effective safety training. Effective safety training hinges on many other aspects of the safety system.

5. *Adults have clear expectations about training.* Adult learners will bring a variety of expectations and assumptions with them to the training session. These will largely be based on their previous training experiences. The designer has the task of planning what can be done early in the training to clarify

expectations and to meet or modify them as appropriate.

6. *Adults learn in a variety of different ways and have preferences in learning styles.* Adult learners have a variety of preferences that affect the way they learn. The challenge for training designers is to appeal to and engage a variety of different learning styles so that participants can learn in ways that are best for them. This is, or course, a bit easier if the trainer knows the audience. However, in discussing expectations about training early in the session, adjustments can be made if a variety of methods are planned and organized that meet the objectives developed.

TRAINING OR EDUCATING?

Training and education are very closely bound and often used interchangeably. However, there are distinctions that are important to best practices in OHS. Milano and Ullius (1998) explain the distinction between education and training as follows: "Education focuses on learning about; training focuses on learning how." In OHS, do companies desire trained or educated employees? Perhaps, they want both. Organizations often focus on giving employees OHS skills or traditional training. *Training* in hazard communication typically might focus on how to read MSDSs and labels, handle common chemicals in one's work area, and recognize upset situations within the process. *Education* in hazard communication could focus on a historical perspective, and on examining case studies of OSHA fines on hazard communication in similar industries. For an example of historical perspective, an educator could utilize the 1984 Bhopal disaster as a case study to highlight current needs in hazard communication. Poor communication about the released methyl isocyanate resulted in medical intervention problems and distrust in the community. Training is more immediate, skills-oriented, and focused on application as compared to education, which is the process of building a knowledge base (Milano & Ullius 1998).

Educating employees and managers about OHS management systems, historical events, and current trends can assist the overall organization to mature in OHS thinking. Consider Appendix B in the ANSI Z-10 standard, where roles and responsibilities are set forth. For the system to work, each person within the organization needs to understand his/her roles and responsibilities (AIHA 2005). The standard lists roles and responsibilities for the President, CEO, or owner; executive officers, VPs, or senior leadership; directors, managers, and department heads; supervisors; employees; and the OHS department. Since most other professionals do not have a formal background in OHS, by default it becomes the OHS professionals' responsibility to educate the rest of the organization on how to properly manage and carry out their OHS roles and responsibilities. Therefore, it is important for OSH professionals to stay current on issues through continuing education, personal research, and the quest for lifelong learning. In order to educate, safety professionals must first know what they are talking about. OHS professionals must ensure they are qualified to educate others within the organization—that means staying current and being humble. When engaging with adult learners, trainers/educators should reflect upon their own lifelong learning and open-mindedness. Safety professionals and readers of this book come from very diverse backgrounds. In their careers, they will be called upon to train and educate on a wide and diverse range of topics. There is no way they can be experts on all of them. Consider how many professionals still quote Heinrich and talk about safety as purely a people problem. Individuals are encouraged to reflect on their own career, their expertise, and where they need to learn more as a best practice. The actions and philosophies of lifelong learning and staying humble will translate into becoming a better educator and trainer.

ORGANIZING AND MANAGING THE TRAINING PROCESS
Strategic Planning

Senior management's commitment to strategic planning is critical to business success and long-term viability. Proactively committing an organization to a carefully planned course prevents organizational drift, competitive mediocrity, and lackluster results. A strategic plan helps mold the decisions and actions of various divisions within the organization into a coordinated, compatible whole (Thompson and Strickland 2001). The International Safety Equipment Association (ISEA) is an example of how an organization can use a strategic plan to chart a growth path and target priorities. The ISEA identified and used the major trends and issues affecting the safety equipment industry as background for developing its strategic plan. The ISEA has committed to making regular plan updates to reflect changing conditions, past performance, and its mission (ISEA 2004):

> ISEA has published a Strategic Plan every year since 1985. The plan establishes a broad set of strategic priorities, generated by the membership, that provides ISEA its guiding principles. Each year a planning task force consisting of the ISEA Board of Trustees and Planning Committee meets to discuss and refine the Strategic Plan. This meeting is an organized and wide-ranging examination of the economic and public policy environments, the effects of globalization and industry consolidation, and market issues unique to safety equipment. The task force looks at the core competencies of the association, how well it's performing, and what it can do to return value to its member companies.

Crafting a business strategy to achieve corporate objectives is one element of strategic planning. Properly completed, a safety and health strategy establishes the managerial plan for running the safety and health program in support of the company's overall business strategy. The safety and health strategy shows how activities will be managed to achieve the company's safety and health objectives and missions.

A safety and health plan often identifies how training is integrated into the overall safety and health strategy. An example is the annual safety and health plan of Canadian Pacific Railway (CPR). In addition to stating its long-term goal of being recognized as the safest railway by its customers and stakeholders, the CPR plan includes specific measures of success, how these strategies will be accomplished, and how CPR management supports the health and safety plan. One of the ten strategies in the plan includes safety and health training. In 2003, nine specific safety and health training tactics were established for integration into day-to-day operations, including providing management safety training to all levels of management and supervision, ensuring employees and managers receive the training necessary to perform their jobs safely, and conducting accident investigation training (CPR 2003). Lower-level or local health and safety plans can be prepared to reflect implementation of the training tactics; for example, identifying the categories of supervisors to be trained on specific health and safety topics, and when that training will occur during the year.

TYPE OF TRAINING	DESCRIPTION	SPECIFIC RECOMMENDATIONS
Team coordination training	Includes an awareness phase (classroom training), a practice and feedback phase, and a continual reinforcement phase (refresher training).	• Effective even with teams that do not have a fixed set of personnel • The training addresses a particular set of nontechnical skills
Cross-training	Each team member is trained in his or her duties and those of their teammates.	• Team has a high level of interdependence between members • There is a lack of knowledge about the roles of other team members
Team self-correction training	This type works on the premise that effective teams review events, correct errors, discuss strategies, and plan for future events.	• Team has a high level of interdependence between members • Low staff turnover
Event-based training	This approach systemically structures training by tightly linking learning objectives, exercise design, performance measurement, and feedback.	• Useful when there are problems with a particular subset of tasks, and the tasks can be simulated.
Team facilitation training	This approach is designed to help leaders stimulate learning by creating on effective learning environment, supporting more formal training, and encouraging team discussions.	•There are limitations in training resources

FIGURE 1. Approaches to training (Flin et al. 2008)

In this section, Fanning (2012) provides excellent information for comparing various training models. For a best-practice training strategy regarding training techniques to be utilized, the OHS professional will need to assess the issues to be addressed, the resources available, and the makeup of the team to be trained (Flin et al 2008, p. 250). Flin offers recommended approaches based on the types of training shown here in Figure 1. OHS professionals should consider these approaches.

ANSI Z10:2005 OCCUPATIONAL HEALTH AND SAFETY MANAGEMENT SYSTEMS

The American National Standard Institute's (ANSI) *Standard for Occupational Health and Safety Management Systems* (OSHMS) recognizes education, training, and awareness as a key component of the implementation and operation of OHSMS. The standard requires organizations to (AIHA 2005):

1. Define and assess the OHSMS competence needed for employees and contractors.
2. Ensure, through appropriate education, training, or other methods, that employees and contractors are aware of applicable OHSMS requirements and are competent to carry out their responsibilities as defined in the OHSMS. The standard provides examples, such as training for engineers in safe design, incident investigation training that includes identifying underlying OHSMS deficiencies, and training for procurement personnel on how their decisions impact OHSMS.
3. Ensure effective access to, and remove barriers from, participation in education and training as defined in the organization's OHSMS. Barriers include disability issues, training on uncompensated time, scheduling, the training environment, and literacy and language issues.
4. Ensure training is provided in a language that trainees understand.
5. Ensure that trainers are competent to train employees. Competency is achieved through

one or more of the following: education, training, mentoring, experience, certification, licensing, and performance assessment.

The ANSI Z10:2005 standard provides training resources, including those from the American Petroleum Institute (API), the International Association of Oil and Gas Producers (OGP), ANSI Z490.1-2009, and OSHA. The latter two are described in other chapters of this section.

OCCUPATIONAL SAFETY AND HEALTH MANAGEMENT SYSTEM STANDARDS

The Occupational Safety and Health Administration (OSHA) developed the 18000 family of standards known as the Occupational Health and Safety Assessment Series (OHSAS), which include OHSAS 18001:2007, *Occupational Health and Safety (OHS) Management Systems Specification*, and OHSAS 18002, *Guidelines for the Implementation of OHSAS 18001*. OHSAS 18001 was created from the *British Standard for Occupational Health and Safety Management Systems*, BS 8800:1996, and other documents from international standards bodies (BS8800 OHSAS and OHSAS Project Group 2007). The 18001 standard was designed to enable companies to control their OHS risks and to demonstrate their commitment to providing a safe working environment, protecting their employees, and improving their performance. OHSAS 18001 was developed to be compatible with the ISO 9001 and 14001 management system standards. To allow for easy integration into a company's quality and environmental management systems, many OHSAS sections and subclauses are similar, such as management review, document control, and corrective and preventive actions.

OHSAS 18001 Section 4.4.2 addresses training, awareness, and competence (OHSAS Project Group, 2007):

The organization shall ensure that any person(s) under its control performing tasks that can impact on OH&S is (are) competent on the basis of appropriate education, training or experience, and shall retain associated records. The organization shall identify training needs associated with its OH&S risks and its OH&S management system. It shall provide training or take other action to meet these needs, evaluate the effectiveness of the training or action taken, and retain associated records. The organization shall establish, implement and maintain a procedure(s) to make persons working under its control aware of:

a) the OH&S consequences, actual or potential, of their work activities, their behavior, and the OH&S benefits of improved personal performance;

b) their roles and responsibilities and importance in achieving conformity to the OH&S policy and procedures and to the requirements of the OH&S management system, including emergency preparedness and response requirements;

c) the potential consequences of departure from specified procedures.

Training procedures shall take into account differing levels of:

a) responsibility, ability, language skills, and literacy;

b) risk.

Selecting the Training Staff

Finding health and safety trainers who can provide the training results desired requires the definition of selection criteria and careful evaluation of trainer candidates against those criteria. Selection criteria need to be specific to the training technique being used and the training results desired. Needed attributes of a trainer providing traditional style training will differ from those for role playing or case-study training styles, but will always include the ability to make the training relevant to students. Having the ability to encourage adult learning is another needed attribute, and trainers should be required to demonstrate proficiency with the adult education technique to be used (NIEHS 1998).

Trainers should be considered professionals who, like all professionals, need specialized skills and education. This may dictate the use of subject-matter experts like firefighters to conduct fire extinguisher training, the use of electricians to conduct lockout/tagout training, and the use of a chemist to provide chemical safety training. Safety and health training does not need to be restricted to professional trainers or safety practitioners, but should always be performed by persons with appropriate training skills. Furthermore, subject matter experts also need to be good communicators and teachers. If trainers have poor interpersonal rapport or communication skills, they will not be effective trainers.

While many companies use safety experts or other subject-matter experts to deliver safety and health compliance training, some have had success using worker-trainers. A worker-trainer is defined as a trainer who has a common work background and/or experience with those being trained (NIEHS 1998). Trainees typically view the trainer as a peer. Such persons may be employed as full-time or part-time trainers, and methods range from the classroom to on-the-job training. One of the best worker-trainer examples is in the delivery of hazardous materials training (40-hour Hazwoper). More than 1000 worker-trainers provide Hazwoper training under the NIEHS-supported hazardous worker training programs. NIEHS reports that employers have found that the use of hazardous materials workers

Questions about the trainer's qualifications and experience
- What experience do you have in training adults in the workplace?
- What experience of workplace health and safety issues in this industry do you have?
- What experience do you have of training adults who come from non–English-speaking backgrounds?
- What qualifications in health and safety do you have?
- What qualifications in training/ teaching do you have?
- How long have you been a consultant in health and safety?
- How do you keep your knowledge up to date?
- What other businesses or organizations have you provided health and safety training to and could they give me a reference?
- What are your areas of expertise/specialization?

Questions about how the trainer will train and assess people in the organization
- What will I or my employees be able to do as a result of this training program? (What new skills and knowledge will we be able to put into practice in the workplace?)
- Where and when would you provide the training?
- How do you plan to assess whether the people doing the training have achieved the outcomes of the program ?
- How will the training contribute to the management of health and safety in this organization?
- As a small organization, we do not want to be totally dependent on health and safety consultants to provide us with the information and training we need. In the training you provide, how will you ensure that we gradually take control of our health and safety training?
- As an employer, I am keen to be involved in the health and safety training that takes place. How will you involve me in the process?
- What sort of training material and records do you supply to employers to keep for future reference?

FIGURE 2. Questions to ask when selecting a health and safety trainer (*Source:* Commonwealth of Australia 1996, p. 20)

as trainers increases the quality of the training since it allows for the application of practical knowledge and direct experience. Worker-trainers have the ability to use personal experiences to illustrate the training, making recipients more receptive to the message.

The Commonwealth of Australia (1996) suggests the following knowledge and experience attributes should be expected of health and safety trainers:

- applicable health and safety codes
- hazard identification, risk assessment, and risk-control approaches to health and safety training
- principles of safety management
- health and safety issues specific to the work assignments and industry of those being trained
- student competency evaluation skills
- adult training skills

Questions to ask when selecting a health and safety trainer are presented in Figure 2. The questions relate to qualification and experience, the conduct of training and training assessment, and related business practices.

Suggested guidelines for worker-trainers have been identified by NIEHS (1998) and include an understanding of adult education training methods and techniques. NIEHS (1994) identifies three principles that need to be addressed to meet the needs of adult learners:

1. Physical environment
   - How are the chairs, tables, and other learning stations arranged in the classroom?
   - How does this arrangement encourage or inhibit participation and interaction?
   - Can the arrangement be changed easily to allow different kinds of interaction?
2. Social environment
   - Are warm-up activities or "ice breakers" used to put people at ease?
   - Do trainers allow participants to say things in their own words, or do they translate what is said into other words or jargon?
   - Are participants encouraged to listen carefully to each other?
   - Are they encouraged to respect different points of view?
   - Are they encouraged to use humor?

3. Differing learning styles, backgrounds, and experiences
   - Do the learning activities in the training program provide participants with an opportunity to listen, look at visuals, ask questions, read, write, practice with equipment, discuss critical issues, identify problems, plan actions, and try out strategies in participatory ways?
   - Is the program sensitive to literacy differences?
   - Do the trainers check privately with anyone having reading and writing difficulties?
   - Is reading aloud or writing in front of the group only voluntary and never mandatory?
   - Are all instructions and other required material read aloud?
   - Do the materials incorporate enough visual aids and props?
   - Do the trainers repeat out loud anything they write on a board or flip chart?

Goetsch (2005) suggests that safety and health trainers understand the principles that explain how people learn. Based on those principles, he suggests that trainers can do a better job of facilitating learning if they have the capability to incorporate the following practices:

- Trainers need to spend time motivating learners, including letting them know how they will benefit from the training.
- Start each learning activity with a brief review of the preceding activity.
- Train in a step-by-step manner that proceeds from the simple to the complex, and from the known to the unknown.
- Classroom presentations are most effective when followed by application activities that require the student to demonstrate understanding by doing something.
- The more often students use what they are learning, the better they will remember and understand it. Infrequent tasks may require more frequent training to maintain skill levels.
- Organize training into segments that are long enough to allow learners to see progress, but not so long as to be boring.

- Give students immediate and continual feedback on learning performance.

The subject of trainer qualifications can become contentious. For example, the workers' bargaining unit represented by the Ontario Public Service (OPS) has suggested that health and safety training be delivered only by workers who have faced actual workplace hazards and who, it claims, better understand workplace health and safety challenges. The OPS Employees Union (OPSEU) Health and Safety policy prohibits its local unions from agreeing to have workers trained by employer-based trainers, has suggested its members file grievances when training is provided by employers, and directs local unions to remove employer-trained workers. It is clearly in the interest of employers and their employees to develop and deliver appropriate health and safety training. Sometimes, the delivery of such training must be managed within the constraints of collective bargaining agreements (OPSEU 2001). The goal, however, should always be the delivery of accurate and effective training.

Petersen (1999) proposes that the supervisor should be responsible for training workers, and that this is particularly important at the front-line supervisory level. If the supervisor is held accountable for safety training, along with other OHS responsibilities, this can be more effective than giving the new employee to an experienced employee. The National Safety Council (NSC) (2010) developed the Supervisor's Safety course that teaches supervisors how to integrate OHS aspects into their daily management process. If supervisors are to be involved in safety training and have other safety responsibilities, it is the organization's OHS professional who will need to educate and train the supervisors, deliver to them the tools necessary to be successful, and develop proper accountability systems.

TRAINING RESEARCH
National Institute for Occupational Safety and Health (NIOSH)

The NIOSH Centers for Disease Control and Prevention (CDC) and participating Institutes and Centers and the National Institutes of Health (NIH) accept grant applications for research related to occupational safety and health. NIOSH research programs support priority areas identified in the National Occupational Research Agenda (NORA) and other significant programs related to occupational safety and health.

NORA represents a research agenda for occupational safety and health in the United States. Using an industry-sector-based approach to develop research agendas, NIOSH is the steward of the NORA program for the nation. There are ten sectors:

1. Mining (except oil and gas extraction)
2. Oil and gas extraction
3. Manufacturing
4. Healthcare and social assistance
5. Wholesale and retail
6. Transportation, warehousing, and utilities
7. Public safety
8. Services
9. Agriculture, forestry, and fishing
10. Construction

OSH training and education is a separate construction-sector strategic goal, and training is included in all other sectors as intermediate and activity goals. Noteworthy is that, in addition to worker training, management and supervisor training is listed frequently within the sector's agenda. NORA has also granted awards for training-effectiveness research. Examples include the effectiveness of computer-based training for vineyard workers carried out at the Oregon Health Sciences University (OHSU) and training and reinforcement in the use of hearing-protection devices done at the University of Washington (NIOSH 2006). In the OHSU study (Anger et al. 2009), workers' knowledge significantly increased after the training. They found that retention in the long term is an issue, and training must be frequently updated.

CONCLUSION

This chapter offered additional strategies in developing best practices in occupational safety and health training, while supplementing previous chapters in this section. Readers are encouraged to benchmark within their own industries and professional circles, and to learn more beyond the field of occupational safety and health training. One can generalize from other disciplines. For example, in engineering education, Richard Felder provides interesting insight on learning styles and student preferences in his model. He categorizes student learning styles and preferences in one of four dimensions (Felder and Silverman 1988, Felder 1993):

1. sensing or intuitive
2. visual or verbal
3. active or reflective
4. sequential or global

Training is just one method for problem solving in the safety and health professional's toolbox. Proper utilization of the hierarchy of controls in problem solving should be thoroughly investigated. Training can be utilized in conjunction with other controls to enhance their effectiveness. Organizations need to understand their population and the population's learning style.

REFERENCES

American Industrial Hygiene Association (AIHA). 2005. *American National Standard for Occupational Health and Safety Management Systems*. ANSI / AIHA Z10-2005. www.aiha.org/ansicommittees/html/z10committee.html

Anger, K., L. Patterson, M. Fuchs, L. Will, and D. Rohlman. 2009. " Learning and Recall of Worker Protection Standard (WPS) Training in Vineyard Workers." *Journal of Agromedicine* 14(3):336–344.

Brauer, R. 2006. *Safety and Health for Engineers*. 2d ed. Hoboken, NJ: John Wiley and Sons.

BS8800 OHSAS and OSHA Health and Safety Management Group. 2002. *OHSAS 18001 Made Easy*. www.osha-bs8800-ohsas-18001-health-and-safety.com/ohsas-18001.html

Canadian Pacific Railway (CPR). 2003. *2003 Health and Safety Plan*. Calgary: CPR Safety and Health Management Committee, pp. 1–24.

Centers for Disease Control and Prevention (CDC). 2000. *Healthy People 2010*. www.healthypeople.gov

Commonwealth of Australia. 1996. *Organising Health and Safety Training For Your Workplace*. Canberra, ACT: Commonwealth Information Services.

European Agency for Safety and Health at Work. 2000. *Facts 7: Future Occupational Safety and Health Research Needs and Priorities in the Member States of the European Union*. www.agency.osha.eu.int/publications/factsheets/7/en/facts7_en.pdf

Felder, R. 1993. "Reaching the Second Tier: Learning and Teaching Styles in College Science Education." *Journal of College Science Teaching* 23(5):286–290.

Felder, R., and L. Silverman. 1988. "Learning and Teaching Styles in Engineering Education." *Engineering Education* 78(7):674–681.

Flin, R., P. O'Connor, and M. Crichton. 2008. *Safety at the Sharp End: A Guide to Non-Technical Skills*. Burlington, VT: Ashgate Publishing Company.

Goetsch, D. 2005. *Occupational Safety and Health for Technologists, Engineers, and Managers*. Upper Saddle River, NJ: Pearson Prentice Hall.

Institute of Nuclear Power Operations (INPO). 2002. *Analysis of Significant Events* (INPO 02-005). Atlanta: INPO.

International Safety Equipment Association (ISEA). 2004. *2004 Strategic Plan*. www.safetyequipment.org/plan2004.pdf)

Milano, M., & D. Ullius. 1998. *Designing Powerful Training: The Sequential-Iterative Model*. San Francisco: Jossey-Bass/Pfeiffer, A Wiley Company.

National Academy for Nuclear Training (NANT). 2003. *The Objectives and Criteria for Accreditation of Training in the Nuclear Power Industry* (ACAD 02-001). Washington, DC: NANT.

National Institute of Environmental Health Sciences (NIEHS). 1994. *Interpretive Guidance to the Minimum Criteria for Worker Health and Safety Training for Hazardous Waste Operations and Emergency Response*. Research Triangle Park, NC: NIEHS.

_____. 1998. *NIEHS Worker-Trainer Programs: Suggested Guidelines for Success*. Research Triangle Park, NC: NIEHS.

National Institute of Occupational Safety and Health (NIOSH). 2006. *Office of Extramural Programs Annual Report, Fiscal Year 2005*. www.cdc.gov/niosh/oep/pdfs/Annual-Report-2005.pdf

_____. 2001. *National Occupational Research Agenda (NORA)*, Publication No. 2001-147 Cincinnati: NIOSH.

National Institute on Deafness and Other Communication Disorders. 2004. *Research*. www.nidcd.nih.gov/research

_____. 2006. Office of Extramural Programs. "Annual Report, Fiscal Year 2005" (retrieved May 16, 2006). www.cdc.gov/niosh/oep/pdfs/Annual-Report-2005.pdf

National Safety Council (NSC). 2010. "Supervisor Safety Training" (retrieved June 16, 2010). www.nsc.org/PRODUCTS_TRAINING/TRAINING/WORKPLACE-SAFETY/Pages/SupervisorSafetyTraining.aspx

OHSAS Project Group. 2007. "Occupational Health and Safety Assessment Series, Occupational Health and Safety Management Systems – Requirements." ICS 03.100.01; 13.100. July 2007. London, UK.

Ontario Public Service Employees Union. 2001. *Update on Workplace-Specific Hazard Training*. www.opseu.org/hands/certificationupdate1.htm

Petersen, D. 1999. *Safety Supervision*. 2d ed. Des Plaines, IL : ASSE.

INDEX